My Life of Crime

Essays and Other Entertainments

Tyler C. Gore

Sagging
Meniscus

Thanks to the following publications and journals, where many of these essays
(and other works) first appeared: *The American in Italia*, *Exacting Clam*, *The Fire Island
Express*, *Literal Latte*, *MeThree*, *Opium Magazine*, *Rosebud*, *The South Shore Express*,
StatORec.

Set in Mrs Eaves XL with LaTeX.

ISBN: 978-1-952386-37-4 (paperback)
ISBN: 978-1-952386-38-1 (ebook)
Library of Congress Control Number: 2022933766

Sagging Meniscus Press
Montclair, New Jersey
saggingmeniscus.com

For Leigh, my partner in crime

—and—

In memory of my friend Fay Webern (1927–2019),

author of

The Button Thief of East 14th Street

Contents

MY
LIFE
OF
CRIME

INTRODUCTION

"**M**EDIOCRE ARTISTS BORROW; great artists steal." That's the line as I first encountered it, as a college freshman in the mid-80s. It was fondly circulated by pretentious students like me, and always attributed to Pablo Picasso (whom no one, in those days, ever called an asshole). But these days, as I discovered when sitting down to write this introduction, the quote is far more often attributed to Steve Jobs, in a slightly blander formulation: "Good artists copy; great artists steal." Jobs duly credited Picasso for the line, but that tends to get overlooked; all sorts of memes, inspirational posters, and other cultural detritus attribute the quote directly to Jobs, who's probably more admired these days than Picasso. As I fell deeper into this Googley rabbit hole, I found—exactly as I expected to—that it's even more complicated than that. T.S. Eliot, Igor Stravinsky, and William Faulkner all uttered variations of the line, and possibly Picasso stole it from one of those guys before Jobs stole it from him. An even earlier variation appeared in "Imitators and Plagiarists," an 1892 essay by W.H. Davenport, who, in writing about Tennyson, expressed a decidedly less punkrock version of the sentiment: "great poets imitate and improve, whereas small ones steal and spoil." Twenty-five years later, Eliot (who was always dipping into someone else's porridge) stole Davenport's line and subverted it to bad-boy modernist sensibilities: "Immature poets imitate; mature poets steal."

Or so the Internet told me. Sweeney guards the hornéd gate, but only algorithms guard the gates of Google. The content-filler articles I gleaned seemed cribbed from one another, reproducing whole passages with only slight changes in wording, leading me to believe that their authors had researched the matter exactly as I had, by spending a few minutes typing phrases into a search engine. Digging deeper only confused matters. An article posted on Artsy.net ("Four Iconic Quotes Artists Never Said") makes the claim that not only was Picasso *not* the originator of the maxim, but that it was Jobs who first falsely attributed it to Picasso, thus inadvertently creating a modern myth. I find this notion disturbing to contemplate, because it suggests that when I was a pretentious student back in the 80s, I hadn't been quoting *Picasso*, I'd been quoting *Steve Jobs*.

But regardless of who said what version of it first, it's easy to see why Picasso's dictum has enjoyed currency for over a century. If it were stated more honestly, the maxim would simply be: "Artists steal"—leaving the self-justifying matter of greatness aside. People get unreasonably upset when their favorite artists turn out to be kleptomaniacs. We moderns tend to fetishize *originality*—the laughable notion that great works of art spring forth, fully formed, from brilliant, singular minds—although in recent years the fetish has shifted towards *authenticity*, with crimes and misdemeanors determined by subtle nuances of identity and "lived experience," and much handwringing over what, exactly, constitutes cultural appropriation. (Either way, no one is sure if it's still okay to listen to Led Zeppelin.) But alas, there's nothing new under the sun, and human beings propagate ideas like bees propagate pollen. Artists steal because there's just so much good stuff lying around for the taking, and the most celebrated artists are often simply better thieves.

I can't say I'm a particularly clever thief, but I've done my share. I'm not talking about out-and-out plagiarism, of course. That's just typing, and where's the fun in that? But when you're a thief and you're invited to someone's home for dinner, it can be hard to resist the urge to sneak off to take a quick peak at the jewelry box on the bedroom dresser. I have many amusing friends, and when they say something amusing, I take mental note of it, in case I'd like to repurpose it later. (Indeed, I've become so brazen, I'll actually pull out my notebook and commit it to paper on the spot.) I'm a bit of a magpie in more ways than one, with a mind as cluttered as my apartment, filled with shiny little baubles that have caught my eye while reading or watching television and these things sometimes wind up, partially digested, in my writing. Usually this is intentional—premeditated larceny, if it pleases the court—but not always, and that's what worries me. I like to know what I've done, so I can confess ahead of time if I'm in danger of getting caught.

Which brings us to Todd McEwen. The earliest essay in this collection—"Stuff"—was written over the course of a week in a sustained outburst of despair. I was in my late 20s, living in my mother's house while I completed my unfinished undergraduate degree at City College. That fall, I'd signed up for a graduate-level nonfiction course with Claudia Dreifus, a journalist for *The New York Times*. The only assignment for the course was to complete a single, substantial work of nonfiction. We were asked to float proposals with her during the semester, and everything I came up with was returned with a variation of the same response: *There's no story here.* By December, with just a week left to go, I knew I was in trouble. I desperately needed a topic, any topic, to write about, and sitting there in the depressing squalor of my childhood bedroom, trapped in the town I'd grown up in and had never particularly wanted to come back to, the topic presented itself: *write about this.*

As those in my intimate sphere can readily confirm, I've always been very good at complaining. Upon the occasion of some small, petty irritation, I am more than capable of channeling my rage into a full-blown jeremiad, a blistering whirlwind of invective, packed with unnecessary literary and historical allusions, and laced throughout with black, seething irony entirely disproportionate to the offense. Oh, with the despair of my current living situation compounded by an impossible deadline—for which I had only myself to blame—I had all of that frothy, splenetic fury bottled up inside me, ready to be tapped, but I didn't quite know how to capture it on the page. I immediately thought of a writer who did.

Years earlier, when I'd lived in Boston, a friend with excellent taste had brought me a novel she'd found in one of the many used bookshops she frequented. It's the funniest thing I've ever read, she told me. The book was Todd McEwen's 1983 debut, *Fisher's Hornpipe*, and my friend was right: it was the funniest thing I'd ever read. The novel takes places in Boston and follows the spiraling trajectory of William Fisher, who, in the opening scene, steps out on Walden Pond in December, where he stumbles upon Henry Thoreau himself, trapped below the frozen surface, pounding on the ice and angrily gesticulating for help. Backing away warily, Fisher slips and cracks his head on the ice. He winds up with his head in bandages for the entire course of the novel, which, of course, encourages everyone he subsequently encounters to interpret his characteristically misanthropic behavior as evidence of a brain injury. Hilarity ensues. Fisher's madcap adventures are an unhinged delight, but what had drawn me back to the book again and again was McEwen's extraordinary style, the way he skids through sentences like a motorcycle stuntman—by turns loose and furious, or scathing and precise—with a Joycean scorn for the conventions of punctuation. All that and the book is *funny*, packed with all the loopy absurdity and savage wit of a Marx Brothers movie.

At some point, I'd also acquired the issue of *Granta* (Issue 41, "Biography") which contained "A very young Dancer," McEwen's superb personal essay about his estranged sister, which had much the same stylistic qualities as *Fisher's Hornpipe*. McEwen provided an excellent model for how to write an extended *rant*. I wanted a style like that for my own extended rant. I wanted *his* style. I think I had in mind a kind of ventriloquist trick, as if I could channel McEwen's voice like a charismatic Christian speaking in tongues. This was a ridiculous aspiration, but I had a deadline.

I turned to those two sources repeatedly while writing "Stuff" over the course of a week. It was like running a marathon in sprints. Writing is, after all, performative. I'd block out a section I wanted to work on, and then—a few minutes before sitting at the keyboard— psyche myself up by re-reading passages of McEwen that captured something of the feeling I was shooting for. Of course, cloning another writer's style is no more possible than cloning someone else's personality. But at some adolescent point in our lives, we've all tried to do just that: attempted to model our personalities on some much cooler kid, trying on alien character traits like a pair of borrowed shoes, assimilating what fits and discarding what doesn't. Through this imperfect process, we become ourselves. I didn't succeed, of course, in channeling McEwen's voice; instead, I learned how to channel my own. The essay I'd written came out sounding more like me than anything I'd written before, but I'd needed to revisit *Fisher's Hornpipe* to get there.

Here's how I expressed my gratitude. One of the quotations McEwen had used as an epigraph for *Fisher's Hornpipe* was a passage from Thoreau's *Walden*, almost uncannily well-suited for an essay about household clutter. I typed it up and slapped it atop of my own essay. Is it a crime to steal an epigraph, something that is already a direct quotation? It sure felt like it, but I couldn't resist. It was there for the taking.

I passed the class, I graduated, I moved back to the city. I didn't want to go back to the kind of shitty office job I'd always worked. I managed to get a job teaching English as a Second Language, primarily to young foreign adults who needed to satisfy their student visa requirements in order to stay in the States. I loved that job—the students were close to my own age, and we often went out drinking together—but it didn't pay well, so I eventually quit and got a shitty office job. I had a group of old college friends—with better jobs—who rented a house together in Fire Island every summer, and they invited me to join them, as they did every year. In the past I'd always declined because I couldn't afford it, but that year I had a brilliant realization—I could afford it *if I didn't have to pay rent in the city.*

For a couple of months, I focused on saving money, and at the end of May I quit my shitty job and moved out to Fire Island for the summer. It was there, on a rainy weekend, that I ran into Kevin Fitz on the ferry dock—a local chef turned publisher—handing out copies of *The Fire Island Express*, which he'd just started a few months earlier. I asked him if he needed writers, and he told me to drop off some samples at his office in the village. And just like that, I had a regular column, which I called "Lost at Sea." I insisted on being paid, and he reluctantly agreed, although most of his writers wrote for free. He couldn't afford to pay me much—once, when he was short on cash, he offered me a small bag of marijuana in lieu of payment, which I happily accepted—but it supplemented the meager savings I was living on. I became something of a *de facto* editor (later, an official one), and he published not only my column, but virtually any piece of writing I gave him. After the summer, he adapted to the off-season, and began publishing *The South Shore Express,* which he distributed in Long Island. By then, I'd moved back to the city, and soon started graduate school, but I continued writing for him, changing the name of my column to "Metropolis."

Here's where the theft came in. I've always been a procrastinator, and I'd often find myself scrambling to compose my column a few days before the deadline. They were never quite how I wanted them to come out, but I needed to get them in. So, after they were published in the *Express*, I'd rewrite them and submit the refined pieces to various literary journals—especially *Literal Latte*, where I was becoming something of a regular. Like so many other crimes, you could get away with stuff like this back then. It was the dawn of the digital age—personal email was still a novelty—and most publications existed only in print, so it was very unlikely that the readers (or publishers) of a literary journal would discover that an earlier version of a piece had been first published in a local Long Island magazine. These days, I suppose that practice would come under the rubric of self-plagiarism, but that wasn't such a big deal in the dial-up era. The concept of separate markets still existed in the days before the Internet swallowed up everything up into one big searchable world-wide repository.

Oh, and there's something else I need to get off my chest. I've been worried for years about William Saroyan. In his classic coming-of-age novel *The Human Comedy*, there's a sequence concerning Henri Rousseau's *The Sleeping Gypsy*, which had resonated with me, because I love that painting. Although I read it long ago, and hadn't owned a copy of the book for decades, it surely had been on my mind when I wrote my own description of the painting in "October's Rain." After it had been published in *Rosebud*, I began to worry that I might've inadvertently lifted whole lines, verbatim, from Saroyan. But I didn't own a copy, so this worry sat festering in the back of my head for many years. Had I plagiarized Saroyan? While I was putting together this collection, I knew I had to resolve this issue. After much Googling, I finally located the passage in question in an online copy of *The Human Comedy*, and, heart thumping, began to read. I was shocked. The passage was not at all how I remembered it. It's a short dream sequence—just two sentences—and the painting isn't even named. Other than noting a few defining elements of the painting (mandolin, jug), and the peacefulness of both the lion and the gypsy, it had little in common with my own description. I'd thought

I'd ripped off Saroyan, but I hadn't. It was all me. *Phew.* My most successful crime ever: the one I didn't even commit.

By the way, I've always assumed that gypsy in the painting is a man—swayed, I suppose, by the oafish, masculine-looking feet—but that's apparently wrong. The gypsy is a woman. But Saroyan made the same mistake, so I'm in good company.

※ ※ ※

With all this confession of theft, you might wonder if I'm a liar, too. Are my true stories true?

Yes, they are. But there's a *but*.

(I'm not speaking, of course, of the three "other entertainments" sandwiched between "Stuff" and "Appendix"—as, I guess, a kind of intermission—which bear little resemblance to my life, or to reality.)

These aren't journalistic pieces; they are personal essays. They are akin to the kind of stories a friend might tell you over a pint. A grain of salt, a pinch of hyperbole. For the sake of narrative, timelines get compressed and sometimes slightly rejiggered; conversations are reconstructed from memory. To protect the innocent (and maintain my friendships), names and places are often changed, identifying details blurred or omitted. But I didn't just make shit up. Everything that happened in these essays happened.

The pieces in this collection, written over a span of decades, have been arranged—like tracks on an album—but they are not in any particular chronological order, not in terms of when they were composed or published, nor in terms of when specific events occurred in my life. (For example, "Stuff," the earliest piece, was composed in the late 1990s, but is placed relatively close to "Appendix," the most recent work, completed in the fall of 2021.) So you can read them in any order you like. That goes for this introduction, too. As Steve Jobs famously remarked, "I like to save the introduction for after I've finished the book." So if you've already skipped this one to jump right in—well, that's no crime.

My Life of Crime

"NO ONE LIKES a practical joker," my mother had often warned me—but, hey, my mother was out shopping. We lived in suburban New Jersey. It was a dreary day, rainy and cold like that day in the beginning of *The Cat in the Hat*, and there was nothing to do. None of my friends were home. So I picked up the phone and ordered a pizza for my neighbor across the street.

I walked to the front window where I could peer at my neighbor's house from behind the curtains. But there is no instant gratification with this sort of prank, and patience has never been one of my virtues. So, after about five minutes, I got up and ordered another pizza from a different shop. Then—either to kill time or to satisfy some vague sense of proportion—I called a third pizzeria. This time, under the assumed name of Andre Breton, I ordered *two* pies, one with sausage and one with mushrooms and green peppers.

Then I went back to wait at the window.

When the first delivery truck—from Dominos—arrived and the driver trudged up the walk carrying the pie I had ordered, I felt a familiar rush of excitement, the giddy thrill of the voyeur. I had a relationship with this man wetly slogging up the walk, but he didn't know it. I had secretly orchestrated his mission, and knew something about how it would end—that is, *in disappointment*. (It occurred to me that this was exactly how God must feel all day long.) Now I watched my neighbor open the door, and even from that distance I could see his puzzled expression as he shook his head and slowly closed the door.

Like Sisyphus trudging down the hill for his rock, the Dominos guy returned to his truck with the noble, dejected air of one who knows that in spite of all his efforts, the fates have singled him out for misery. He pulled his truck into the road just as the truck from Tony's Pizzeria arrived. The Dominos guy slowed down for a moment, as if to assess the situation, but then apparently decided to wash his hands of the whole thing and continued on his way. The

Tony's guy got out, paused for a moment to cast a long, perplexed gaze at his competitor's truck, shrugged, and removed a pie from the passenger side of his own truck.

When my neighbor opened the door, I observed with fascination how quickly his expression could change from mild surprise to extreme irritation. He shook his head emphatically, and then peered over the driver's shoulders, as if looking for a hidden camera. It was at that moment the third truck arrived, pulling up right behind the other truck.

My neighbor, who has a short temper—believe me, I know—pushed past the Tony's guy and stormed out towards the third truck, gesticulating angrily. Then he suddenly stopped in the middle of his lawn and, mute with rage, intently scanned the houses around him, as if dormant psychic powers might help him locate the culprit. For a tense moment, his gaze passed directly over my window, and I held my breath.

The moment passed, the drivers were dismissed, and after my laughter subsided, I considered calling another place. Sure: why not make a day of it? In the heavily Italian area where I grew up there are more pizzerias than, um . . . I don't know . . . something. Starbucks. Fire hydrants. Chinese restaurants. Whatever. There are a lot. And I was prepared to arrange for every single one of them to visit my neighbor. But just as I reached for the phone, it suddenly rang all by itself.

I picked up the phone and a man said, "Hello, Mr. Breton, this is Ray's Pizza. Did you order two pies for delivery about half an hour ago?" His tone was suspiciously smug, the way it is when someone asks a question that they already know the answer to.

Uh-oh, I thought. I'd given them a false callback number, so how did they know to call me here? But I kept my head. "This is the Duchamp residence," I said calmly. "You must have the wrong number."

He laughed snidely, and my heart began to pound. "No, I don't think so," he said triumphantly. "You see, we have *caller ID*."

Oh Jesus. I had forgotten all about caller ID. It hadn't existed the last time I'd done this. I think it's probably important to explain that the events in this narrative took place at the dawn of the digital era. Cell phones were the size of bread loaves and were used exclusively by stockbrokers; the Internet ran on tin cans and string and was used exclusively by nerds. A phone was a landline phone, period, a stationary object hardwired into the guts of your house, or, in this case, my mother's house. Caller ID was the gee-whiz technology of the day, and I had completely forgotten about its recent proliferation.

This was not good. My mother was due to arrive home within the hour, and I didn't want her to find out how I'd spent the afternoon. It wasn't that I was afraid of *punishment*. It was *shame*. I was really getting too old for this kind of thing. After all, it's one thing when your ten year old finds it amusing to play games with the telephone. But when your son is a twenty-eight year old man . . . well, the first word that comes to mind is *disturbed*.

There was an urgency, then, in getting rid of this guy. As an experienced prankster I knew the rule about getting caught: *no matter how incriminating the evidence, deny everything*. And I knew the corollary of this rule: *believe your own lies or you won't sound convincing*.

I took a deep breath, summoned up an appropriate sense of righteous indignation, and replied, "Listen, buddy, I don't care what your *caller ID* says. I didn't order any pizza." With shaking hands, I hung up the phone and exhaled.

Then the phone rang again.

"Hello, this is Ray's again. Look, maybe *you* didn't order the pizza, but someone from your line did. Do you have any children?"

What I said next was very stupid.

I said yes.

I suppose I was trying to play the part of the indignant suburbanite to the hilt—in fact, I was imagining that I was my neighbor across the street—and, after all, *he* had children. "But," I added quickly, "Josh wouldn't do something like that." Of course, the phrase *something like that* implied that I knew more about this scheme than I was letting on, but the man seemed not to notice. He was more concerned with my son—my son!—Josh. He was sure he'd found the culprit.

I was now burdened with defending the honor of a son I didn't have. I began to panic, and my usual reaction to nervousness is to start babbling. Somehow, during our conversation, it became established that Josh was eleven, a good student, that he hadn't been home for at least an hour, that he was playing with someone named Benjamin. I was beginning to have trouble remembering it all, so I tried to turn the conversation away from Josh Duchamp by disparaging the supposed merits of caller ID. I claimed to have seen an episode of *60 Minutes* in which the accuracy of caller ID had been tinged with doubt.

"Oh yeah?" the man countered. "Well, I've never any problems with it."

"Well, now you have," I said, and hung up again. Five minutes passed, and I decided I was off the hook. Then the phone rang again. It was like a leak I couldn't plug.

It was a different person this time. "This is Officer Antonelli of the Closter Police," a gruff voice said. I was now in such a panicky state that I didn't soberly consider the extreme unlikelihood that I was speaking to an actual police officer. I began to wonder if ordering pizza under false pretenses was a punishable crime.

I tried again to blame the caller ID, but the alleged policeman claimed to have expertise on his side. "These are very sophisticated machines," he told me. "In my experience they are 100% accurate." He certainly sounded like a cop, or at the very least like someone who had watched a lot of cop shows. The topic of conversation turned back to the character of my fictional son Josh, and I was beginning to doubt that Josh was innocent.

I began to lose hope. I was going to jail, and Josh would grow up fatherless. I took advantage of a pause in our conversation to make a desperate bid for freedom. I sighed dramatically, and in a weary voice, I said, "Well, I guess we're going to have to take this to *court*. Give me your badge number and I'll have my lawyer contact you."

There was a long pause on the telephone. Clearing his throat, the would-be cop adopted a kind of blustery boys-will-be-boys tone and said, "Well, Mr. Duchamp, there's no need to go *that* far. I'm sure you believe your son didn't do it, but I think you should talk to him when he gets home. Oh, and I'm sorry to say that Ray's won't accept any more calls from this number."

Yeah, his bluff was called, but I felt no sense of triumph. I quickly agreed to the offered terms and hung up the phone. For a long time I sat quietly in the kitchen, unhappily considering the current trajectory of my life.

❀ ❀ ❀

Alright, I admit that this was not my finest moment. Ordering pizzas for the neighbors is childish and immature, a temptation that most adults probably have little trouble resisting. But try to understand my state of mind. I was in my late twenties, and after years of living on my own, I'd moved back home to save money while finishing my long-neglected undergraduate degree in the city. At the time of the pizza incident, I'd been living at my mother's house for nearly a year, and life in the suburbs was beginning to unhinge me. It's not true that you can't go back home, but it *is* true that when you do, you revert to the mental age you were when you last lived there. You complain that there's nothing to eat, you watch a lot of TV and feel bored all the time, and that's when you start remembering how you entertained yourself when you last lived here.

❀ ❀ ❀

As a teenager I was a consummate prankster. From the ages of nine to sixteen, I logged many, many hours on the phone, annoying random strangers. My favorite gag was to call someone in the small hours of the night, and when they groggily answered, I'd say perkily, *Hi! I got up for a sandwich . . . What did you get up for?* This never failed to provoke a gratifying string of four-letter words. During those school years, my neighbors received many unwanted pizzas, magazine subscriptions, Franklin Mint products, and unscheduled visits from plumbers.

Another favorite, of course, was Ring-n-Run, which has surely existed as long as there have been doors. My compadres and I tried all the variations on this childhood classic, including, of course, the infamous *burning bag trick*. You know the one—you place a bag of dogshit on your neighbor's doorstep, set it on fire, ring the doorbell, and hide. In theory, when your neighbor opens the door, he will see the fire, shout "Good heavens, there's a *fire* on the *doorstep!*" and stamp it out in a hurried panic—thus baptizing his shoes with crap. It's a brilliant, elegant scheme that never worked once. Either the fire would go out two seconds after I lit it, or—worse—no one would answer the door and I'd have to go stamp it out myself and spend the next two hours sitting on the curb with a sharp stick, scraping shit out of my sneaker treads.

The pranks got more sophisticated as I got older. I developed an unusual (and I believe unprecedented) stunt involving an egg. From grammar school on, my friends and I had spent every winter merrily hurling snowballs at cars, but there was no summertime equivalent of this happy sport—except for hurling *rocks*, which was too heinous even for us. So one June day, while we were hanging out at my friend Paul's house, I tossed a length of kite string over a powerline that traversed our street. I then took an egg, wrapped it in a paper towel, and tied it to one end of the string. With the other end of the string, I hoisted the egg to dangle about four feet above the road, or roughly the level of a car's windshield. I secured the loose end of the string by tying it to a telephone pole, and then we all ran into Paul's garage, shut the door, and stood by the windows to await the results.

Paul and I lived on Winston Road, a slow residential street. Cars were rare and cautious. The first few cars confronted by the mystery of what closely resembled *a scrotum floating above the road* slowed down to a halt, and then carefully drove around it. No one got out to investigate. They didn't know what it was, and they didn't *want* to know what it was.

We were getting bored with the whole thing when we heard it: the sound of a car roaring up Winston at what must have been sixty miles per hour. We crowded around the windows in anticipation. A white Ferrari flashed past us and whipped straight through the egg in a glorious burst of yellow goo—*and just kept going.*

We stared after the car in awestruck wonder. Was the driver not in the *least* concerned about what had just splattered across his windshield? Did he think it the droppings of an enormous pigeon? The spattered body of a grotesquely large insect? We pondered the matter silently as we gazed at the forlorn sight of a gooey paper towel undulating at the end of a string.

For a few weeks, we became obsessed with this egg business, moving the site of our experiments to Danny's house on Grant Road, one of the busiest thoroughfares in town. There, we suspended all sorts of things above the road: not just eggs (although they remained the favorite) but also grapefruits, stuffed animals, and once, a plastic baggie crammed full of oatmeal. There was a much greater likelihood of getting caught on Grant Road, so whenever we were in the process of setting everything up, we made sure to carry a physics textbook, a clipboard, and a pad of graph paper crawling with elaborate trigonometric diagrams. If caught, we planned to say that we were conducting a science project for school, that our construction was *intended to demonstrate the properties of angular momentum on objects of varying masses*. I can't imagine what on earth made us think that anyone—especially a cop—would have bought this sorry-ass excuse for creating what was literally *an accident waiting to happen*.

I really don't know if the other kids in town devoted such enormous efforts towards irritating other people. It seems to me that my circle of friends was particularly driven towards this anti-social form of entertainment out of a deep, aesthetic revulsion to the suburbs. We subconsciously sensed, in the keep-off-the grass, keeping-up-with-the-Jones's mentality of our town, a kind of Puritanical ideology which passionately embraced both boredom and passive consumption, and which harbored deep suspicions of any form of entertainment outside of sports and lawn maintenance. We longed to escape, but until the day when we could, we devoted ourselves to heroic, quixotic efforts to bring magic and life into this dead world by annoying the hell out of the people who lived there. Many years later, I discovered that a similar impulse had fueled anarchistic art movements throughout the twentieth century, and sensed a kindred spirit in the subversive antics of the Dadaists, the Surrealists, the Diggers, the English punks. Not so long ago, I came across the Situationist slogan painted on Parisian walls during the General Strike of May 1968: *Down with a world where the guarantee that we won't die of starvation has been purchased with the guarantee that we will die of boredom.* Upon encountering those words, I wished I could travel back in time to deliver that slogan to my teenage self, along with a nice can of red spraypaint.

Eventually, of course, we all got our wishes and left for college, a rite of passage so taken for granted that we didn't even understand what a luxury it was, made possible by the middle-class values that we all held in such contempt. You'd think life away from the suburbs would have freed me at last from my sociopathic tendencies, but alas, it was not so. A dormitory is a nicely encapsulated version of the suburbs, and living among six hundred students and a handful of scared adults lends itself easily to a prankster mentality. Indeed, this was the period when I formed a new group of like-minded friends, and devoted myself to what I will euphemistically refer to as *drunken hijinx.*

It's a pity, really. I wish we'd channeled our anger and energy into more productive pursuits—but don't we always wish that of our younger selves? Many of the friends I knew in college remain among the smartest, most interesting people I've ever met. They were well-read, creative, and capable of in-depth discussions on nearly any topic with great energy and wit. Literary, musical, and artistic interests cross-pollinated among us with the feverish intensity of the very young. We were hipster snobs who sneered at the frat houses, but our eggheaded, nihilistic romance with booze and drugs often led us to engage in exactly the kinds of stupid, destructive acts that occasionally earn fratboys a spot in the evening news, as the anchors slowly shake their heads in disgust. We seemed incapable of distinguishing *youthfully rebellious* acts from those that were *pathologically criminal.* Spending an evening strolling around the city while carrying a naked, life-size inflatable sex doll is kind of funny. Drunkenly hurling a heavy chair off a dormitory rooftop is not. There's a certain subversive charm to defacing random buildings with a spray-painted stencil of Mickey Mouse sporting a huge erection—although, in retrospect, I worry that those stencils may have prematurely destroyed the innocence of some young Disney fans. Considerably less charming would be placing a smoke bomb with a delayed cigarette fuse behind a public toilet in a crowded urban cafe. Well, actually, even thinking about it now, it *was* just a teensy bit funny when that woman came running out of the bathroom—mysteriously billowing with white smoke—and breathlessly exclaimed, "I don't understand it! I was just sitting there and the toilet burst into *flames!*"

Yeah—well, maybe you had to be there.

(Please, kids, for Christ's fucking sake, do not try this stunt yourselves. Not only is there the *totally unacceptable* risk that you may incur the hospitalization or actual death of other human beings, but you will almost certainly wind up being arrested as an arsonist, or worse, a terrorist. And also, this is *exactly* why no one likes a practical joker.)

Actually, common sense dictates that I should now officially declare that, um, I am *making all this up*—and given my ignorance of the statute of limitations and other legalities, it's probably best to cut short this self-incriminating Catalogue of Shame. Suffice it to say that my grades began to suffer, and I eventually dropped out for several years.

I can think of one incident during this time, however, that's worth relating. A female friend of mine—who occasionally dabbled in garden-variety college feminism—gave me a bunch of small, rectangular stickers emblazoned with the slogan THIS INSULTS WOMEN. You were supposed to stick them on beer advertisements featuring women with large, sexist breasts.

I put them in my wallet and forgot about them until, one day, I happened to be in the lobby of a K-Mart where there stood an array of those vending machines for kids—the kind where you put in a quarter and get a plastic bubble containing a toy worth considerably less than a quarter. Among the machines was a very unusual apparatus. A glass booth enclosed a mechanical chicken surrounded by brightly colored plastic eggs. When you put in a quarter, the chicken jerked around, cackled once or twice, and a plastic egg containing a toy popped out of slot below. The second I saw it, I whipped out a THIS INSULTS WOMEN sticker and placed it on the center of the glass.

Oh God, it was perfect.

When I later told my friend what I had done with her sticker, she laughed in spite of herself, and observed, "What's funny about it is that it's now *the sticker itself* that insults women."

For a long time, whenever I was feeling the melancholy gnaw of depression, I would remember that chicken and its double insult, and feel a little better. Years later, when I moved back to the suburbs to finish my degree—that is, around the same time I was ordering pizza as Andre Breton—I was inspired to print up stickers of my own, all variations on the THIS INSULTS WOMEN theme. On my computer, I printed up dozens of different labels:

THIS INSULTS SEXISTS

THIS INSULTS JUNKIES

THIS INSULTS AQUATIC MAMMALS

and finally, the all-purpose

THIS INSULTS YOU

I'd stick them on billboards in the subway while I was in the city to attend classes and to work at my part-time crappy job to pay for those classes. No matter how absurd my slogans became, I always found a poster that seemed to scream out for a particular sticker.

But my favorite one involved, once again, a chicken. As part of New York State's campaign against deadbeat dads, there was a clever poster in the bus terminal with the legend WHAT DO YOU CALL A FA-THER WHO FLIES THE COOP? Below this was a picture of a chicken wearing sneakers.

I reached into my bag of tricks and plastered the billboard with a sticker that read: THIS INSULTS POSTAL WORKERS.

I passed that billboard every evening on my dreary commute from school back to the suburbs, and it never failed to cheer me up.

A DAY AT THE BEACH

ON THURSDAY, I took a water taxi out to the Fire Island lighthouse museum with Lucy and her family. The museum was closed, but the park ranger was nice enough to let us into the lobby to watch a video about the lighthouse. "It's very homemade," she warned us as she popped it in the VCR, thus defusing my *sneering cynicism* before I could even get it started. Afterwards, Lucy and her family took the water taxi back to Ocean Beach, but I decided to walk, lured by rumors of a nude beach in the vicinity.

Sure enough, it was there. It was rather cold to be naked, but I suppose that naked sunbathing, like all competitive sports, has its diehard aficionados. There were more naked men than women. I noticed that there were two broad categories of people. The first were those who'd obviously invested a lot of time, labor and money in sculpting their bodies and were eager to show them off, regardless of the weather. The second category consisted of fat old men with greying pubic hair above their uncircumcised wienies; no longer in any sort of competition, they were happy to spend their golden years wallowing butt-naked in the sand. I saw only a few representatives of the middle class of good looks, and I suspect they were of the hippy-ish sort who find in public nakedness some kind of obscure social virtue.

Paradoxically, I felt self-conscious in my clothing: only my hands and face were uncovered. I felt that I must look as if I had come only to ogle naked bodies, which, of course, was true, but I didn't want to appear that way. I wanted to appear as a simple beach-stroller who happened to have wandered into a section of the beach where people didn't bother to cover their genitals. As my concession to free-spiritedness, I took off my shoes and socks. I removed the Bic lighter from the front pocket of my blue jeans, lest its tube-like shape be mistaken for arousal. Strolling around, I tried to affect a nonchalant air, a semblance of *cheerful indifference to the unclothed*.

But affecting all this nonchalance made it a little difficult to leer, which is what I really wanted to do. All the naked people were sun-bathing at the top of the beach, far away from the water, and I really couldn't think of any plausible reason to walk along the top of the beach. I saw a threesome of beautiful unclad women frolick-ing there, and briefly entertained the idea of asking them for the time, but I was wearing a watch, and undoubtedly, none of them were. There was a lovely woman near the sea, naked and crouching in the sand, but I averted my eyes. She was with her buff, tanned, long-haired boyfriend, and I felt a little ashamed to look in their direction. They might as well have belonged to a different species. Radiant with fitness and health, they were both magnificent exam-ples of the sublime beauty of the human physique in peak condi-tion, whereas I was a scrawny, chain-smoking, unnatural product of a modern lifestyle which had conditioned me to view the unclothed human body as an object of lust.

The whole experience was decidedly unerotic; a withering ex-perience, you might say.

The worst part is that I knew it would be this way. I'd been to nude beaches before.

All this gawking about in the nude beach was actually leading me in the wrong direction. I needed to walk east, not west. I re-versed direction and speedily trudged away from the naked ones. Once among the clothed, with whom I felt an renewed kinship, I be-gan to trudge slowly, the way trudging ought to be done. I walked with my feet in the freezing tide, in order to numb them against the miles of broken shells and sand through which I planned to trudge.

☼   ☼   ☼

Except, of course, for nude beaches, there is really nothing to see at the shore. There's the ocean, majestic and rolling, but once you've seen it, you've seen it. It's not going to *do* anything. The same with the beach itself; there isn't that much variation, after all, in the qual-ity of *sand*. So you start looking down, like everyone does, at the treasures tossed up by the sea, the shells, the rounded sea glass and stones, the driftwood, the Twinkie wrappers and beer cans and used condoms.

I saw a beautiful stone, almost perfectly round, streaked with an unusual, rhythmic pattern of translucent rose and white quartz. I picked it up and admired it as I walked. Then I saw another stone, wide and flat and lovely, spotted with black granite like a leopard. I looked at my old stone. It was starting to dry and didn't seem so beautiful anymore. I regretted picking it up. I coveted the other stone, the *leopard stone* (I had already named it) but the rule is you can only take one stone, otherwise you will wind up with pockets of crap when you get home. *You're so greedy*, I told myself. *You had to pick up the very first stone you saw.* I wanted to drop it, and get the leopard stone, but I knew that I would just see another stone I wanted later on. I put the first stone in my pocket, and trudged on, feeling its nagging, insistent heaviness weighing me down, reminding me that I had *picked the wrong stone.*

But soon I was to feel another nagging insistence. As everyone knows, there are no bathrooms on Fire Island's beaches. I had forgotten about the frequent demands of my kidneys when I so cavalierly decided to forgo the water taxi. I had no idea how far I had to go. I tried not to panic. I had been walking for quite a while; I was probably fairly close to Ocean Beach.

"Excuse me," I said to a woman walking her dog. "How far is Ocean Beach?"

"*Ocean Beach?*" she said, incredulously, as if I had asked her for directions to Osaka. "Oh, you have *quite* a way to go."

I nodded morosely, and watched her and her dog slowly recede towards the west. I looked around. To the east, there were the tiny forms of children prancing around in the surf, and farther on, a few prone bodies in the sand. To the west, the lady and her dog. Behind me, though, were the forbidding windows of a half-dozen beach houses; who knew what condemning eyes gazed from within?

Oh what the hell, I thought. I unzipped my trousers and opened the floodgates. Right into the foamy sea. No need to feel any guilt, I thought. It's not like it's a swimming pool. Emptying my bladder took a little longer than I'd anticipated. I could see a jeep coming towards me from the east, possibly a police car. *Come on, come on*, I said to myself, pushing with muscles I don't even know the names of. I zipped up in time to watch the police car roll past me. They waved. I waved. They moved on. I moved on.

Farther on, I found a horseshoe crab on its back, just beyond the reach of the tide, its articulated legs squirming in the air. I stared at it in horrified fascination. Its spiny tail wobbled futilely. *I will save this creature of the sea*, I resolved, *in spite of my revulsion to it*. The problem was that I didn't want to touch it. I looked in vain for a nearby piece of driftwood. Finally, I took one of my shoes out of my bag. Holding the shoe at arm's length, I gingerly attempted to flip the crab right side up. I got it partway over and slipped. The crab panicked and tried to cushion its fall by bending its pointed tail into the sand. Now it was propped up by its tail, forming a kind of crustacean lean-to, legs wriggling furiously. I tried again and this time managed to flip it right side up. It immediately began to crawl in circles. "No, no," I told it. "The sea is *that* way." Round and round it went. I began to wonder if I had somehow *broken* it. But I didn't know what more I could do to return it to its ancestral home. Some people approached, and I guiltily abandoned the crab to its own devices.

By the time I saw the blue water tower of Ocean Beach in the distance, my feet were raw, eroded, as it were, by the surf and sand. I decided to put my shoes on, seemingly a simple operation, but nothing is simple at the beach. I wanted to get the sand off my feet before I put them in my shoes, which involved the complicated operation of sitting on my butt, sticking my feet into the very edge of the tide, and then drying them off with my sock. The problem was that the rising tide came in so quickly that I barely had time to wipe off my foot before I had to scuttle back to avoid getting soaked. I was also distracted by a nearby woman sitting cross-legged, apparently attempting to meditate. I worried that my butt-scuttling presence was somehow corrupting her spiritual growth. I eventually managed to get one foot shoed and socked, and then, while holding the finished foot in the air, clumsily dressed the other. I hoped the woman would think I was practicing some form of yoga.

As always, I felt much happier in my shoes, and though I walked near the edge of the water, I was careful to avoid getting my feet wet. I finally spotted a landmark I knew, an elegant wood-paneled house with a large circular window featuring a telescope. I knew that house, not only because it was near the entrance to Ocean Beach, but also because I coveted it. I thought that if I lived there, I would learn *the secrets of the stars*. While I was standing there looking at it, the tide sloshed over my shoes, and my feet made sad, squishy noises all the way home.

NEIGHBOR

HAT IS IT about the word *neighbor* that fills us with such moral ambivalence? (Ah, the age-old dilemma: *love thy neighbor* or *drunkenly urinate on his doorstep at three in the morning?*) In the abstract, we use the word "neighbor" as if it refers to something more than the stranger who happens to live near us. *It's the neighborly thing to do* we say of our good deeds, as if moral virtue bubbles forth wherever random human beings happen to eat, sleep and shit in rough proximity. A neighbor is not a relative or a friend, but neighbors are commonly thought to inspire a warm and fuzzy camaraderie—as in Mr. Rogers' creepy invitation, *Won't you be my neighbor?*

On the other hand, the word *neighbor* is also invested with a peculiar paranoia, as in *What will the neighbors think?* I heard this a lot as a child because we had a lot to hide. It was a function of the social geometry of the suburbs—the inside of the house is for *us*; the outside is for *them*, The Neighbors. The Neighbors got the washed car, the mowed lawn, the friendly wave from across the street. *We* got the crusty unwashed dishes, the overflowing stacks of ancient newspapers, the dingy underwear strewn across the furniture. The Neighbors got my father leaving for work in a three-piece suit and tie, his face neatly shaven, his keys swinging smartly in his hand as he approached the gleaming car. *We* got the early morning performance of my father raging through the house in nothing but a pair of sagging jockey briefs and a single black sock, shouting violent and obscene threats against the *other* black sock (the *missing* sock, the stupid goddamn *cocksucking* sock) as my mother followed in his wake, hissing *Lower your voice—The Neighbors!*

Who were they, really, The Neighbors? They watched us like the eye of God, silent, patient, anonymous, ready to expose us all to scandal and ruin; they kept the primordial fury and squalor of our house sealed up tightly behind the orderly façade of lawn and car. But who exactly were they, these Neighbors? I knew most of the people who lived near us—crazy Mrs. Coogan, who collected antiques and stray cats; the compulsively neat Borowitz family, whose son actually ironed his *blue jeans*; the red-headed Metzger family with their ugly twin daughters—but surely these halfwits and incompetents, the subjects of much derision under my roof, weren't The Neighbors, that mythical entity talked about but unseen.

At times, the oppressive force The Neighbors exerted upon us seemed so darkly malevolent, so otherworldly, that I felt I compelled to launch a formal inquiry into the matter—which is to say, I spent some time sneaking around at night, spying into people's windows, conducting investigations of the burning-bag-on-the-doorstep variety—but all I could ascertain of the secret lives of the families around us was that they ate, watched television, and raged at each other in hushed and strained voices. They lived as we did—in a private universe of shame. On weekends, they made enormous efforts to impress one another, they mowed their lawns and bragged about their children. Between fighting and lawn maintenance, when did anyone have time to get together and discuss the shortcomings of my own family?

But then it came to me one day, standing by our chain link fence as my mother chatted with Mrs. Radeki (who lived next door) and the subject turned to Mrs. Coogan (who also lived next door, but on the other side of our house). In hushed tones, they systematically maligned every facet of Mrs. Coogan's existence—her cats and antiques, her delinquent son, her slutty daughter, her absent husband, her wretched taste in clothing, her fly-infested compost heap. Though I was a child, I could see that this character assassination infused my mother and Mrs. Radecki with a pleasure almost sexual; they practically rubbed their hands with glee. And I knew then what I should have known all along, that *we* were The Neighbors, that all of us who lived on that street were The Neighbors, that the only relief for the secret humiliations of family life lay in publicly heaping shame upon the other families, and that this network of furtive malice was, in fact, what made us a Neighborhood.

✿ ✿ ✿

As soon as I came of age, I escaped to the anonymity of city life, but something of the old suburban paranoia endures within, and I find myself compulsively speculating about the lives of my neighbors. Neighbors are different in the city, though. They live in your building, you see them by the mailboxes in the hall, but you rarely exchange more than brief greetings before shuffling back into the cramped seclusion of your apartment. There's little opportunity for gossip and, since no one knows anyone else, there's nothing to gossip about.

I have moved many times, and I've had many neighbors who've occupied my thoughts. I find every neighbor as mysterious as an uncracked nut. I wonder about their enigmatic comings and goings. I wonder about the odd noises and unpleasant smells that issue from their apartments. I have lingered in the corridors, and I have pressed my ears against the walls, but I never figure anything out.

Lately I've been thinking about the pretty Chinese girl who lives in the apartment above me. Since there's no intercom system for the building, she has one of those remote-control buzzers you can buy at Radio Shack. It's a little doorbell-like thing that is supposed to be attached near the entrance of the building, and when you press the button, it rings a wireless speaker upstairs. But the buzzer keeps falling off. Nearly every day, it seems, I go outside and find it lying on the sidewalk like a squashed insect. I bring it inside and set it on the mail table in the foyer. Usually, by the next morning, I'll see that she's stuck it back to the doorframe. By the afternoon, though, I'll notice that it's fallen to the ground again. On the doorframe itself, I often see evidence of her attempts to fasten it securely: scotch tape, masking tape, blotches of dried glue.

Sometimes I feel a little guilty about bringing it back inside. I've wondered if she subconsciously *prefers* to having it lying on the ground since it winds up there so often. I try to think about the situation from her point of view: every morning she attaches the buzzer to the doorframe, and every evening she comes home to find it inside the building on the mail table. It must be very frustrating. Perhaps she doesn't know that the buzzer falls off on its own. Perhaps she thinks that someone pulls it off, out of malice, and then brings it inside. But she can never be sure—does it fall off on its own, or is it being *pulled* off? Are her neighbors good Samaritans, who nobly rescue her faulty buzzer from the sidewalk, or are they petty vandals, who find a strange delight in making her life a little more miserable?

I imagine that this is why the Chinese girl is so shy when I pass her in the hall. She is in a constant state of uncertainty about the character of her neighbors.

The buzzer falls off because she uses inferior materials to fasten it to the doorframe. She's using the wrong type of glue. I think about buying a small bottle of superglue and leaving it on the mail table next to the buzzer. Then she would know that we, her neighbors, are good Samaritans, and not the petty vandals she sometimes suspects us of being.

But I don't buy the superglue, because I can see where it will lead. I know the perversity of my soul. If she uses my superglue to fasten the buzzer to the frame, I know that then I will be tempted to yank it back off and lay it on the mail table in the foyer. The Chinese girl's state of uncertainty will reach a fevered pitch. She will be in a kind of agnostic purgatory, in which she must doubt either the goodness of her neighbors or the power of superglue.

She looks so sweet and shy in the halls that I just can't bring myself to plunge her into this sort of neurotic limbo.

I guess I'm just not that kind of neighbor.

October's Rain

Yet how much room for memory there is
In the loose girdle of soft rain.

—Hart Crane

ETWEEN THE DROWSY, EROTIC MONTHS of summer (when the long days pass us by too quickly, like a chain of broken promises) and the sterile gloom of winter (when it seems that darkness and cold will never leave the world again), lies October, the loveliest month in all the pages of the calendar. We speak of Autumn as if it were a proper season but Autumn is only a short passage between the seasons, a brief and melancholy interlude that spans a few scant weeks in October, lovely October, when the air is crisp with the sharp, sad smell of woodsmoke and decaying leaves. That earthy, sepia smell is to me the smell of nostalgia, because Autumn is not so much experienced as remembered. Every Autumn is every other Autumn, winding down the staircase of my years, so that I can no longer remember whether it was last week or last year that I spent that wonderfully sad, rainy Saturday in October, walking around the city with a broken umbrella.

It was windy and rainy, that drizzly, cold rain which seems to fall sideways rather than down, and threatens to last for days—a terrible day to be out, but I was lonely in my cramped little apartment, where nothing ever happens, and I wanted to go out into the wet world. The instant I stepped outside, I was ambushed by a blast of windy rain, the tails of my overcoat whipping out behind me like a fluttering cape. I struggled with the spring mechanism on my umbrella, and it finally popped open; but the wind caught it at once and popped it inside out, so that I was now holding a useless object resembling either a very small broom or a very large exclamation point. With some effort I managed to make it look more like an umbrella, but several metal spokes now protruded from the ripped canvas like menacing, skeletal fingers.

I leaned into the wind and began to walk with great determination, as if I had somewhere to go. Wet candy wrappers and plastic bags hurled past me, eager to flee the city, and the slender, bare branches of New York City trees pitched violently in the wind, reminding me of my umbrella, which was not really much of an umbrella any more, just some steel spokes with a bit of black material hanging between. I was reminded then, of that line in a Yeats' poem, the one where he says

> *An aged man is but a paltry thing*
> *A tattered coat upon a stick*

and just as I thought of it, a tiny old man stumbled past me, dragged along by his enormous umbrella, which he clutched desperately as the wind pulled him down the street like a sailboat. *That poor old man*, I thought, *he'll be swept away like the candy wrappers and newspapers, and no one will ever know what happened to him.*

And then I thought: someday, I too will be old, and my wife of many years will sit in vain in our dingy apartment, waiting for my return, and the cup of tea she has made for me will grow cold as she sits waiting, waiting by a drafty window in October for her husband, who loved poetry, and used to read her those poignant lines from Rilke's "Autumn Day"—

> *Whoever has no home now, will never have one*
> *Whoever is alone will stay alone,*
> *will sit, read, write long letters through the evening*
> *and wander on the boulevards, up and down,*
> *restlessly, while the dry leaves are blowing.**

Yes, that's sad, I thought. *The old man is sad, and I'm sad, too, a sad figure in a soggy overcoat with a sad umbrella which is really just a metaphor for my sadness.* Over and over again I ran this sad and useless train of thoughts through my sad old head, until I became bored with it. The word

---

*Excerpted from *The Selected Poetry of Rainer Maria Rilke*, edited and translated by Stephen Mitchell.

sad, however, reminded me of my roommate in college many years ago, who liked beer and hated Ronald Reagan with equal measures of passion, and who (I now recalled) showed up at the dorm cafeteria one Saturday morning in October wearing black eyeliner, and when we asked him why, he replied, *Because I'm sad today.*

My roommate made sadness seem as beautiful as a Charlie Chaplin movie, and now I remembered how he and I used to stay up all night drinking beer, listening to the Throwing Muses, to that strange, jarring song which contained the line *Like an old man in a dress*. I never knew what that line meant, but *Like an old man in a dress* now seemed to bear a certain similarity to *Like a sad man with a broken umbrella*, so it suited me fine.

Like an old man in a dress, I thought to myself, holding my broken umbrella before me like a tattered shield. As I passed other people fighting their way through the wind and the rain with their own tattered umbrellas, I would smile a melancholy smile and think, *Like an old man in a dress*.

I stopped in front of the dirty, rain-streaked window of a music store to gaze at some expensive electric guitars, and they seemed lonely and forlorn. They were too expensive for anyone to buy. Now I passed the Hells Angels Club on Third Street, and even the motorcycles seemed dejected and cheerless. No one would ride them on a day like today, not even *an old man in a dress*.

As I passed a wire trash can, I stuffed my broken umbrella into the heap of wet refuse. It was a terrible act of betrayal, we had been through a lot together, but enough was enough. As I walked away I heard it whispering my name, *Tyler, Tyler*, in the gloomy, metallic voice of a squashed insect, but I chose to leave it in its sorrow, and carry on alone in mine.

I now found myself, soggy and cold, at the intersection of street and avenue, unsure which way to go. It didn't matter which way I went, because I wasn't going anywhere in particular, but still I couldn't decide. *Yes, it's always like that for me*, I thought, *I'm like a leaf tossed about by the wind*. I gazed up the avenue and I gazed down the street. Candy wrappers and little old men blew every which way. I realized I was standing in front of a cafe, and looked through the window.

The room looked warm and inviting: under the coppery glow of incandescent bulbs, people sat chatting and reading books at dark wooden tables as they drank coffee from steaming porcelain mugs and munched their buttered croissants and muffins.

In the back of the cafe, a mottled brick wall housed a fireplace, and above the mantel hung a print of a painting I knew well: Henri Rousseau's *The Sleeping Gypsy*. I also own a print of this painting, and it has hung above my bed in every apartment in which I have ever lived.

But seeing it on the brick wall inside of a cozy cafe as I stood outside in the cold October rain was different than seeing it in my bedroom; it was as if I saw it for the first time: the gypsy in his multicolored robes, sleeping peacefully on desert sand under a pale moon in a deep blue sky. Beside the gypsy lies his mandolin and water jug, and behind him stands a lion, huge and startling, bending his head to sniff the robes of the gypsy. What a strange moment! The lion has come upon the sleeping man, but the man, because sleeping, displays no fear to startle the lion. The lion has never seen such a man, a man at peace. This is a night when the lion can stop being a lion long enough to contemplate the ways of men. Yes, under such extraordinary circumstances, the ancient enmity of lions and men becomes irrelevant; the lion's attitude is one of curiosity, not aggression, and so the gypsy sleeps undisturbed. I wondered now, as I had long ago when I'd first seen the painting, about the gypsy. In his peaceful sleep, was he at all aware, even in his dreams, of this magical, dangerous encounter? I have always thought the painting captured the floating, surreal mood of *a moment of suspension*, that sudden instance of peace and wonder which comes to us odd and unsummoned in midst of our tumultuous lives, that fleeting moment when we see ourselves as if from outside, as if in a dream. But what if the man were to awake?

With some melancholy, I realized that I had not really looked at the painting for years. I had once loved it so much that I bought a print to hang above my bed, but it had quickly become familiar to me, and finally invisible. And now I stood outside the cafe, wanting to be in that place that seemed as magical and inviting as a painting to me, but I thought, If I go inside, I will no longer be in the rain, and the cafe will become familiar and ordinary to me, like the print of *The Sleeping Gypsy* that hangs upon my bedroom wall. Surely the cafe was more beautiful, and sad, from the outside looking in.

I had stood there a long time when an attractive woman inside the cafe gestured to me, as if to invite me in. I stared at her in wonder, certain that there must be some misunderstanding, when her face suddenly shifted and became a face I knew: a woman I had known for over ten years, our friendship formed during that sepia-toned era of interminable evenings spent drinking beer to the sound of the Throwing Muses. There she sat, alone at a little wooden table, a newspaper and mug of coffee set before her, and I forgot my sadness, my bittersweet, wonderful, October sadness, and walked inside.

JURY DUTY

I KNEW IT WAS A MISTAKE to vote. There's something un-American about voting, after all. I mean, sure, it's great that we *can* vote, but to actually go through with it—to get hold of one of those hard-to-find registration forms, fill it out, wait for your voting card in the mail and then show up on a workday at some high school you never heard of and stand on line to pull a lever on those ancient machines—well, if you ask me, it all smacks of some kind of nutty European socialism. But I'd done it—even though I knew my vote was more or less meaningless, that at any rate the Electoral College (whatever *that* is) would cast the *actual* votes for one of two schmucks—and *that's* how they must've gotten my new address.

Jury duty. Dreaded words, like *April 15th* or *Department of Motor Vehicles*. You could defer it for six months, but why put off the inevitable? Besides, I had nothing better to do. So, at 7:30 a.m., I flopped out of bed and dragged myself down to the courthouse, navigating my way through the maze-like corridors of the mayor's concrete barricades until I found a bland, squat building, as brown as a turd.

So I had somehow managed to arrive, bleary-eyed, at the appointed hour. Well, not exactly. I was about fifteen minutes late, and when I got inside—to a dark, cavernous room that looked vaguely like a movie theatre, with rows and rows of seats—a video was just beginning on the TV monitors that hung over the room. I couldn't find a seat, so I stood by a wall to watch.

The video vaguely resembled an infomercial. Several Ordinary People—a black construction worker, an Asian lawyer, an Hispanic woman pushing a stroller—testified about their real feelings towards jury duty. "I mean, how could I judge someone else?" the woman was saying. "I didn't think I could do it." An elderly black man, leaning on his cane, chuckled ruefully and confided, "Jury duty is a real pain in the neck." We all laughed. *Tell it like is, brother.* At least they had a sense of humor about it. But then, to my surprise, Ed Bradley from *60 Minutes* came on the screen, looking very grave.

He told us that jury duty was indeed a so-called pain in the neck, but it was also the *very foundation of our judicial system*, and *an essential component of our democracy*. A shot of the Acropolis appeared on screen, and Bradley's disembodied voiced continued, "You see, it all started back in Ancient Greece . . ."

Everyone groaned.

After the video, an officer of the court came to the front of the room and announced that certain people were automatically excused from jury duty, and that if they fit into the following categories they should line up in the left aisle to have their notices stamped. "Non-US-citizens," he called out, and several people got up. "Parents who are the sole caretakers of their children during the day. People who have doctor's notes. People who have airline tickets for any flight during the next three days." Various people stood up, beaming with delight. We looked at them enviously. I wondered if there were categories like *People who have houseplants* or *People who just feel kind of tuckered out*.

The officer continued. "Anyone who has ever been convicted of a felony." There was a short pause, and then several people shuffled to their feet, looking sheepish, and took their place in line. I noticed a grizzled-looking old man with long hair, wearing a shirt emblazoned with a big marijuana leaf, advertising a newspaper called *The Daily Buzz*. On the back of the T-shirt was the legend MEAN PEOPLE SUCK under a caricature of Rudy Giuliani. In my mind, I nicknamed this man *Snuffy McGoo*, and wondered if he was one of the convicted felons. I could imagine Snuffy McGoo talking to his friends through a haze of pot smoke: "Yeah, I once got called for jury duty, but *The Man* wouldn't let me serve."

After the unwed mothers and felons left, the officer explained that *People who didn't have employers*—that is, people like me—would be paid forty dollars a day by the state. I was very happy to hear this. Forty dollars a day was forty dollars more than I would have made if I'd stayed home. I now began to feel differently about jury duty. I began to think of it as a *job*.

We were told that we would eventually be summoned to serve on a particular case and to just wait patiently until that time. We were supposed to sign out if we left the room. We were allowed to use laptop computers if we had them (I didn't), but had to go into the hall if we wanted to use cellular phones. The officer left, and everyone settled into a comfortable funk.

I now discovered that there were two small rooms adjacent to the main room: a reading room, with a big desk in the middle and a lot of little desks to the side, very much like a college library, and a TV room, which was exactly the same, but with a TV. I found a desk in the reading room, feeling a certain smug superiority to the TV people. I imagined that we, in the reading room, would make far better jurors than those slack-jawed yokels watching Jenny Jones in the next room. A woman's cellphone rang, and the rest of us rattled our newspapers and glared over our spectacles until she left the room.

About an hour passed before the officer returned, announcing that he was going to call out the names of several people, who were to report to a courtroom where some lawyers would select or reject them for the actual jury. He stressed that even if you weren't actually picked for the jury, it had nothing whatsoever to do with you personally. I felt a flush of anticipation. I wasn't like that Hispanic woman in the video: I *knew* I could judge someone. In fact, I can be *very* judgmental, and I wanted to put my talent to professional use. But as the officer began to read the list of names, I suddenly knew that I wasn't going to be picked. I wasn't. I was rejected before I even had a chance to be rejected. It was just like grammar school.

I trudged back to the reading room, but just as I took my seat, the officer announced that we should all take a half an hour break.

Outside, the day was sweltering and humid, and the security guards were wearily smoking cigarettes, trying to keep themselves awake. I went to a deli across the street to get something to eat. There was a family—a mother, a father, and two small children—wandering around the salad bar, taking turns sampling from the bins. "Mommy, this is *good*," the little girl said, stuffing something that looked like sliced beets into her mouth. "Well, if it's good, then shut your mouth and eat it," the mother retorted.

While I was paying for my food, the Korean woman behind the counter suddenly leaned forward and shouted past me, "Sir! Sir! You haven't paid for anything yet!"

The father looked up and dismissed her with a wave of his hand. "We ain't finished getting our food yet, lady," he protested around mouthfuls of bread.

The Korean woman scowled. "They eat like that for half an hour already," she told me in despair.

"These things happen," I observed, uselessly.

There was a park next to the court building, and I sat down near the entrance to eat. The park was full of a strange variety of people. Two men sat across from me chatting amiably, but whenever a woman passed—any woman—one of them would rise to his feet, shout, "God bless you! God *bless* you!" and then resume his conversation (which seemed to be about good places to go fishing). Nearby, a well-dressed man sat on a bench, conversing intensely with a shabby old woman surrounded with bags, while his baby daughter toddled after a pigeon, arms outstretched. The pigeon easily managed to keep one step ahead of her, but then suddenly—as if weary of the whole futile exercise—came to an abrupt halt. Confused, the little girl skidded to a stop. Here was the object of her desire, presenting itself at last, and she didn't know what to do. She shook her head, dashed towards her father, and threw herself in his lap. *There's a lesson in that*, I thought, but it was too hot to figure out what it was.

Two people I'd seen in the courtroom—a pretty young woman, and a clumsy-looking man in his early twenties—emerged from the park. The man was speaking animatedly, but as they passed, the girl looked at me desperately and rolled her eyes. I then realized that they had probably met in the courtroom, and the young woman had made the mistake of speaking with this guy and now couldn't shake him off. It had been a mistake the way speaking to a stranger on an airplane is a mistake.

I followed them into the building, where we stood in line to go through the metal detector. For some reason, the clumsy young man kept setting it off. He divested himself of keys, wallet, coins, watch, but it kept going off. They pulled him to one side, waved one of those wands over him, and let him through.

At the elevator bank, he kept talking about it. "That was really weird," he said over and over again, flushed with excitement, as the

girl nodded wearily. *Perhaps it's the plate in your head*, I thought. I secretly gave him the name *Boris Bonehead.*

When I returned to the courtroom, I found that the reading
room and the TV room were packed with carpetbaggers who had
taken advantage of the short break. In despair, I looked around the
main room for a seat, finally settling down next to an extremely old
man, who, implausibly, had rollerblades tucked under his seat. I
had already consumed all the good parts of my newspaper, and now,
out of boredom, prepared to read the business section.

After about forty-five minutes, the court officer emerged and
told us we could break for lunch but would have to be back by two.
By two! It was only noon! I wandered back out into the heat, and
meandered aimlessly around lower Manhattan for two hours.

Soon after I returned, the officer came out and read another list
of names. Mine wasn't one of them. I saw Boris get up with his companion. *He'll make a terrible juror*, I thought. *He has a plate in his head.*
As they were leaving the room, another young woman spotted them
and dashed over to join them. Delighted exclamations all around,
followed by hugs. So this was a chance encounter between friends,
and since this new woman was clearly well-acquainted with both
Boris and his companion, I had been wrong about the accidental
nature of their relationship. They'd already known each other. For
some reason, this plunged me into despair. If I was wrong about
Boris Bonehead, I could be wrong about anything. I would be a terrible juror. It was just as well they didn't call me, I thought miserably.
I didn't know how to judge anyone.

The room had emptied out quite a bit now. An hour or so passed
very slowly. Some more people were called to serve on various ju-
ries. I didn't get called. Time took on an almost palpable quality, like
a thick, gooey sauce. Row after row of people sat in various states
of decomposition, snoozing behind their newspapers, draped over
their chairs like rag dolls. No one spoke. I was so bored I got up to go
to the men's room, although my need was less than urgent. While
I was in there, I noticed a sandwich lying on the floor of the stall. I
bent down to look at it: it looked like ham and cheese, with one bite
missing. Back in the reading room, I tried to imagine various scenar-

ios in which a half-eaten sandwich might wind up on the floor of a bathroom stall. It seemed like the work of Snuffy McGoo.

I yawned. I decided to go have a cigarette, even though I didn't particularly want one.

Bizarrely, everything outside was exactly as it had been several hours ago. The guards were smoking, the little girl was with her father and the bag lady, the two men were still blessing women and talking, only now they were talking about *Star Trek*. I began to wonder if someone *paid* all these people to sit in the park. If they were, I don't know, *municipal extras*. I mean, who sits in a park for five hours on a sweltering hot weekday?

Across the park, I saw a homeless man throwing bread at pigeons. He wasn't throwing bread *to* the pigeons—he was taking great hunks of what seemed to be stale Italian bread and hurling them *at* the pigeons with all his might. The pigeons exploded into flight, circled once and floated back to the ground, where the man was waiting for them with a fresh hunk of bread. Another homeless man, apparently an acquaintance, dashed up and angrily grabbed the bread out of the first man's hand. Shaking his head in disgust, he tossed the bread into a trash barrel. The first man glared at him, fished out the bread, and furiously hurled a piece at a nearby pigeon. The second man wrestled the remaining pieces away from him, and they stood there arguing. Finally, they sat down on the bench together, as if they had reached some sort of truce.

I'd finished my cigarette. It was 4:30 in the afternoon. Back in the courtroom, the officer was speaking to everyone, and I sat down to hear what he was saying. We were done, he told us. We could go home now, and, he assured us, we wouldn't be called again for four years. He thanked us for helping sustain the American system of justice, and with a sigh of relief, we all rushed out of the building, eager to return to the rich, vibrant tapestry of our lives.

CLINTON STREET DAYS

WHEN I FIRST MOVED TO NEW YORK, some fifteen years ago, I rented a tiny cockroach-infested studio on Clinton Street on the Lower East Side. I loved it. Living on Clinton Street was like living in a foreign country. Nearly everyone who lived there was Puerto Rican or Dominican and all the store signs were in Spanish. There were only three sorts of businesses on Clinton Street: bakeries, bridal shops, and heroin dealers. (These last operated out of storefronts half-heartedly stocked with laundry detergent and dusty old cans of Alpo.) This mysterious three-sided economy made the neighborhood seem even more exotic to me.

Even during working hours, the street bustled with activity. People rushed up and down the street, calling to each other in Spanish over the blare of a dozen radios blasting salsa and merengue music. Although much of the neighborhood seemed to be unemployed, there was nonetheless a great sense of industriousness everywhere.

I particularly remember the man who used to sweep the street. Scruffy and tattered, he always wore a dirty white T-shirt over a pair of ragged blue jeans held up by an actual piece of rope, like a cartoon hobo. He had the cheerful, weather-beaten face of a chronic drunk, and yet he always seemed to be up by dawn. When I'd go off to work in the morning, I'd see him out there in the middle of Clinton Street, sweeping with the ecstatic, maniacal fury of a whirling dervish, as if God had chosen him alone to single-handedly clean the entire city in one giant, demented effort. Cars piled up behind him, blaring their horns, or swerved dangerously around him, but nothing could break his fanatical concentration. I have never seen a man so utterly devoted to his work while so utterly ineffective. Although he labored all morning without rest, he never actually swept anything into a pile. He just pushed it back and forth, all over the street.

One day, I found he had switched occupations. He was as ragged as ever, and still in the middle of the street, but now he'd set a policeman's cap at a jaunty angle on his greasy head, and had tied a two-by-four to the rope around his waist as a makeshift nightstick. Around his neck, he had fastened a tin whistle with a bit of string. He directed traffic with the same deranged intensity he had applied to street sweeping. He blew his whistle furiously and snapped out his arms with triumphant abandon as he attempted to guide traffic onto the sidewalk.

I developed a certain fondness for the man. I found myself impressed by his sincere, if somewhat misapplied, sense of social responsibility, and I admired the gusto with which he threw himself into his tasks. He certainly worked harder than I ever did. My enthusiasm lessened, however, when he took to sleeping inside the foyer of my building, in a cardboard box tucked under the stairwell. He didn't make a mess, and he was always back out in the street by morning, but I resented having to tiptoe up the stairs in order not to wake him.

I don't know who had set him up there, but I suspect it was the super: a fat, irritable Dominican woman who had many unsavory relatives. Whether or not the street-sweeper was one of them, I never figured out for sure, but several others lived in or near the building, and would periodically gather *en masse* to cram themselves into her tiny studio apartment for food, music, and loud arguments. Her relatives were always traipsing in and out of the building, but the one I'd see the most often was her nephew, a slovenly derelict who lived in the building—in an actual apartment—but who preferred to spend his days hanging around on the stoop as a kind of *de facto* doorman. Whenever I'd enter or leave the building, I'd find him waiting there, grinning moronically, as if there were no one in the entire world he'd rather see. "Heya, Papi," he'd say, disconcertingly spreading that stupid smile a little wider across his unshaven face.

One evening he came knocking at my door around midnight. Not entirely happy to see him there at that hour, I asked what he wanted.

He smiled hopefully. "Papi, you got a dollar?"

I stared at him. "What?"

He scratched his head and broadened his smile. "All I need's a *dollar*," he said, shuffling his feet like some bashful six-year-old. The effect was entirely repulsive.

I was annoyed. "Why don't you go to your aunt?"

"Well . . ." he said, sheepishly, "she's sleeping." He shuffled about a bit more, and then switched tactics by adopting an earnest man-to-man expression. "This is how it is, Papi," he explained. "I want to get a beer and she don't like me to drink."

He didn't get the dollar.

Some weeks later, when I ran into him at his usual spot in front of the building, I immediately noticed something different about him. A long, nasty-looking slash, bristling with stitches, ran down the left side of his face. He wasn't smiling anymore.

"What happened?" I asked.

He shrugged and looked at the ground. "I got some problems with some people," he mumbled. He didn't want to talk about it, but it was easy to guess what had happened. In that neighborhood, a slash down the face meant that you had stiffed a drug dealer, and had been marked as a bad customer.

❀   ❀   ❀

Actually, I think everyone but me who lived in the building was related to the super, with the exception of the punkrock couple who lived in the apartment directly above me.

Physically, they made a strange match, as if they'd been paired by God to demonstrate the versatility of the human form and its wide range of model designs. She was a short, dumpy white girl with bleached blond hair, and he was a tall, lanky black guy with dreadlocks. At night, I'd hear them screaming at each other with murderous fury, but whenever I met them in the hall they always smiled and said hello.

Once they invited me up for a beer. I've certainly never been a paragon of clean living, but even to me the squalor in which they lived was utterly appalling. Empty beer cans and heaps of garbage—burger wrappers, half-eaten slices of pizza, rotting containers of Chinese food—lay strewn around a ripped-up mattress occupying the center of the room. Someone had knocked large gaping holes through the plaster of the walls, apparently at random, and the words MISSING FOUNDATION had been spray-painted above the window. Roaches swarmed all over everything.

"It's the mattress," my hostess explained matter-of-factly. "I don't know why but they love it."

She sounded almost affectionate. A sudden wave of queasiness forced me to turn my attention away from the floor. I noticed that someone had haphazardly glued several egg-cartons to the surface of the walls and the door, and I asked why.

"Soundproofing, man," the boyfriend said. "I used to play the drums, you know?" By way of illustration, he drummed the air frenetically, but then suddenly stopped and frowned. "Yeah, but I had to sell them," he said, gloomily. "You know how it is."

I nodded, as if I did.

Although they invited me up again from time to time, I always managed to excuse myself. But one night, at about three in the morning, a sharp insistent rapping at my window jolted me out of my sleep. With bleary eyes, I stared into the dark night, and made out the ghoulish face of the punkrock girl peering into my room from the fire escape. With her pale skin and heavily mascaraed eyes, she looked exactly like a vampire.

I squinted at her hazily, partly convinced that I was having a nightmare, but then she banged again on the glass and I bolted up from the bed, heart pounding. "Jesus Christ, what are you *doing*?" I shouted.

"Relax, man, it's *okay*," she said in a tone of distinct annoyance, apparently put out by my bug-eyed reaction. Her voice was muffled by the windowpane. "I just need to use your *phone*," she explained.

"My *phone*?" I repeated, baffled. She made it all seem so ordinary, like knocking on the door for a cup of sugar.

"Yeah," she said, nodding. "Can I use your phone?"

"Right *now*?" I asked, with a helpless gesture that was meant to encompass the entire situation—the darkness of the room, the distance from my bed to the window, the late hour, the unusual and creepy proximity of the punkrock girl to the interior of my fifth-floor apartment *from the outside of the building.*

She shot me a withering look of disgust. "Oh, just forget it, man." She shook her head at the uncoolness of it all, and crawled back up the fire escape.

❀ ❀ ❀

It wasn't much later that I decided I'd had enough of Clinton Street, and found a new place on Avenue C. At the time, this seemed like a vast improvement, to get away from the wedding boutiques and bakeries. Avenue C had an even more limited economy consisting primarily of barber shops. These were always packed with young men standing around waiting for a turn in the elevated chair. It seemed to me that the same young men also took turns doing the actual haircutting, and I eventually gave up trying to distinguish customers from barbers.

My window came equipped with a heavy accordion gate. Still haunted by the memory of the punkrock girl, I made sure to lock it every night. But I never had any nocturnal visitors in that apartment—or indeed, any unexpected visitors at all—except for the time the former tenant showed up at my door. He said he wanted some things he'd left behind. I thought this a strange request, since I had already been living there for nearly six months.

Furthermore, the items in question were junk—a large plywood cable spool that served as my dinner table, a few plastic dishes, a single place-setting of cheap silverware, a dish-drying rack, and a nearly-collapsed foam couch that could be unfolded, with some difficulty, into a mushy sort of mattress.

I didn't want to surrender these worthless items because I used them on a daily basis (especially the awful couch, which was my bed), but I felt it politic to keep things civil. When I'd first moved in, the super had mentioned that the former tenant was a boxer, and now that he actually stood at my door, I could see it was true. Although lean enough to be a featherweight, his tattooed arms rippled with knotted muscle, and he wore an intensely anxious expression that seemed ready to ignite into open hostility at the slightest provocation.

So I told the boxer that he could have the stuff, but explained—with the ineptness of an unpracticed liar—that this was "an inconvenient time." I couldn't think of *why* this particular Saturday afternoon was such an inconvenient time, so I just left it at that and nervously asked if he could come back next week. I was nervous because it was obvious that only the thinnest veneer of social convention restrained him from simply walking in and taking whatever he wanted.

But surprisingly, he readily agreed to the arrangements I'd proposed, and left promptly. I figured that if he showed up again I simply wouldn't open the door, and so for a few anxiety-tinged weeks I waited for a knock at the door. But it never came. After a month had passed, I realized that no one was going to take away my foam couch or wooden spool.

For a long time I wondered about the encounter, about why he had shown up after all that time, and why he had never returned, and eventually came to suspect that I had met him in the midst of a bad domestic situation that had since somehow been repaired. The life of a boxer is a lonely one, fraught with difficult challenges and strained relationships, as I knew from that Simon & Garfunkel song.

Anyway, by then I had my own domestic situation to worry about. I'd fallen behind in my rent.

At first it was only a month. I'd been going out a lot and somehow spent most of my paycheck on beer and restaurants, and didn't have enough left for the rent. I decided to head over to Fourth Street to visit my landlord, a strangely cheerful Korean whom I'd met briefly only once before, when I'd signed the lease.

In his office, a cramped, poorly lit storefront, layers and layers of dingy keys on hooks cascaded down the walls like some strange metallic fungus. As my eyes adjusted to the dim light, I saw that keys clung, insect-like, to every available surface: the sides of rusty old file cabinets; the backs of doors; had accumulated in boxes and buckets around the room; lay scattered, randomly, across the floor. In the midst of all the keys, behind an ancient steel desk (overflowing with keys), sat my landlord, Buddha-like, his expression benign and patient, as though he had been awaiting my arrival for untold aeons, during which the keys had spawned and proliferated with lusty abandon. A coppery smell pervaded the room.

Nervously, I explained that this particular month had been tight for me (I neglected to mention the bars and restaurants), but I'd be able to pay him half of what I owed with next month's rent, and—

He waved me off before I could finish. "No problem," he said in heavily accented English. He smiled serenely. "Take your time. You pay me later."

I stood there for a moment, waiting for him to lay out some kind of arrangement, but that seemed to be all he had to say, so I quietly let myself out, leaving him alone with his keys.

I left with the best intentions, but my landlord's saint-like response to my late payment only encouraged my negligence. When the next month rolled around, I not only failed to make a payment on my last month's rent, but I failed to pay the current month as well. I didn't have the courage to return to the Temple of the Keys. I was afraid that his enigmatic tranquility might mask an equally formidable capacity for rage. In dread, I waited for the phone to ring, but he never called. Eventually, I wound up owing three months rent, and I knew something had to be done. After much thought, I decided to cut my losses and move out altogether. As a gesture of goodwill, I left behind the mushy couch and the plywood spool.

❀　❀　❀

After I left Avenue C, I sublet an apartment on Sixth Street near Avenue A from a young filmmaker who had decided to move back in with her parents for the summer in order to save money for a documentary she was making about dominatrices and their clients.

"Who *are* their clients?" I asked her, as she gathered up a few last items to take with her.

She closed the lid of the box she'd been packing, and sighed. "Mostly lawyers," she said, sounding weary of the entire subject.

I liked living in someone else's apartment. Although tiny, and cheaply furnished, the filmmaker had made the place pleasant and orderly in a way that I never would have been able to achieve on my own. She had an excellent library, which was like the library I might have accumulated in a parallel universe—all books exactly suited to my own eclectic tastes, but most of which I'd never heard of. I spent my evenings plowing through them at random. Just across the street stood the famous Sidewalk Café (which had an excellent breakfast special), and I was delighted to be only a half-block away from the bustling freak parade of Avenue A.

The filmmaker hadn't been sure whether she was actually allowed to sublet her apartment, so she'd instructed me to pretend I was her cousin in the event that I ran into her landlord, upon whom life had bestowed the unfortunate name of Pincus Plod. One Sunday afternoon, after I'd been living there for a few weeks, he showed up.

I'd been sitting in bed reading when I became aware of a soft but persistent knocking at the door, almost like the steady tapping of old heating pipes in the winter. I didn't know how long it had been going on. I opened the door, and gazed down at a tiny, bent-over old man, with a great round head like a turnip sparsely decorated with a few tufts of white hair. The turnip-head looked peeved and irritable. I knew without a doubt that this could only be Pincus Plod.

In a quavering, Yiddish-inflected voice full of outrage, he sputtered out a barrage of questions. *What, you don't hear me knocking?* (Sorry, I was reading.) *Reading! Who are you?* (The tenant's cousin.) *Her cousin! Where's the rent?*

This turned out to be a more complicated question. My arrangement with the filmmaker was that I'd send her the rent, and she'd mail a separate check to the landlord. Earlier that week, I'd found in my mailbox a mysterious letter addressed to "Sixth Street Corporation," which had been returned in the mail for lack of a zipcode; I'd assumed it was something the filmmaker had sent before leaving. I spent a few harried minutes rummaging through the apartment, and now produced the crumpled envelope. With shaking hands, Mr. Plod tore it open, revealing a check. He gave me a long meaningful stare that somehow made me feel guilty, as though the filmmaker, the post office, and I had all conspired to make an old man's life a little more miserable. Without another word, he turned away and shuffled down the stairs.

We would encounter each other in the halls a few more times, and eventually I worked up the nerve to ask him if any other apartments were available. He shook his turnip-head apoplectically. "We're very busy now. Very busy!" During a later encounter, however, he abruptly asked me what I did for a living.

"I'm a word processor at a law firm," I told him. "A temp."

"What?" he cried in fury. "I can't understand what you're saying!"

"A typist," I said quickly. "I'm a typist!"

My answer sent him into a long period of deep contemplation. His shaggy eyebrows drew close, and a long furrow divided his broad forehead. He suddenly opened his eyes and demanded to know how much money I made a week. I told him, and he said, to my surprise, "We may have something for you." He held up a gnarled finger before I could reply. "Not yet. I'll let you know." With a dismissive wave, he shuffled away. He was halfway down the stairs when I distinctly heard him mutter, "Cousins!"

The only other person who came knocking at my door that summer was the morose Swedish girl who lived just above me. I had first met her when she came by with a girlfriend, and asked if she could use my window to climb up the fire escape because she had locked herself out of her apartment. I found that if strangers were going to use my fire escape, I preferred this direction of egress. On that occasion, she had rushed through the apartment so quickly that I'd barely caught a glimpse of her pudgy, bespectacled face before she and her friend were out the window. I didn't see her again until about a month later when she came by to ask for a cigarette.

She told me she'd quit smoking earlier that year, but she'd just made a pot of coffee and, "Well, sometimes a cigarette is so *nice* with a cup of coffee." But she certainly didn't seem as though she were looking forward to a nice cigarette with her coffee—she seemed, in fact, on the verge of bursting into tears. Behind the thick lenses of her glasses, her eyes were red and puffy, and her lower lip trembled as she spoke. The moment I gave her the cigarette, she mumbled her thanks and rushed out of the apartment.

To my surprise, she returned the next day. "It's coffee time!" she said in a bright, chipper tone that so completely belied her miserable expression, I felt a momentary desire to take her into my arms and tell her that everything would be okay. Instead, I hunted around for a pack of cigarettes and told her to help herself. This time, before rushing back out to her troubled life, she introduced herself. Her name, she said, was Jim. I suppressed the urge to tell her that she had the same first name as my father, feeling that this would only add to her sorrows.

I didn't see her for about a week or so after that, but when she came by it was not to ask for a cigarette but a hammer, and she seemed angry rather than tearful. I dug around the place and found a hammer, and asked what she needed it for. "My fucking dumb boyfriend," she said. "He won't wake up."

I wondered if I was about to become an accessory to murder, and debated with myself whether I should try to take back the hammer, or if it was just too much trouble. Thankfully, she elaborated. She had put a kettle on the stove, but then stepped out of the apartment and locked herself out. Her boyfriend was inside, but he'd gotten high and had passed out on the couch. She'd pounded on the door, but neither that nor the shriek of the now boiling kettle had made any effect on his narcotic slumber. The fire escape was no use; she'd put an air conditioner in that window. "So I'll try the hammer," she explained. "I should think that will wake up the idiot."

A few moments after she left, my ceiling began shaking with the bone-jarring clatter of someone upstairs relentlessly smacking a steel door with a claw hammer.

It went on for a long, long time.

Jim came back to visit me only once more, to return the hammer, and she must have started smoking again, because she didn't ask for any cigarettes. Towards the end of the summer, though, I found her sitting on the stoop outside the building, where she presided over a small pile of shredded paper between her feet. She seemed to be trying to set the pile on fire, but the wind kept blowing out her matches. She explained that she had kicked her boyfriend out, and she was burning his letters. "That stupid junky," she said bitterly. "When I have done burning all his asshole writing, I will put the ashes in the toilet because I don't want a pigeon to eat this and die of poison." I began to speculate that pigeons were unlikely to be tempted by ashes, but she interrupted me and said, "Of course, if I flush them in the toilet, it is so toxic, it will probably kill all the fishes and crabs." With shaking hands, she lit another match, and it blew out. All at once, tears spilled out of her eyes, and she looked up at me plaintively. "Do you have any matches?" she asked.

I didn't see Jim after that. I was nearing the end of my arrangement with the filmmaker, and had already begun the tedious process of finding another place to live, circling ads, pulling flyers off the walls of cafes, vainly hoping that Pincus Plod would come through for me in the end. Then something bad happened late one night, when I was returning from my second-shift job at the law firm. When I arrived at my building, I found a young guy sitting on the stoop. He looked a lot like a Spanish guy who lived in the building, so I said hello, but he said nothing and sullenly turned his head away. Asshole, I thought, and reached over him to unlock the door. Big mistake. Immediately I was forcibly shoved into the foyer of the building by another man, a big guy who'd apparently been hidden in the shadows of the doorway of the next building. From behind, he tightly gripped the back of my arm, rammed me into the row of mailboxes, and hissed in my ear, *Don't say anything and we won't hurt you.*

Time slowed down, the way it does when you skid in a car, or whenever you believe that you are about to suffer severe physical trauma and possibly death. A split-second cracked open to reveal a momentary eternity, and I found I had time to consider the situation. An entire chain of logical possibilities unfolded in my adrenaline-soaked brain. The basic existential fact flashed as brightly as a neon sign: these two men were here to rob me. But if I acquiesced and put myself under their power, they might do more than rob me. They might cut up my face for spite, the way the super's nephew had been cut on Clinton Street. Or they might smash in my skull with a pipe and leave me lying in a bloody coma. Or they might shoot me, if in fact they had a gun. Of course, if I tried to get away, they might still do these things, but wasn't it better to get hurt trying to escape than simply surrender to these stupid scumbags? Yes it was, I decided, with more conviction than any decision I've ever made in my life: better to escape or die trying to.

Time began again, and my memory of what happened next remains blurred and impressionistic. They had told me not to say anything, and this suggested my first course of defense—I began yelling my head off. It's amazing how well you can project when you think you are about to die. *Help!* I shouted in a voice so loud my throat would be sore for a week. *I'm being mugged! Call the police!* And then, realizing the cynical nature of most New Yorkers, I added, *This is not a joke!*

I struggled as I shouted, and to this day I can't reconstruct exactly how it happened, but somehow I had switched places with my assailant: originally he had shoved me against the mailboxes, but now it seemed our positions were reversed—*he* was against the mailboxes, and, free of his grip, *I* was shouting directly into his face *Call the police! I'm being mugged!* Our eyes met then, and I'll never forget the expression on his face. He looked *annoyed,* as if I were being a bad sport and ruining a perfectly good mugging.

I stumbled backwards over his partner (the one who'd been waiting on the stoop) but had the luck to fall on the stairwell, where I managed, while sitting on my butt, to propel myself upwards and backwards with uncanny speed, all the while shouting for help. At the top of the stairs I scrambled to my feet just in front of my apartment door, but I didn't want to risk attempting to open it when they were so close behind, so I kept going, up flight after flight of stairs, banging on every door I passed.

The building only had six floors. I quickly reached the top, and with great trepidation peered down through the narrow gap of the stairwell.

"Are you all right?" a voice called up. It was one of the tenants, a guy who lived on the ground floor. "They're gone. You did the right thing by yelling, they ran away."

My legs shook so hard I had trouble climbing back down the stairs.

Someone had called the police, and they eventually showed up, but they were useless. "Technically," one of the cops told me, "it's not an assault. You didn't see a weapon, and they didn't rob you." I rolled up my sleeve for him. On my upper right arm, where I'd been grabbed, was a dark and ugly bruise in the exact shape of a hand. The cop shrugged. "Well, you can come to the precinct and make a statement if you want." I asked if it would do any good. "Probably not," he conceded. "But it might make you feel better."

The cops may not have considered it an assault, but the incident affected me more deeply than I could admit to myself at the time. For the first time since I had lived in New York, I became afraid of the city. In New York, there's an important and universal sense of personal space, a well-defined but highly intuitive bubble that New Yorkers surround themselves with as they navigate the city. Without even thinking about it, New Yorkers fluidly steer past one other in public areas, careful not violate anyone else's space by, for example, approaching someone too quickly from behind. On the subway, and in other tight circumstances, the bubble shrinks, but the rules are still in play—you are careful not to jostle other people in a crowded train, and if you do, you automatically apologize.

After the attack, my personal bubble expanded significantly. I didn't like it when a stranger—any stranger passed within three feet of me on the sidewalk. I couldn't stand hearing footsteps behind me. I avoided passing near loitering males, no matter how well-dressed they might be. I didn't like being outside at night. The whole social contract of the city had crumbled for me. I distrusted everyone.

In retrospect, it's not so surprising that I decided to leave the city—I was suffering from some mild but insidious form of post-traumatic stress disorder. At the time, though, admitting that I had become afraid endangered my pride, my self-identification as a street-savvy New Yorker. Everyone I knew was mystified when I turned down a great apartment I'd found near Tompkins Square and opted to move back to the New Jersey suburb where I'd grown up.

I found two excellent excuses for leaving. First of all, my father had recently been diagnosed with terminal lung disease, and (though our relationship had not been a close or happy one) I needed to be near him to help out with his care. And secondly, I wanted to go back to school—I had never finished my undergraduate degree and thought that the attendant financial pressures would be lessened if I lived at home. Although both of these concerns were entirely reasonable, I now think that if I hadn't been attacked, I never would have left the city.

Over beers one evening, a friend of mine urged me to reconsider. "You won't be happy out there," he said. "You love it here."

"It won't be all that different," I replied, trying to hide my own anxieties. "Anyway, it's not like I'm moving to Nebraska. I'll be just across the Hudson River."

His reply was ominous, and memorable. "It's a big river," he said.

After I moved to New Jersey, I had ample time to think about this rejoinder. It *was* a big river. I commuted into the city for work, and later, for school, but it wasn't the same. I was busy with my father and my studies, and besides, it was a pain to find parking. I couldn't go out drinking because I had to drive home. I seldom visited my old haunts, and gradually lost touch with my friends in the neighborhood.

My exile in the suburbs lasted nearly three years. I had stayed through my father's illness, and remained for almost two years after his death. It was one of the most unhappy and lonely chapters in my life. By then, my fear of the city had faded—the risk of being attacked had come to seem more attractive than enduring another year in the cultural and social wasteland of the burbs. As soon as I got my degree, I moved straight back to the city. I quickly found a sublet in heart of the East Village, on Third Street and Second Avenue.

I think this last location was my favorite in the East Village. I lived in a beautiful old 19th-century building surrounded by relatively cheap Italian restaurants and Irish bars. The 6 train was just around the corner, St. Mark's just up the avenue, and it was a mere ten-minute walk to Greenwich Village, SoHo, or Chinatown.

But there were downsides, too. The drag queen who lived below me had a predilection for blasting operatic heavy metal whenever he felt sad or lonely, sometimes so loudly that my windows would rattle. Those same windows, I should note, looked out on the recreation yard of a halfway house whose residents began their day at six in the morning, and it was a constant annoyance to be jerked out my dreams by the sound of some two hundred and fifty recovering addicts chatting loudly over their morning coffee and cigarettes. And speaking of addictions: I shared my railroad apartment with a morbidly depressed hairdresser, who—as I discovered after I'd moved in—was spiraling into a deep and probably irreversible relationship with heroin.

Heroin, again. We know from a thousand maudlin arthouse movies that heroin destroys the lives of talented, beautiful hipsters who die in the photogenic bloom of their youth to a really cool soundtrack. What a load of crap. The tragic pop mythology of heroin, with its romantic aura of death and glamour, is probably exactly what attracts new users in the first place. Someone should make a film from the outsider's point of view instead, about how fucking annoying it is to live anywhere in the vicinity of junkies, what a royally *unglamorous* pain in the ass they are. How they climb down your fire escape in the middle of the night or mug you at your doorstep, or how, if you happen to live with them, they eat all your peanut butter, steal laundry money from your change jar, and leave tiny plastic bags floating in the toilet. It's probably no coincidence that as the bags proliferated, my roommate kept raising my share of the rent, until one day I could no longer afford to live there.

That was the last place I had in the East Village.

It still seems strange to me, but I've now lived in a modest walkup on the Upper East Side for nearly eight years, the longest I've ever remained in one dwelling in my entire life as an adult. My wife and I live in a sunlight-drenched apartment with wooden floors in the richest, snobbiest neighborhood in all of New York City, and yet our rent is far lower than any place I'd ever be able to find in the East Village these days, and that probably goes for Williamsburg too. It's too expensive to live in Bohemia in an era in which everyone wants to be cool. I just can't compete with the corporate attorneys, pharmaceutical marketing directors and trust-fund kids who enjoy artsy cafes and quaint, seedy dives just as much as I do. A strange paradox of New York City is that down in the Village, rich hipsters will shell out big bucks to live in crappy little holes that face air shafts, but up here, the market is driven by luxury high-rises with uniformed doormen—which means that underemployed writers like me can sometimes still find a bargain in some of the less well-maintained walk-ups.

I had a long and slightly bitter period of adjustment to the Upper East Side, but over the years I've found many things to like about my neighborhood. I'm not far from Central Park and the museums, and I don't have to worry much about unannounced visitors on my fire escape. I've found a few local dives I like, although I don't spend as much time in bars as I used to. In the summer, I like to go running along the East River, where there's a beautiful esplanade overlooking Ward and Roosevelt Islands. If I step out late at night for a carton of milk, the possibility of being mugged by some asshole junky is relatively remote. But every so often, while walking through the streets of this clean, well-heeled neighborhood, and staring into the smug, empty faces of my wealthy neighbors, I find myself longing for the lively pageantry of Clinton Street, where the unexpected often came knocking at my door—or my window. But the Clinton Street I knew has already slipped away into the sepia haze of nostalgia, and it may be that I just miss my youth.

Abnormal Psychology

*L*ATELY, I'VE BEGUN TO REALIZE the profundity of a theory proposed years ago by my best friend in college. Most of the world, he speculated, can be divided into two sorts of people, *dirtbags* and *psychos*. Let me explain.

Psychos masquerade as normal people—the sort of people, let's say, you might see portrayed in a L.L. Bean catalogue. In fact, it's more accurate to say that psychos *are* normal people, and vice versa, and as such, they are also obsessed with *appearing* normal—even to themselves—because they have to keep a tight lid on their malfunctioning psyches, which are putrid, frothing sewers of repressed hatred, lust, and animal greed. Psychos live life in a permanent state of denial, but Freud will not be denied. You can only cram so many bad feelings and unpleasant truths into the subconscious before the pressure builds and the lid pops open and everyone stares agape at the gnarled, twisted little soul inside.

Psychos are fond of clothing that requires dry-cleaning, and you generally meet them in offices and in any locale featured in the Lifestyle section of *The New York Times*. Psychos run the world.

And then there are the *dirtbags*. They repress nothing because they have no inner life to repress. They are entirely driven by their appetites: beer, cars, domestic violence. They tend to congregate in packs, and when dressed for play demonstrate a disproportionate fondness for expensive baseball caps, heavy gold chains, and apparel festooned with Abercrombie & Fitch logos.

Dirtbags are dangerous because they harbor a deep rage against the psychos they work for. You can easily find dirtbags at sports bars, construction sites, and beauty salons. Dirtbags don't run anything but get revenge on the world by overcharging for parts and labor.

My friend allowed for a narrow third category which he called *people like us*, by which he meant overeducated neurotics (characterized by their slovenly appearance, obscure aesthetic tastes, and bitter cynicism) who spend their tormented lives trying to avoid both psychos and dirtbags. But there are far more of *them* than there are of *us*, and there are casualties. Wearied by the struggle against the blandly smug and the militantly vulgar, some of the *people like us* stop being mere cranks and eccentrics and succumb at last to the refuge of being *plain fucking nuts*.

Of course, like all great systems of wisdom, my friend's theory of human behavior is prone to being misunderstood or abused. Do not ask yourself which category you belong in. Only a psycho or a dirtbag could be so completely out of touch. The truly self-aware, the *people like us*, ask instead: what category do *other* people belong to? This is the path of enlightenment and personal freedom.

Test your understanding of the principles outlined above. I offer, for your edification, a day of my life.

The buzzer for my apartment is marked "Superintendent" although I am not, in fact, the superintendent. Consequently, a lot of people I don't know buzz my apartment, and to make matters worse, the intercom itself was apparently installed sometime during the First World War, and is slightly less comprehensible than the announcement speakers on the subway.

It was one of those mornings when you have woken mysteriously and suspect some loud noise occurred while you were sleeping, except in my case there was no mystery because moments after lifting my weary head from the pillow, the buzzer rang *BZZZZZ BZZZZZ BZZZZZ BZZZZZZZZZ* again and again, like an angry hornet. I had no intention of answering it, but lay in bed wondering how long it would take for whoever it was to give up and go away.

This turned out to be a surprisingly long time. I was beginning to think I might actually have to get out of bed when I finally heard the outside door click open, meaning that someone else had let the bastard in. Thank God. I could now savor the last peaceful, bladder-filled minutes until I had to get out bed, urinate, and go to work.

But I was wrong. Whoever was at the door was unsatisfied with being granted general access to the building and wanted specific access to *me*.

BZZZZ BZZZZ BZZZZ! I couldn't stand it; I broke policy and pressed the talk button on the intercom. "Who is it?" I demanded. But what came out of the intercom downstairs was probably something like "Hmxpxh zxxt sch?"

I did not need to press the "listen" button for a reply, because I could hear the man shouting from downstairs, "It's Con Ed!" He could have said "It's Ted Bundy," and I would have let him in. I pressed the door button, holding it down again and again for long periods to convey my displeasure.

To my surprise, my buzzer rang again. Downstairs, I could hear someone yelling "Supah! *Suuuupaaaaah!*" Christ. I wasn't going to give in. I sat down to my morning cup and tried to achieve that state of mind peculiar, perhaps, to New Yorkers, whereby all outside stimuli—jackhammers, fire engines, gunshots—can be utterly ignored.

I could not achieve it. The buzzer and the man's shouts were syncopated like a demented drum solo: *BZZZ! BZZZ!* Supaah! *BZZZZ! BZZZ! BZZZ!* Supaah! Supaaah! It was awful, like hearing a baby cry. This Con Ed guy sounded so forlorn, as if he were lost and cold. In pity I finally opened my door and saw him standing in the vestibule at the bottom of the stairs, with his finger on the buzzer and an almost tearful look of frustration on his thick young face.

"I'm not the super," I told him.

He looked up in surprise, as though God had personally appeared in response to a prayer, only to deny His own existence.

"But the buzzah says supah," he said accusatorily, as if I were holding out on him.

"I know it does, but I'm not the super," I said patiently.

"It *says* supah," he repeated to himself. Obviously he had to reevaluate the entire situation. He accepted it; he had a new idea. "Do you know how to get in the basement?"

"How do I even know that you're from Con Ed?" I countered.

He pointed to the laminated ID hanging from his coveralls. "It says I am right here."

"You know," I said, "I think you place too much value on labels. The Buddhists say that only insofar as one is free from words does one really understand words."

The Con Ed man stared. I coughed. It was an awkward moment. "Anyway," I added, "I don't know how to get in the basement. I'm only a subletter, not the super." He nodded slowly, and I gently shut the door behind me.

It was an annoying way to begin the day, but it got worse. Later that afternoon, I found myself at the 77th Street Station, waiting in line to refill my MetroCard. The No. 6 train pulled in just as I reached the subway clerk. "Ten dollars," I said, pushing the card towards her.

"*Ten* dollars?" she asked. I guess it's an odd amount to request, since it doesn't result in an exact number of trips. But I didn't want to get $15 because that was all I had and I didn't want to get $6 because I would run out of fares too quickly.

While she was punching numbers into the computer, I noticed the whiteboard hanging behind her, on which she had written: MONEY IS NOT THE MOST IMPORTANT THING IN LIFE. Broke and underemployed, I found myself in solidarity with this revolutionary sentiment. Right on, Sister, I thought. "I like your sign," I said, as she handed back my card.

"Thank you," she said, smiling.

Just then, the train pulled out of the station. "Aw, shit!" said the businessman behind me.

I went down to the platform to wait for the next one, when suddenly there was a commotion up the stairs by the turnstiles. "Fuck! Fuck fuck fuck!" someone was yelling. It was the businessman, who had just come through the stile. He slammed his briefcase repeatedly against stiles, and then, for emphasis, hurled it violently against the floor, screaming obscenities all the while. Everyone stared: you don't see a man in an charcoal suit behave like this every day.

"Ten dollars! Ten dollars!" he screamed. He picked up the receiver of a payphone and banged it loudly against the metal casing. "I like your sign! I like your sign!" he raged, in a mocking sing-song voice.

I began to feel extremely uncomfortable.

He ran down the stairs towards me, and I felt a wave of panic, but then he hurtled right past me to deliver a violent kick to a trash barrel. Everyone gave him a wide berth. Hair flying back, he kicked it again with a loud clang.

Then his rage began to sputter out.

"Whew!" he shouted, as if letting us all know that this frightening display had alleviated his stress, that all this screaming and briefcase-bashing had not been in vain.

"Whew!" he shouted again, and drew his hand across his forehead to demonstrate his relief, his dissipated tension.

"Whew." He said it less emphatically and smiled, as if feeling slightly foolish. Then he kicked the barrel again, but this time more softly. Then his face darkened and crumpled, passed through various stages of anxiety and annoyance, and settled somewhere between *extreme irritation* and *smoldering rage*. Clutching his battered briefcase, he fell into an energetic pace along the edge of the platform, muttering "Ten dollars!" to himself.

Although the businessman had never directly acknowledged me as the source of his grief, I felt a bit injured by his mockery. My feelings were hurt. He would have missed the train anyway, I thought resentfully. Having temped for many years in big financial firms, I felt that his bizarre behavior exposed the true inner nature of businessmen everywhere: irrational, bullying, insane. I wanted to taunt the other businessmen on the platform with their defective colleague. *You suits are all the same.* I wanted to kick the angry businessman in the butt, and hiss, *Money isn't everything, you know.* But when the train arrived, I made sure to get in a different car.

All the way downtown, I stewed, resentfully dreaming of a glorious revolution in which impoverished writers and subway clerks would get to shoot and hang corporate executives. I glared at the other business people on the car, shooting out psychic rays of hate as they sat quietly reading their financial bulletins. *When the Revolution comes*, I thought, you'll *be working for* us. *You won't get to wear suits anymore—we'll make you wear diapers. And funny hats. In the shape of vegetables. Carrot hats, and broccoli hats. You won't care so much about your appointments in a broccoli hat.*

Still steaming, I got out at Bleecker Street, and trudged home, vaguely wondering if I'd find the Con Ed guy still ringing my buzzer.

On Third Street, to my amazement, I saw an angel on an enormous bicycle pedaling down the narrow residential street, dragging a wooden cart upon which sat a huge golden harp, festooned with colorful streamers. Instantly I forgot my revolutionary fervor. The angel wore pink and blue feathers on his head, his eyes were shadowed with glitter, and his great sparkling wings of silver and pink satin fluttered against his back as he cycled.

Taxi cabs, bottle-necked behind him, impatiently blared their unholy horns, but the angel remained unperturbed, looking neither to the left nor the right, and maintained a leisurely pace towards the Bowery. I ran after him, weaving in and out of the honking taxis.

"Wait a sec! Wait a sec!" I shouted as loudly as I could. And then he stopped.

When I had caught up with him, he looked down at me from his heavenly perch, and asked me in a coy tone if I wanted to pay him to play the harp for me. I admitted I didn't and felt ashamed.

"Then why are you pestering me?" the angel snapped irritably. I stared at my feet and shrugged. He shook his head in disgust, and pedaled away.

But just as the angel reached the Bowery intersection, I thought of a response. "Hey, angel! Mr. Angel!" I bellowed at the top of my lungs. He slowed down. "I just think you're cool!" I shouted, giving him a thumbs-up. He paused for a moment, as if weighing the merits of my remark, shrugged, and resumed his surreal journey up the Bowery.

I was left standing on the side of Third Street wondering why I had chased him in the first place. Perhaps I had wanted a some sort of blessing, a benediction to protect me against the evil forces of corporate executives and Con Ed, but I think it was something more. I think I saw in him divine possibilities that I had denied myself. Perhaps it was time to go all the way, to stop being *borderline* and actually cross the border. Life might be more enjoyable in a costume. A lifestyle that said *crazy as a loon and I don't care* might free me from my irony and cynicism, allow me to rise above the need to label others as *psychos* and *dirtbags*; indeed, might allow me to rise above the psychos and dirtbags *themselves*, and float away on angelic wings, free at last of the earthly encumbrances which deform and twist us all into creatures we'd rather not be.

STUFF

> I had three pieces of limestone on my desk, but I was ter-
> rified to find that they required to be dusted daily, when
> the furniture of my mind was all undusted still, and I threw
> them out the window in disgust.

> —Henry David Thoreau, *Walden*

*E*VERY TIME I'VE EVER MOVED—nineteen times in eleven years, to be exact—I've lamented the amount of *stuff* I had. All those crates of books—the weight of my *useless knowledge*—to be lugged up stairs. The ungainly and grimy futon. The boxes of myste-rious papers and the dented file cabinets in which they will never be filed. The knick-knacks, the whatnot, the bric-a-brac of the years.

And then I went back to school and, driven by the economics of higher education, moved back home, Gen-X style, to live with my mother and brother and sister in the New Jersey suburb I thought I had long ago escaped, where my stuff was finally united with all the stuff of my family and, of course, all the stuff I had conveniently left behind when I moved away at eighteen. I do not exaggerate when I claim to be *drowning in a sea of stuff*, sinking into the flotsam and jet-sam of possessions, the swirling detritus of our collective lifetimes of collecting which chokes the closets and crowds the passageways and congests the bureaus and shelves and clogs the nooks and crannies of the House of Gore. I fear the day when we will all have to move to make more room for our stuff.

Well, you say, it can't be *that* bad. It is that bad. Actually, it's worse, because I haven't mentioned that my mother now owns two *other* houses—one that belonged to my grandmother, and one that was my father's before he died—and they are worse, far worse than my mother's house. The phrase *packed to the gills* is ridiculously insuf-ficient to describe them.

"Cluttered" might describe the house I live in. It doesn't, but it will have to do. "Messy" is the word my family has traditionally used, the shameful reason why no one is allowed in. Really, I guess it's a combination of both. Both cluttered *and* messy. They go hand in hand, cluttered and messy, because when you have too much stuff, there's no place to put the *new* stuff. And when it's already messy, why bother putting anything back where it belongs?

The heart of the home is the hearth, and the kitchen can serve us here as the essence, the Platonic form, of my family's neurosis.

The kitchen is the most actively used room in our house, the hub of dysfunctional family interaction, mostly because it contains the television and the food. That's where we—me, my mother, my brother, and, occasionally, my estranged sister—gather to argue, complain, eat and watch TV. On any given day, the table is piled high with paper plates *and* real dishes, paper cups *and* real glasses, dirty flatware, frozen food boxes, paper towels, mail, catalogues (they come in by the dozen every day), boxes of breakfast cereal, empty milk cartons, darkening banana peels and squashed grape-fruit rinds, and hundreds of little tiny pink pieces of paper upon which are scribbled notes to each other and cryptic phone numbers belonging to various unnamed parties. You might think it's hard to fit all this on one table. Well, it is. Things tend to be pushed towards the middle in a crusty heap as little clearings are made at the edges so we can eat while we watch TV. Why do we live like this? This is one of things we argue about at the table.

For one thing, it's because we have too many dishes. When all the dishes are clean, they must be stuffed precariously into the cabinets, wedged into a kind of ceramic jigsaw puzzle, so that the care-less removal of any one dish may cause an avalanche of the others. It is a system that discourages anyone from putting away all the dishes. There is a similar problem with the flatware, of which we have several sets, enough for a small restaurant. My family has adapted to the surplus of dishes by using the dishwasher as an extra cabinet: when the dishes are done, they are left in the dishwasher and used until the dishwasher is empty, meanwhile accumulating on the counter, the sink, and, of course, the table. The dishes are sometimes reloaded at that point, starting the cycle over, but more often, we move on to the cabinets and use *the rest of the dishes.*

Then there are the paper plates and cups, liberally employed throughout the whole process in a pitiful attempt to avoid using real dishes, which will, after all, only have to be washed. Paperware (if such an awful word even exists) has the advantage of being disposable, but we tend to leave it all on the table with everything else. This is because the only garbage container we have is a small 4- or 5-gallon plastic container, about the size of a wastepaper basket, stored under the sink. In a house where each day we use enough paper products to deplete a personal-sized rainforest, this small container is filled almost instantly. It is apparently too much effort to change it daily (and really it would need changing several times a day anyway), so once it is full, the garbage is left on the table. I have repeatedly suggested that we purchase a large 55-gallon garbage can so that waste is a little easier to dispose of, but this plan is always met with hostility by my mother, who doesn't like the unseemly idea of *having a garbage can right in the middle of the kitchen.*

I don't think we always lived like this. I can't remember—I was away for ten years, preoccupied with moving my own possessions all over the Northeastern United States. But it seems to me that the paper plates were an innovation introduced in my absence. As were the frozen food packages, which modern supermarkets now offer in great abundance and variety, since nearly everyone owns a microwave oven. (Except us. For some reason, we don't have one.)

When I was a kid, we mostly ate canned SpaghettiO's, accompanied by glasses of Tang (which I mistook for orange juice until I was around thirteen). But I seem to remember that the cans were thrown away, and the dishes were washed on a semi-regular basis. (Even then, though, my mother had perversely used the dishwasher as a spare cabinet.) Back in those days, if memory serves, my mother made a sincere and regular effort to clean the kitchen. As a matter of fact, she did *all* the housework, picking up after her grubby children and husband and daily finding places to put all the stuff everyone had already begun collecting. She made many futile attempts to recruit the aid of her children, but we followed my father's example, who believed that it was my mother's job to clean up, and his job to make sure that there *was* something to clean up. Driven to the point of despair, she finally gave up, and began buying paperware.

Well, it happened something like that, anyway.

When I first returned to this house, I decided I would help my family break out of this terrible dish-and-garbage cycle. I suggested the large garbage can, and finally, surreptitiously, I bought a *small* garbage can, with an attractive lid that could be opened by means of a foot pedal, and placed it in a discreet corner of the kitchen. It has never been used, and has become yet another useless object taking up space in our house.

The other suggestion I made was to pack away half of the dishes and glasses and put them in the attic. This idea, which I had thought sensible and sane, provoked even more hostility than the garbage can idea. *Now you don't want me to have dishes?* my mother cried in disbelief. Admittedly, a reaction colored by my incessant and obnoxious pestering for her to get rid of certain other non-dish items in the house.

Most of them, really.

The childhood games and toys, for example, the sad, battered boxes of Chinese Checkers and Life and Connect-4, the ancient Atari cartridges, the Stretch Armstrong, the wizened stuffed animals and their missing eyes, the broken crayons, the rumpled Twister mat, its optimistically colored circles now pathetic with neglect. The bright playthings that started us all on the road of acquisition now lie (for some reason) in a melancholy heap in our basement, the junkyard of our childhoods. Some of them my mother hopes to give to her future grandchildren, although this hope recedes a little farther with every passing year. Some of them have too much sentimental value to throw away, and my brother and mother consider my suggestion to cart them all off to the Salvation Army a blasphemy and a betrayal. Others still, the ones that are missing pieces, or are too broken for the unborn grandchildren, are being saved for the garage sale my mother has been planning for years.

And there's more, more, more, in the family room, the attic, the vestibules, the bedrooms, more stuff, more *things* that I find just too disheartening to name. I don't where all this crap came from, or why we have it. I wander through the wreckage of our house pondering the mystery of it.

I've begun to think that there must be some sort of syndrome behind our cluttered lifestyle, something worthy, perhaps, of the Rikki Lake show. There are others like us, I know. Tolstoy said every family is unhappy in its own unique way, but I think this is only partially true. I think there must be categories of unhappiness, a set number of family types, like signs of the Zodiac. I have a friend in Massachusetts who, for many years, refused to let me visit his family's house, and I knew he must be one of us. But gradually, as I shared the shameful secrets of my own family, he opened his doors to me. I was right, of course; no need to describe his house: I've already described mine. He is also currently living in his childhood home, and we call each other up to swap war stories—a kind of group therapy in miniature—and already I have begun to detect certain patterns, certain recurring motifs. Maybe I'm on to something. Maybe this is the great purpose in life that has eluded me for so many years: I was born to describe, dissect, and analyze *the psychology of stuff.*

We tend to take our family members for granted—especially once we escape them—but lately I've been taking a closer look at mine.

Perhaps to make up for her general suspicion and distrust of other human beings, my mother is sentimental about objects. She feels pity for objects. She feels that they can be betrayed. I remember when I was a kid I had cut out some pictures of raccoons and such from my issue of *Ranger Rick's Nature Magazine* to put on the wall. When I proudly showed my mother what I had done, she sadly pointed to the remainder of the magazine and said, "But now you can't look at the pictures on the *other side* of the pages." I tried to tape them back in but it wasn't the same. I'd hurt the magazine and there was nothing I could do about it.

My mother's sentimentality makes her a *saver*. Once an object has visited our home for a little while, it seems to her cruel to send it back out into the streets. So we must live with the Fisher-Price wooden giraffe with wheels that I sat on at the age of three. She will not part with the cracked plastic jack-o-lantern that the kittens used to play in. (Have I mentioned the cats? We have thirteen of them. Do you begin to see the pattern here?) The plastic mice that came with some Carvel's ice cream cake in the late Seventies. Christmas cards, written in italicized verse by a Hallmark computer, personalized only with the scrawled signature of someone she has not seen in years and cares about not a whit. The notes scribbled in haste from us to her: *Mom Im going to a party at Wiggies, P.S. I took your car.* The days of the present are crowded with the minutiae of the past.

There are things she doesn't want, but these too must be saved. Remember? *Someone can use this.* God gave us all this stuff and none of it must be wasted. This is not as frugal as it sounds. I don't want to give the impression that my mother lives *in harmony with the earth*: the paper consumption in our house easily puts to rest any notions of environmentally sound living.

And, of course, there are the things she doesn't want *now*, but she may find a use for *someday*. Buckets of screws, trinkets, buttons, bits of plastic and string. Stacks of newspapers and magazines, still unread, ready to kill us all should a fire ever break out.

❊　❊　❊

Her mother—that is, my grandmother—was more or less the same, except that she lived in a house in western Maryland 400 miles away, and her stuff is a lot older than my mother's. I say "is" because we still have it all. My grandmother was also fond of saving cans of food, sometimes for decades, even as they menacingly bulged from the shelves with botulism. My mother spent the whole summer and part of the fall attempting to empty out my grandmother's house so that it could be rented. "My God!" she told me over the phone. "Grandma saved *everything.*"

My mother did not manage to clean out the entire house, but managed instead to get very sick with the dust, the heat, and the effort of it all. I feared for her health and urged her to come home, but she insisted on coughing her way through September, held hostage by her mother's stuff.

My brother has inherited, or learned, the maternal line of sentimentality. There is an entire room in our house that I think of as *the museum of my brother's childhood.* Toys, books, notes from schoolmates, awards from third grade, novelty items won at carnivals, Matchbook cars, all on display and kept in more or less the same arrangement as the day when he moved out of that room and into the room that had been my father's before my parents divorced. It's eerie. The room looks like one of those rooms people keep after someone has *died.*

He is also a *collector,* which is different from a *saver,* although both manias often seem to inhabit the same person. Many of his collections date from his childhood. A vast collection of Star Wars toys and promotional paraphernalia, which is now, I begrudgingly admit, probably worth something. A large collection of novelty keyrings, which is probably not. A collection of art books, which I covet. A collection of obsolete video game cartridges, which I do not.

My sister, by the way, is also a collector: she collects clothes she never wears and CDs she never plays. But she lacks the fastidiousness of my brother. She is driven more by greed than obsession. It's the bulk that matters to her, not the individual items. And she lacks any sentimentality for objects at all, frequently purging her room of unwanted possessions with a ruthlessness that frightens my mother, who shakes her head and says, *With her, it's easy come, easy go.*

I admit that I have thus far presented myself as the only rational member of my family, the one who rises above stuff and its terrible allure. Well, it's true in some ways. I have learned from my family and seen what stuff can do. I've tried to save my family—admittedly in the face of great resentment—from being consumed by their own possessions. But nonetheless, I am a member of this family, and its odd genetic demons work in me, too. I possess a vast and unwieldy library, eclectic in a way that probably only reflects badly on my taste. I once read of an author who remarked that his appetite for the printed word was restrained only by the volume of his house. This is also true of me, and this is a possible reason why I am so anxious to purge the house of the things which are not books. I am irrationally proud of my books—many of which I have never read, and many more of which I never will—because I think they make me look smart. I have, as a female friend once remarked, *book macho*.

But I am not blind to the connection between my books and my family's terrible addiction to objects. I've tried to get rid of a few—I recently pushed my entire *Planet of the Apes* series onto an unwilling friend. But I can't help but feel that books are . . . well, *books*. They represent learning, scholasticism, the monasteries of Europe, the Library of Alexandria, *curling up by the fireplace*, red leather chairs and glasses of port, an older way of life disappearing under a cultural avalanche of MTV videos and Sega games and proliferating cable channels. So I will feel no shame for my books, even though my family feels they belie my hypocrisy.

But anyway, it's not just the books. I collect other things, too. Useless and bizarre things, things which I find on the street and am compelled to bring home with me. This was a terrible problem when I lived by myself in New York. My wretched little apartment on Avenue C was stuffed with rusted parts of cars, odd bits of discarded kitsch, mannequin body parts, gears and tools (I particularly like things made of metal), shiny bits of beach glass, plastic toys. My prized possession was an enormous rusted steel spring, six inches wide, a foot and a half long, weighing around eight or nine pounds. I have absolutely no idea what its function had once been—its only function in my apartment was *to get in my way*.

I left most of these things behind when I moved. I usually do, although I sometimes miss them. (I often pine for that giant spring. I know I'll never get another.) It doesn't matter though, because in our over-productive culture, I know I'll always find more.

When I lived with a girlfriend in Nyack, I drove her crazy with this habit. "But what do you *need* that for?" she'd say, pointing to (for example) a sheaf of industrial blueprints I'd rescued from a dumpster and proudly held up for her approval. "I don't know," I admitted. "I just thought you'd think it was *cool*." Our living arrangement did not last long.

I don't know, to be honest, why I am driven to bring these things home. I think it is my way of short-circuiting my genetic destiny: by collecting useless junk, I am under no obligation to keep it, although I often do for many years.

I have a friend who does the same thing, which I only discovered recently. I have known his family for years and they are not subject to same neuroses as my family. But they are very wealthy, and are obsessive in displaying their wealth. They are *conspicuous consumers*—yet another breed of acquisitiveness. Sax Fifth Avenue coats, luxury sedans, objets d'art, trips to Paris litter the family landscape. So collecting junk may be a kind of rebellion for him too. Just as I must collect objects without meaning, *objects devoid of sentimental value*, so my friend must collect objects without status, that is, objects devoid of *material* value.

As it happens, of course, these are the same sort of objects, the sort which can be found in alleys and garbage bins.

My friend differs from me, though, in that he never throws out his junk—he crams it all into boxes. This is a problem, because my friend travels all over the world—he is a respected student of anthropology etc. with a sizable bank account to boot—amassing rubbish from the streets of Calcutta, Bangkok, Tokyo, London and Paris. All of which he stuffs into crates and boxes and ships back to his mother's home in New York at great expense. She doesn't know what it is in the boxes and he tells her they contain various items important to his important discipline but she is beginning to catch on. Lately, he told me, necessity has forced him to begin storing boxes in other people's apartments, all over the world.

✿ ✿ ✿

It is a sickness, a disease of the soul, we need a Freud or, better yet, a Dante to describe its twisted permutations. Yes, and if there were a circle in Hell waiting for all of us, my father would surely occupy its center. The Archdaemon of Stuff.

He lived in a house not far from my mother's house—in fact, the house I had lived in as a child. For years, he wouldn't even let us in the house. On my rare visits, he'd open the door just a crack—just enough to let an unidentifiable yet unpleasant smell waft out—and then he'd squeeze out with his jacket and coat and take me to a diner. But then, two years ago, he became sick with a slow and fatal disease none of us had ever heard of, and we began spending many, many awful hours on the other side of that door.

Words fail me here. Pictures failed us too, when out of some carnivalesque need to document this perversion of human behavior, we brought a camera into the house while he was in the hospital for a few weeks. 4 x 6 color shots could not capture the awful splendor of it, we needed SurroundVision. We needed Smell-O-Rama, to capture that thick odor which still cannot be identified or purged.

You will not believe me—it *cannot* be believed—but you can only gain an understanding of my father's house if you visualize the entire town dump of a medium-sized suburb crammed into a three-bedroom house. Somewhere underneath was the dilapidated furniture, collapsing from the weight of it all. A narrow path had been cleared in order to get from one room to the next, but it was too tight for us to pass through, and my father was a large man. To get from one room to another, he must have *climbed* over his stuff.

While my dad was in the hospital having his ravaged body explored for disease, we decided to undertake an excavation of the house. There were several layers of stuff, and, like archaeologists at a dig, we had to clear away the top layers of garbage before getting to the actual *things* embedded near the floor. We wore masks and rubber gloves to scoop up the cardboard boxes, food scraps, dirty dishes, rumpled magazines, used tissues and paper towels, destroyed clothing and fast-food packaging, and crammed it all into Hefty bag upon

Hefty bag. The process took days, and squat, green, overstuffed plastic bags gathered on the front lawn like a surreal army of malignant dwarves.

Discouragingly, under the wreckage, we found a desperate abundance of cleaning supplies, enough to stock the shelves of a grocery store aisle, bespeaking of resolutions made and forgotten.

And then, underneath it all, we got to the *real* stuff.

My dad had at least one of everything that has ever been manufactured by the human race, and usually four or five spares. Tools, stationery, compact discs, bottle openers, windchimes, board games, video tapes, office supplies, antiques, books, gadgets, doohickeys, thingamajigs. Widgets. I think he lost things among the chaos and bought more to replace them. We found the guts of a Wurlitzer jukebox. An original Edison phonograph with wax spools. A three-foot tall robot from Radio Shack, its function obscure. 10,000 plastic parts of a deluxe model Mercedes Benz scattered throughout the house, each waiting to be found in its own quirky little hiding place.

And all manner of things electronic: VCRs, monitors, computers, cables, soldering irons, integrated circuits, professional sound editors, manuals, mice, software, disk drives, ham radios, oscilloscopes, capacitors, resistors, transmitters, transformers, transmogrifiers.

For electronics were my father's lifelong passion, the soul not only of his business, but of himself, his digital soul. My father had always collected machines, had always repaired and built and puttered around with them, but the advent of the personal computer cranked up his voltage considerably. All in all we found about eleven computers and enough parts to make many more. A computer is not one machine but an infinite number of them. What the Philosopher's Stone was to alchemists the computer is to technophiles. There are a million and one stupid things you can do with a computer and my father had to do them all. His consumption of software was frightening, and apparently continued up to the week of his death; we later found, stuffed into his armchair, recently dated mail-order receipts from Egghead for such arcane items as *Street At-*

las USA v. 3.0, Visual FoxPro 2.6 and *The Better Homes & Gardens CD-ROM Complete Guide to Gardening.*

※　※　※

It has been a year since my father died, and we are still clearing out his house. I think my father's maniacal appetite for stuff has shaken us all up a bit, has pointed to unpleasant future possibilities for all of us. My mother has begun to toss out the old magazines, the childhood clothing. I can tell it pains her, but I admire her resolve. My brother recently presented me with a box of junk culled from his room, containing, among other things, a chain made of beer pull-tabs, a rubber chicken and a genuine Brunswick bowling pin. (Shamefully, instead of hurling these things out the window, I stashed them in my closet.) I recently disposed of a store dummy—a prized possession for ten years—by leaving it standing at a bus stop in Fort Lee, one arm posed in the air, waiting to flag the next ride anywhere, straight the hell out of my life.

My father died of a degenerative illness called interstitial pulmonary disease, in which the lungs progressively scar until they can no longer absorb oxygen. It is a rare disease, but not unheard of. Its exact cause is still undetermined, but the accumulation of foreign particles in the lungs is suspected. My father had smoked for much of his life—although he had quit ten years before he died—and undoubtedly this habit played a major role in the contraction of his illness. But while cleaning out my dad's house, we all developed hacking coughs, and our noses became clogged with dust. The sheer mass of objects in his home offered an enormous surface area for dust to gather upon. It is just possible that my father was killed by his own stuff.

THREE INTERNATIONAL RECIPES

EXCERPTED FROM

The Larder is Bare:
Low Expectation Recipes from Around the World

Deep-Fried Cheezy Snacks

An American Classic

INGREDIENTS

2 12 oz. bags of cheese puffs
4 slices American cheese
1 cup microwave cheese-food sauce
3 tbsp cheese spread
2 tsp salt
1 cup cottage cheese (lowfat if desired)
4 cups Crisco oil
1 cup bacon bits

METHOD

Mix cheese puffs with cheese-food sauce and salt. Place in microwave-safe bowl. Microwave at high power for 3 minutes. Let cool slightly.

Shape mixture into meatball-sized balls. Bring Crisco to a boil in large pot. Drop cheese balls into pot; let fry for two minutes. Remove with fork.

Let balls cool and harden. Place on microwave-safe serving dish. Cover balls with slices of American cheese. Microwave at high power for 30 seconds.

Top with alternating layers of cheese spread and cottage cheese, sprinkled generously with bacon bits. Serve with cans of beer.

Serves four unemployed friends.

Gloomy Raisins

An Olde English Treat

INGREDIENTS

2½ cups water
1 tsp mossy treacle
3/4 cup cornstarch
¼ tsp mint jelly
2 cups old raisins
dash of biscuit crumbs
1 cup overcooked rice
½ cup confectionery sugar
1 raw egg, beaten
3 tbsp solidified cream (optional)

METHOD

Preheat oven to 350° F. Bring water to a boil and mix in cornstarch. Stir until tired.

Cover for 3 minutes, until mixture is thick and lumpy, like a hastily cooked porridge. Drop in raisins, one at a time, and then cover for 5 minutes.

Stir in rice and egg. Add mossy treacle and biscuit crumbs while stirring. Boil until hard and grey.

Roll dough in sugar until coated, then mold into greased casserole dish and bake for 1 hour at 350° F, or until mixture feels rubbery to the touch. Spoon into teacups and serve with crusts of solidified cream if desired.

Serves three unhappy companions.

A Very Nasty Squid

L'appel du vide

INGREDIENTS

the squid, *in exile*
½ cup flour
2 tbsp olive oil
a lemon, *bright and dissected*
fresh parsley, *a useless garnish*

METHOD

Its appearance is not pleasant. But the task is set before you, and you know what you must do. With one hand, you must grasp the mantle as you would an alien penis, with trepidation and longing. It is tender, but cold. It is dead. Do not dwell on these things. With your other hand, take firm hold of the head just above the hateful eye.

Wait. Your desire to quickly yank the head out, to get it all over with, is an urge towards denial and bad faith, and will also cause the ink sac to explode. Take responsibility for your reality, and pull with slow deliberation. It separates, smelling of the sea, and procreation, and futility.

Your mind is wandering; take hold of yourself. Seize the knife and decapitate the squid. Do it now! This wretched blob of tissue is captain of nothing now, it is no longer subject but object; offal, garbage, refuse. Throw it away. Squeeze out the beak, glossy and wet as an unwanted fetus.

Now, the finish: chop up the body, the serpentine tentacles, cut it all to bits. The organizing structure of the creature is gone now; you feel enormous relief to disguise the torn remains with flour and toss it all into the pan. You are dismayed to find your mouth watering at the smell of seared flesh. It is the smell of despair.

Serves one, sitting alone at a small kitchen table under the glare of a single bulb.

THE ELDERLY WIDOW PROBLEM

You have been allotted 60 minutes to read the following and solve the questions below. Please write clearly with a number two pencil.

NDER IDEAL CONDITIONS, the number of elderly widows who can be kept spry and witty by a steady flow of sugared tea conveyed via a standard municipal water main is directly proportional to the square of the diameter of the water main, when divided by the average volume of bladder capacity per widow as distributed across the total length of the conduit. In *practical* applications, however, much of the hydrodynamic power generated by an industrial-class tea pump will be frictionally impeded by the subconscious ether that is typically generated in the proximity of any large human population, and this consideration must be factored into your calculations.

If biscuits are provided, you may expect the trajectory of the tea to follow a fairly steep angle with respect to the ground; however, its velocity vector may be resolved into two components: the "smashingly refreshing" velocity and the "unexpectedly crunchy" velocity. Since the digestion of the remaining tea can be estimated by calculating the ratio of widow to hatpin—ignoring the action of gravity—we can ascertain that:

1. in any series of elderly widows, the tranquil enjoyment experienced by each subsequent widow should diminish (in set intervals) as described by Karasovski's Law of Mutual Dissatisfaction; and

2. the ratio of gin to tea, when factored into each widow, should result in an irrational number forming an unsavory square root.

Now, let us suppose that a small consortium of wealthy Chinese businessmen have agreed to fund the construction of a silver and mother-of-pearl water main with a cross-section of 15 meters, extending 200 meters from the spout of a Class 5 nuclear-powered samovar and subsequently channeled through a series of nozzled hoses (each with a diameter of 3 cm) directly into the mouths of 12 elderly widows.

A. Calculate the mean velocity of each widow under the following conditions:

1. the widows are seated in a 42-foot pleasure boat travelling at 30 knots.

2. 11 of the widows are orbiting the first at a distance of 40 km.

3. two widows suffer from bursitis and one suffers from gas.

B. Plot a graph of volume vs. pressure for each widow. (Hint: What pressure would be necessary to expand an elderly widow to a volume of 27.6 cubic meters?)

C. If each widow has already consumed two biscuits and a scone, how much force would be necessary to push a raspberry tart through the combined length of the widows? How much force is ethical to apply?

In providing your solutions, please show all work.

A Sketch of My Childhood in the Country

IN THE HOT DRY SUMMERS of that hard country, my brothers Nemezekial, Proust, Jake and me would amuse ourselves by lathering our buttocks with margarine and sliding down the roof of the house. We thought this great fun. We were always looking for fun, my brothers and me, and consequently, we were always looking for new things to lather over our buttocks.

On the particular day on which my story begins, we had in fact lathered our baby brother with molasses, which was amusing in itself, but which became much more amusing when we carried him into our rustic country dining room, climbed up on our thirty-foot oak-plank table, and stuck him to the ceiling. When we stood back aways to look up at what we'd done, a quiet hush fell over us. With his back stuck fast to a cedar beam, and his little arms and legs left free to wiggle and squirm, our baby brother looked as if he were floating above us, like some divine creature from another world. I waved to him, and he giggled happily.

"Why, I declare," Nemezekial declared, "he looks like one of them fancy plaster cherubim rich folks use to ornamentate their parlors and such."

"Nemezekial," I said, "you ain't never been so right as you are at this here exact moment of time. And seeing as he can't get in much trouble up there, let's leave him be and find some other dumbass way to pass the rest of the afternoon."

So we all ran back outside to play a game of Kick-My-Ass in the sugar fields. This was a simple country game, of the sort city folk could never really understand. The fellow who was "it" would bend over and shout "Kick My Ass!" and the rest of us would run up to kick him in the ass. It hurt like hell. The first person to deliver the kick would get to be "it" next, so there was always quite a scramble, and we often had violent arguments over who had delivered that first crucial kick. I suppose that being country boys in the green of our youth, we all had a pathological obsession with the human butt.

Anyway, on that particular afternoon, we delighted ourselves with this amusement until dusk, when Mama dinged one of those little metal triangle things on the front porch, which signified suppertime. But she always called, "It's suppertime!" just in case we didn't understand what the triangle meant.

Like most farmers, we ate what we grew, but the land was so poor in that part of the country, all we could grow was sugar. Mostly it was just ordinary granulated white sugar, but we also grew brown sugar, spun sugar, molasses, honey, sugar plums, and a bit of aspartame, too. Once in awhile, Pa tried his hand at other crops, such as corn syrup, marshmallows, and saltwater taffy, but our land wasn't suitable for anything but sugar.

So it was no surprise that evening, after we'd all gathered around the table for supper, that Mama started us all off with some great steaming bowls of hot sugar soup, followed by a baked sugar loaf, still warm from the oven, topped with sugar-cubes and sprinkled all over with sugar.

Now I know that city people sometimes get strange notions about country folk, and I don't want you to think we ate *nothing* but sugar. Back in those days, the government would give us these huge blocks of yellow cheese, as big around as a dairy cow, and so heavy that Pa needed the tractor to drag them into the barn, where we generally stored the cheese until Mama had a need for it. Then she'd send a couple of us boys out to cut a big old slab off with one of those saws it takes two people to pull, and like little pallbearers, we'd haul that great big waxy chunk of cheese into Ma's kitchen on our shoulders. In addition to all that cheese, the government gave us these 50-pound bags of powdered eggs, which made for a nice change from the fresh eggs we got from our chickens.

Mama was a mighty fine cook, and highly inventive with our rude country staples. So the main course that evening was fried cheese with sugar, which was one of her specialties. She also knew how to make sugared eggs, sugared eggs with cheese, sugar loaf topped with a layer of cheese and eggs, cheese and sugar omelets, and cheese soup, which she sometimes served with eggs and other times just sprinkled with sugar.

Most evenings, for dessert, Mama usually just gave us our insulin shots. However, on this dusky summer evening—which was significant for reasons I can't tell you yet for reasons of narrative suspense, but which will be shortly revealed—that evening, Mama had a special surprise for dessert. Now you may not know it, but in the sugar trade, early summer is a very special time, because that's when we harvest confectionary sugar, which is the finest, sweetest, most powdery sugar there is. And that evening, Mama set an enormous wooden barrel of it right on the table, and handed each of us a scoop.

Now Pa ordinarily said grace before supper, but that evening he was agitated and got confused because of the soup—he couldn't remember whether it signified the beginning of supper or end, so he didn't say grace but then it turned out to be supper after all. So now, when Mama put that heaping barrel of confectionary sugar in front of us, Pa remembered that he had stuff to be thankful for and decided he'd better say grace now. As Pa always said, there's no sense in getting God any angrier than he already is.

"Dear Lord," Pa began, "thank You for all this sugar, especially the confectionary sugar, which is so powdery and sweet I don't expect we'll see a much better food until we join You in the next world. Thank You for good health we all enjoy as the direct result of our rugged country farm life. Oh, and also," he added hastily, "Thank You in advance for providing for our fambly when we are all homeless and destitute, which as it happens, we are likely to be very, very soon. Amen."

Well, you might say Pa's prayer came as something of a surprise since none of us had the faintest notion that we were soon to be homeless and destitute. I suppose we all had some questions on our minds, but we clean forgot them, for just then we all heard a slight sucking sound come from above, and just as we looked up, the baby came unstuck from the ceiling above us, and came tumbling down smack dab into the barrel of sugar with a great soft *whoof* and a explosion of powder that sent us all coughing.

Hacking and wheezing, Pa reached into the barrel and hauled out the baby. The sugar had stuck to the molasses, so that now the baby looked exactly like a powdered donut, if a donut had arms and legs and mournful, puzzled eyes.

"So that's where he was!" Mama said, clapping in delight. "I was wondering!"

Pa leaned over, stuck out his tongue and thoughtfully licked the baby's head.

"Oh, don't wash him off, Jed, don't!" Mama cried. "He's just perfect the way he is, like a sweet little angel."

Mama left him that way for months, and even took to recoating him with fresh molasses and sugar every morning. The nice thing about having the baby sugar-coated was that you could just stick him to a wall and he would stay there for hours, unless it got real hot, in which case he'd gradually slide to the floor. Sometimes Mama would use him to hold notes to the door of the icebox. But now that I think about it, it must've been Pa who did it the very first time, because the next morning, that's exactly where we found the baby, squirming and gurgling on the icebox door with a note in Pa's hand stuck to his sugary belly.

"Dear Fambly," the note began:

> I forgot to tell you, the reason we are all destined for great poverty is that Mr. Wiggily Pyle, the villainous and evil owner of the Sugar Farmers Loan and Trust Bank, has called in our loan. He has informed me that he will no longer accept powdered eggs or blocks of cheese as payment, so it's pretty much a done deal that we're going lose the farm.
>
> My austere country upbringing leaves me too proud to have my fambly beg for a living, so instead I am leaving to pursue my childhood dream of becoming a particle physicist. I plan to exploit a paradox in the quantum topography of space-time, after which I'll travel fifty years into the past, and file patents for inventions that don't exist yet, like panty-shields and Gummy Bears.

That way, when I return to the present time, we will all be rich and can forget about this whole sorry episode.

But if that doesn't work, I'll just come back with a high-powered assault rifle and kill each of you in turn, followed by a long and tense stand-off with the sheriff and ending with an unsuccessful attempt at shooting myself in the head.

Either way, I'll be back soon.

Fondly,

Your Loving Pa

Appendix

I. Vestigial

> It is curious that I remember well the time when the thought of the eye made me cold all over, but I have got over this stage of the complaint, & now small trifling particulars of structure often make me very uncomfortable. The sight of a feather in a peacock's tail, whenever I gaze at it, makes me sick!

> —Charles Darwin
> Letter to Asa Gray, April 1860
> (The Darwin Correspondence Project)

THE WORD *vestigial* is invariably paired with another word, and that word is *organ*, and the whole enchilada—*vestigial organ*—refers almost exclusively to the human appendix, which is THE vestigial organ: a chubby little worm of tissue dangling off the massive corridor of the large intestine, a celebrated symbol of evolution's occasional failure to rid itself of obsolete developments.

Useless. That's what *vestigial* really means, useless like the dusty VCR wedged into the shelf under your flat panel television even though you no longer own any videotapes and the very thought of even *playing* a videotape—the *chunk* and *whirr* of that oblong plastic brick being slurped into the mechanical maw of the thing—makes you shudder with inexplicable feelings of nausea and sadness. Ah, but back in your college years your mom gave you that VCR when you were home for the holidays, and this magical engine of wonder and delight served you well for many years, conjuring up hours of *Monty Python* and *Star Trek* and all the porn you had the courage to rent from the creepy back room of that Korean video store, and so it remains in your possession, an artifact of a long-gone era of technological innocence, forever blinking midnight.

The appendix, of course, is not the only useless part of your body. The utility of the grub-like pinky toe, with its tough little slab of greenish nail, has been regarded with skepticism. Neither science nor scripture has adequately addressed the mystery of male nipples. If you can live without a gall bladder then why do you need one in the first place? Don't get me started on wisdom teeth.

But what makes the appendix fascinating is not so much that it's useless, but that it can kill you. So, actually: *less* than useless. Its primary function is *to explode without warning.* It's a strange joke of evolution that we are all born with this deadly little time bomb tucked into the bottom shelf of our most important insides, as if the human body had been hastily manufactured by Samsung.

The exploding appendix has always been a subject of special delight for small children, as of course it should be. The bizarre treachery of the appendix is disclosed to children at an early age, because their parents worry that their sons and daughters won't be adequately alarmed if their appendices should suddenly burst inside of them. When I was a child, it was tempting to categorize this as just one more incredibly stupid parental concern, because so many parental concerns are so incredibly stupid. Children often feel this way, that their parents are complete idiots, and I agree with them. Although I have no children of my own, my long years on this earth have given me the opportunity to witness many fine examples of parental idiocy across multiple generations, and it has been both delightful and demoralizing to realize that perfectly sensible children often grow up into perfectly idiotic parents who will perpetuate the same patently dumb shit upon their children that they themselves were once subjected to by their own idiotic parents. This, too, must be evolution at work. Upon successfully reproducing, some genetic switch is flipped off in the parental brain so that the idiot parade can march on in perpetuity. It's the only way to explain how otherwise more-or-less functional adults—like, you know, *grown-ups*, endowed with the minimal cognitive skills required to make mortgage payments or operate a microwave—can continue, generation after generation, to subscribe to variations of the same imbecilic, harebrained notions:

- If you eat that hot dog and jump back into the pool you will get cramps and drown.
- 13-year-old suburban girls wear colored-coded plastic bracelets to advertise their sexual exploits to classmates.
- Those smeary rub-on tattoos dispensed by gumball machines are laced with LSD by drug dealers hoping to hook kids on bad acid trips.
- Such dealers find their most lucrative venues at school playgrounds because there's just no market for selling recreational drugs to adults.
- Every Halloween, some of your neighbors succumb to the irresistible temptation to insert razor blades into apples and distribute them to unsuspecting children.
- An unsupervised child in possession of a large sack of Hershey Bars and Skittles will, nonetheless, prefer to eat an apple which may or may not contain a razor blade.

Philip Larkin was right.* Hysteria builds like a coastal shelf. The thing that kills me is that the same implausible rumors which were circulated by mimeograph at PTA meetings when I was a kid in the 1970s are now circulated by my peers on Facebook and Twitter.

Now, I don't want to get carried away. Pay attention, kids. Some parental fears really *are* based in the empirical universe. You really *shouldn't* run with scissors, or climb into unmarked vans driven by strangers, and acute appendicitis really *is* more likely to occur in children than adults,† and that is *exactly* why whenever you had a pain in your side, your mother would anxiously inquire whether it was the left side or the right, although I guarantee you that every time she asked this question she struggled to remember which side mattered, because no one can *ever* remember which side matters. Even as I write these words, I myself can't remember. This, too, seems part of the evolutionary scheme, the long Darwinian struggle between human and appendix.

---

* Google it. *They fuck you up, your mum and dad . . .*

† At a rate of 80,000 kids per year in the US, appendicitis is the most common cause for emergency abdominal surgery in childhood. *Source:* I Googled it.

In such situations, my own mother would consult the ancient leather-bound medical encyclopedia she had preserved from her own childhood in the 1930s, the era in which 4 out of 5 lung surgeons recommended Lucky Strikes for their patients who smoked. Although modern antibiotics and polio vaccines went unmentioned in this tome, it was otherwise an impressive distillation of mid-20th-century medical knowledge, and thus a reasonably accurate guide to the everyday ailments and maladies of the human body. In this regard, my mother probably held an advantage over modern-day mommies, who are likely to consult Google for medical advice, thus risking exposure to scientifically dubious theories concerning wheat gluten and measles vaccinations.

Mid-20th-century medical science took a dim view of vestigials. Like tonsils or foreskins, the appendix was dismissed as a less-than-essential body part that could be conveniently discarded in childhood with no more thought than you'd give to tossing an empty can of Schlitz out the window of your '55 Buick Roadmaster.

Television writers of the black-and-white era loved appendectomies. If your ratings slipped, and you needed to inject some novelty into the clockwork universe of your bland family sitcom, well, a little *routine surgery* might be just the ticket. Timmy won't eat his French toast, doesn't want to go to school, says he's got a tummy-ache. Mommy lays an anxious hand across the little ankle-biter's forehead, frowns. Dr. Shapiro knocks at the door, black bag in hand. *Oh yes,* he says, folding up his stethoscope. *I'm quite sure. You'll have to bring him in, I'm afraid.* Mommy phones Daddy at the office, who grabs his hat and briefcase. Hospital scene, some lab coats—easy enough to borrow the set from one of the daytime soaps. Toss in your favorite doctor jokes and a pretty nurse and call it a day. You've titillated your viewers with a Child in Jeopardy and a taboo whiff of human mortality, and now you can wrap up the whole thing—routine surgery!—with a happy outcome of so little consequence that no future episode will have to acknowledge it ever happened.

For the sake of variety, broken bones and dental catastrophes could be similarly deployed, but tonsillectomies were especially favored by sitcom writers: an even better choice than appendectomies, since tonsils used to be removed prophylactically. Vestigial! By my childhood in the Seventies, doctors had stopped routinely yanking out tonsils—turned out they might be useful after all—but tonsillitis continued to serve as a tried-and-true plot device on contemporary dreck like *The Brady Bunch*. In such episodes, the humor revolved around enticing a frightened child into an operating room with the prospect of unlimited ice cream to follow.

These shows made surgery seem like an important rite of passage, but like stickball, swimmin' holes, and drugstore soda fountains, perfunctory tonsillectomies were yet another hallowed, character-forming American tradition that had somehow been excised from my polyester suburban childhood of Tang and Saturday morning cartoons.

So I took note of such Very Special Episodes with keen interest. They inspired in me a strange sense of envy. It wasn't the fucking ice cream. I wanted to be injured.

The problem was I didn't play sports, and I was also a coward. Opportunities for broken bones were limited. When I was eight, I did manage to fracture my ankle after I threw a Superman cape over my shoulders and jumped off a one-story ledge onto the concrete surface of our driveway. My superpowers failed. My bravery was rewarded with a genuine plaster cast that could be signed by my classmates, but hobbling around on crutches turned out to be a remarkably shitty way to spend the summer.

By the time I reached adulthood, I'd lost two of my wisdom teeth and my foreskin. (Not in that order.) But I still had my tonsils and my appendix. My mom had been worried over nothing every time.

As a young, newly independent adult, I still felt an obligation to worry whenever I got a pain in my side—I owed my mother that much—although I could never remember which side mattered because I didn't own a medical encyclopedia and Google hadn't been invented yet, and by the time it was, I knew that a persistent pain in your side might be gas, or cancer, or the result of a sexual mishap, but whatever it is, it is definitely not appendicitis.

Except, of course, when it is.

My friend Valerie, whom I've known since my college years, lives a few blocks away in our sleepy Brooklyn neighborhood, and *she* got appendicitis.

So it happens.

And they left her with a *stump*, which I didn't know could happen.

I mean the stump of her appendix, but *stump* is never a good surgery outcome.

She didn't find out until months later that her surgeon, for reasons unknown, didn't quite get the whole appendix out. She just kept getting sick every few weeks, feeling exactly as she had when she'd had appendicitis, and then she'd go back to her surgeon, who said, "Well, of course you don't have appendicitis, you can't have appendicitis, because you only have one appendix and I cut it out of you."

He hypothesized that her suffering was caused by a *phantom appendix*, that she was literally being haunted by the ghost of her severed appendix.

Finally, she went to another doctor, who did some scans and whatnot, and offered a less supernatural diagnosis: *stump.* So then she had to go back to her original surgeon with the diagnosis and scans, who awkwardly glossed over the fact that he'd royally fucked up and scheduled her for another surgery.

So that was how my friend happened to have her appendix removed twice.

I was not envious of Valerie's double appendectomy.

As a middle-aged man, I'd long outgrown all that Cindy Brady crap, the romance of routine surgery.

Indeed, even by the end of my adolescence, as I prepared to leave for college, the only rites of passage I looked forward to involved recreational drugs and casual sex. I'd come to embrace my physical cowardice by then and had acquired a strong distaste for both injury and doctors.

Sometime in my mid-twenties, I wound up losing two more wisdom teeth—four in total, all impacted—but that was fine because good riddance to those fuckers, which would randomly flare up with throbbing infections until I finally paid a dentist to rip them out of my skull.

I'd also lost most of my hair. Not really fine at all, but my good looks and natural charm carried me through the transition. I grew a fashionable goatee.

Otherwise, I still had the rest: tonsils, appendix, gallbladder, spleen, toes, fingers, nose. Nearly the whole collector's set, not exactly in mint condition, but bought and paid for, and all mine. With the passage of time, I grew more and more attached to these personal components. It became a kind of challenge, to see if I could reach the finish line of life's grueling obstacle course with all the equipment still intact by the time I was ready to check out at the rental desk. I avoided activities involving motorcycles or circular saws, declined invitations to bicycle down mountainsides or hurl myself out of airplanes. After many years of relying on public transportation in New York City, I developed an aversion to traveling in automobiles, which I'd come to regard—supported by overwhelming empirical evidence—as the prime threat to my cherished collection of limbs and innards.*

❁ ❁ ❁

*About 40,000 motor vehicle deaths per year in the U.S. alone. About 4.5 *million* serious injuries. Compare this to commercial flying (2016: 303 deaths *worldwide*, 2017: zero deaths, as in *none*). Indeed, compare the risk of automobile travel to almost any other cause of accidental death or injury. The media and Facebook have worked you into a tizzy about all sorts of Chicken Little bullshit—Ebola, terrorists, Mexicans, vaccines, GMO tomatoes, hot dog induced swimming cramps—but face it: you're probably going to die in a car crash.†

†*2020 edit:* A note composed in the Before Times, now imbued with unintended irony. Never mind—let it stand.

Given my distaste for physical risk, I suppose it's strange that I enjoy skiing.

Of course, employing the present participle in this context—*I enjoy skiing*—makes it sound as if I plan my year around pilgrimages to Aspen, or that I spend the winter months parading around the streets of New York City in one of those obnoxious puffy jackets festooned with lift tickets.

The truth is, I have gone on exactly three weekend skiing trips in my entire life, each of which was separated by a span of many years, and most of that activity took place on bunny hills. The last time I went skiing was, um . . . let me think. Well, my niece Jordan had come with us, and she had just turned two . . .

Oh Christ, that was fourteen years ago.

Gah.

Anyway, in early January of 2016, the year in which the story I'm about to tell takes place, a childhood friend invited me to join him on his annual Martin Luther King weekend ski trip in Vermont.

Although I enjoy skiing, I had some hesitation. His brother-in-law, whom I don't know, would be joining us, as well as his brother-in-law's friends, whom I also don't know, and we'd all be driving up in a car from New Jersey, and that sounded like a rather confined space to be spending seven or eight hours with a bunch of guys I didn't know, who all shared a long history which excluded me, and who, liberated from the moderating influence of their wives, might decide to talk about sports, or have a farting contest, or grumble about my frequent bathroom stops and proclivity towards motion sickness. And if my friend was driving, he'd surely be distracted by all that ruckus going on in the car, and I-95 is the worst fucking highway in the universe—from Maine to Miami, it's a veritable *river* of assholes—and then all those crazy switchback Vermont mountain roads caked with ice, and 40,000 automobile deaths per year etc.

And also, and perhaps most importantly, the invitation had come at *short notice*, and while I am definitely an impulsive person, I am sadly not a very spontaneous one.

My life is in constant disarray, I am always losing stuff, I am terrible at planning, and the few good habits and routines I manage to establish are easily disrupted by holidays and trips, and for that reason spontaneous travel plans fill me with anxiety because I am terrified that in my haste to pack and get ready I will forget some crucially important thing like turning off the stove or arranging to have someone feed the cat.

I know this is a character flaw, one that's caused my wife unhappiness over the years, short-circuiting the potential for zany road trips with friends or last-minute romantic getaways, and because I know it's a character flaw, I tried to reconsider, and told my friend I'd think about it.

But what I thought about instead was the last time I went skiing, fourteen years earlier, which also happened to be over MLK weekend. I'd finally acquired enough skill on that trip to get off the bunny hill and managed to glide down the green beginner trails a number of times without falling or crashing into other people, and it was glorious, the silence, the snow-crusted trees, the breathtaking sense of flying through a winter wonderland. *Woohoo! I enjoy skiing!* Then I got cocky and tried a blue intermediate trail, gained way too much speed on a sharp downward slope, hit a patch of moguls, instantly lost control, and missed dashing out my brains on a tree trunk by approximately four inches.

In the ski lodge at the end of that day, as we clomped around in boots and struggled to pull off wet clothes, we learned from a ski instructor that a few weeks earlier another novice skier had made a similarly unwise assessment of his skills, but with far less luck: he slammed hard into one of the steel poles supporting the chair lift. He died instantly.

❁ ❁ ❁

Now that was definitely an unsettling thing to hear about at the end of my victorious ski weekend. But my main takeaway was not to avoid skiing *altogether*, but just to avoid skiing on those mogul-y intermediate trails, at least until I'd had more lessons. And maybe invest in a helmet. Because I'd had *fun*. Because it had been pleasant to discover, in my mid-thirties, an unrealized potentiality in myself, that I could be *a person who enjoys skiing.* So I resolved to solid-ify this new identity with a return to the slopes at some yet-to-be-determined point in the future.

But I didn't. In my mind, that final trip had been just a few years ago. But fourteen years—fourteen winters!—is not *a few years*, it's an *era.* The chubby, adorable two-year-old niece who'd accompanied us on that trip had transmogrified into a smart, snarky, cellphone-addicted teenager who wore knee-high Doc Martens and compul-sively posted selfies to Instagram. The iPhone hadn't even been in-vented the last time I went skiing. So that was unsettling, too, the sobering arithmetic of mortality. That poor guy who slammed into the pole died a long time ago. It was sad for his family and friends, but everyone has moved on by now.

When someone invites you to do something, and you say *I'll think about it,* you really mean *no.* I already knew that I would decline my friend's invitation to Vermont, but I vacillated because my decision made me sad. It made me face the possibility that I might never go skiing again, that I hadn't actually become *a person who enjoys skiing,* and it was unlikely I ever would.

Fourteen winters. Why hadn't I ever gone again?

As with most things, I'd prefer to blame my wife. Natasha grew up in Trinidad in the West Indies, and—as we discovered during that long-ago MLK weekend—she does *not* enjoy skiing. Natasha does enjoy *snow,* which, even after decades in New York, still seems like a miracle to her, a vision out of a fairy tale, and *that's enough for her.* She loves walking through the snow. She loves hurling poorly constructed snowballs that crumble into chunks of powder in mid-air. She even loves flopping herself down into a snowdrift to make an angel, which is quite a charming thing to watch a grown woman do. But she didn't like skiing. She found it scary and cold, and—in terms of enjoying a beautiful snowy vista—unnecessary. Not that she would've objected to me going on my own. But frankly, I'm not much of a self-starter. The only reason I ever leave town at all is because Natasha wants to go somewhere (Turkey! Cuba! Long Island!) and is willing to make travel arrangements for both of us.

I don't know. I think I'm lying to myself about this. It's not Natasha. It's like that time I bought a one-year membership to the Museum of Modern Art and never went. Not once. I had good intentions, took note of events and exhibitions I wanted to see. Frequently jotted *Go to MoMA this week!!!* in the little black Moleskine notebook I carry around. And before I knew it, a full year had passed, and all I had to show for my membership was a heightened sense of shame.

Everyone knows that time accelerates as you grow older. You start to have that panicky sense in your late teens and early twenties, that *you'd better get a move on.* That the summers are no longer a green eternity of freedom, that opportunities have been squandered, that, shit, the final paper you had all semester to write is due on Thursday. You start thinking about how you won't always be this young, and you think you understand mortality. But you don't, because you're young. Evolution doesn't want you to see the shape of mortality yet. It wants you to think you are bullet-proof and that you have all the time in the world. Go ahead, jackass—eat as many hot dogs as you want and cannonball right off the high dive. Evolution wants you to be thoughtless and arrogant, to take stupid risks, so you'll fling yourself out into the world, and, ideally, propagate the species by knocking someone up (or getting yourself knocked-up) before it dawns on you that the absolute freedom of young adulthood—that giddy interval of pure possibility sandwiched between innocence and experience—spans just a few short years and they will be over before you know it.

But the last time I went skiing, I was already past that phase. I was married and in my mid-thirties. That Rip Van Winkle sense of time was getting worse and worse. I could feel *forty* breathing down my neck and tried not to think about it. Already I had an adult understanding of my limitations in a way that I had not when I'd been in my twenties. I understood that I was not the great genius I'd once hoped I might have been. That my potentialities were sharply proscribed and grew more so with every passing year. That I'd never get to experience all the kinky sexual stuff I'd hoped to, and that

I was damned lucky I'd gotten to check off as many boxes as I had. That I was never going to understand quantum physics, or speak Chinese, or start an underground art movement, or become a mysterious traveler.

What I *didn't* know in my thirties was that during the next fourteen years my understanding of time and mortality would become a lot less abstract. In the intervening decade and a half, bad shit seemed to happen with clockwork regularity. Natasha and I tried to procreate, and failed. We went the IVF route—a merry-go-round of needles and hormones—and the doctors discovered she had extensive endometriosis. She had to have surgery, and I was thus first introduced to the exquisite torment of spending an entire day waiting for someone you love to emerge from an operating room. The next year, Natasha had a miscarriage. That same year, one of Natasha's best friends died of cancer. She was only thirty-seven, and left behind her husband and two young children. My uncle died. He lived alone, and a policeman found him in his backyard, lying on the ground near the rock he'd hit his head on. He'd been there for days. Around that time, I started to get a recurring heel injury—plantar fasciitis—which doesn't sound like much, in the larger scheme of things, but it prevented me from running and playing volleyball for months at a time. Those are the only physical activities I do regularly, and I wondered how long it would be before I'd have to give them up altogether. Natasha's endometriosis grew back; she had to have another surgery. A few days before the operation, one of Natasha's closest childhood friends from Trinidad crashed his car into a tree and died. He was forty. Natasha's second endometriosis surgery took far longer than expected—they wound up removing one of her ovaries as well—and I spent the last few hours in an emptied-out waiting room inhabited only by myself, Natasha's mother, two of our friends, and the members of some other patient's family, who spent those hours huddled in a corner with their arms around one another, sobbing. After that second operation, Natasha went on a special form of birth control pills to retard the growth of her endometriosis. Two of Natasha's uncles died, and then her father died. I think that might have been the same year that her young cousin in Canada, who was still a teenager, died of cancer. One September—after a summer of unwisely combining my prescription ADD medication with recreational drugs—I experienced a brief but disturbing episode of psychotic paranoia, during which I became convinced that a neighbor we barely knew was planning break into our apartment to kill our cat. When Natasha found the butcher's knife I'd been keeping in my bedside drawer for protection, she flipped out, and made me go to a psychiatrist. We moved to another apartment, and I stopped using recreational drugs.*

During those years, no less than four of our friends underwent mastectomies for breast cancer. At least two had to have their ovaries removed, too. A friend landed in the emergency room with a broken wrist and cracked ribs when some happy-go-lucky tourist on a Citi Bike crashed into her at full speed. Another friend happened to be shopping with his wife in a Manhattan Home Depot when, just feet away from him, a disgruntled employee shot and killed his supervisor, and then shot himself in the head. Exactly one year prior to my friend's skiing invitation, over MLK weekend, Natasha began coughing up blood. She'd had a pulmonary embolism—an errant blood clot had lodged itself in her lungs. That was pretty scary—a PE can kill someone in minutes—but she was very lucky, and sustained no permanent damage to her health. It was almost certainly caused by the birth control pills, so she had to stop taking them. She had to go on blood thinners for six months, and got a scrip for Xanax because she suffered from mild panic attacks in the evenings, when she was afraid of dying in her sleep. That was when we found out that at least two of our friends were also taking blood thinners. Who knew? Oh, and our friend Valerie had to have her appendix removed. Twice. I began to suspect that any number of our friends suffered from serious health problems, both chronic and acute, and just didn't talk about it much because, well, it's kind of a drag to bring up your clogged arteries or cervical cancer when you're all getting together for drinks and laughs.

So that's pretty much how the whole mortality business was shaping up by the time I was in my late forties. In middle age, you start to see it all with frightening clarity, the beautiful idiocy of your

* Mostly.

wastrel youth and the shape of things to come. Evolution is done with you by now. You've had your chance to reproduce, whether or not you made good use of it, so it's time to start closing up shop. You're last year's model, an obsolete unit taking up valuable shelf space. Software updates are being phased out, the end-of-support date rapidly approacheth. *If you continue to use this product, you agree to do so at your own risk.*

One of the things you don't realize about middle age until you get there is that you'll have a ringside view of what the coming decades have in store for you. Your parents, your friends' parents—if they are still alive—are now fully in the cruel grasp of old age, teetering on the brink of oblivion. It is pretty fucking bleak. The very old are cranky, sick, demented, stubborn, increasingly helpless, angered by their own irrelevance, grieving for lost friends and spouses and a world that used to make sense. Every other month, Natasha and I found ourselves writing sympathy cards to friends who'd recently lost a parent. A whole generation was slipping away, stepping into the void, and taking with them the last living memories of automats and dance cards and triple-feature matinees, radio serials and vacuum tubes and television antennas, live operators and party lines, telegrams and handwritten letters, and human conversations that had once taken place not through a dark glass screen but face to face, self engaging self in the fragile intimacy of a single, shared nexus in time and space.

Reader, I was forty-eight, and it was early January. David Bowie had died a week earlier. The days were cold, the nights were long, and I had much on my mind.

❁   ❁   ❁

"Why don't you just go?" Natasha said. "You always talk about how much you enjoy skiing."

"I don't know," I said. "It's a long drive."

"You'll have fun. You're always saying you never get to do anything fun."

"I don't know. I'll think about it."
I thought about it.

❀ ❀ ❀

If you don't make plans, they tend to be made for you. Unless absolutely forced to do otherwise, I will always defer a decision to the last moment, since by then the default choice will be the only option remaining and all I have to do in the interim is suffer through the vague haze of anxiety that lingers at the back of the skull when you routinely defer decisions. So I dilly-dallied with thoughts of mortality and dudes farting in cars until two days before the trip, when I finally offered last-minute apologies to my friend. So now we had the three-day weekend ahead with no plans in place, which was practically an invitation for fate to slide over and grab the steering wheel.

❀ ❀ ❀

Speaking of steering wheels, dear passenger, you may be wondering where we're going with all of this. Like a road map, titles and opening paragraphs create certain teleological expectations. An itinerary. *Oh, the places you'll go.* When you first buckled in, I handed you a map entitled *APPENDIX* and hit the gas. We're chugging along, passing the expected sights and milestones, when a fork appears in the road and suddenly we veer off towards some random ski resort. Halfway there, another fork beckons, and now you suspect (correctly) that we're heading off in a new, completely unrelated direction which is literally *neither here nor there* and you're staring at the map, wondering if I ever bothered to consult it at all, and who the hell still consults *an actual paper map?*

If you don't feel this way yet, you will.

Let's pull over for a sec.

So I forget—did I tell you I have attention deficit disorder? Confirmed by several therapists. I even have a prescription. Oh, yeah, I think I did tell you. Well, not to worry. Over the years, I've learned to manage it.*

Which is why I can assure you that, yes, this is indeed an appendix story. I didn't forget. Appendix-related events will be happening. I promise. Soon. (Pretty soon. Right after that long-ass section about Luna and cat puke.)

And sure, we could get there faster, but I've always thought that if it's just about *making time*, rushing towards a destination, then where's the *trip?* The Interstate holds no romance for people like you and me. To misquote Gertrude Stein: *there's no there there.* It's all Dunkin' Donuts, Taco Bell, and Exxon. You can't tell whether you're passing through Connecticut or Arkansas, nothing to experience but six sterile lanes of asphalt slashed through a wasteland of corporations and death.

Screw that. We're taking the life-affirming scenic route all the way. In keeping with our theme, this will be an *intestinal journey.* Twisting side roads looping from one damn thing to another and back again, experiences and impressions accumulating like so much hastily masticated salt-water taffy. There will be roadside attractions. (I happen to know there's a sad little karaoke bar just ahead. And just a little farther there's an off-season Christmas Village! Who can resist?) Come on, it will be *fun!* Don't worry—we'll make plenty of bathroom stops.

It's settled. We've been idling in this rest stop long enough and I've sucked all the juice out of this road trip metaphor. You get the point: this thing is digressive. Lots of detours. Time to buckle up, roll down the windows, crank up the tunes. Oh come on—get back in the car. Please? We have a long way to go.

---

* Fun tip: whenever you enter your home, put your keys and your wallet in a bowl by the door. That way, you'll always know where they are!

So where were we? Oh, right. The three-day weekend that kicked it all off.

On Friday afternoon, Natasha called from work and suggested we go into the city to see the Picasso sculpture exhibit at the Museum of Modern Art, and this sounded as a good a plan as any as it avoided potentialities of social discomfort or bodily injury. Actually, it sounded like a lot of fun. You'd think New Yorkers go to museums and gallery openings all the time, but we don't, because we can. Why go now, when you can go anytime you want? Which is why I no longer had a membership when we finally got around to going.

The Picasso exhibit was fascinating, thought-provoking, worthwhile in all the ways it always is whenever we actually bother to do stuff like that, provoking the question we always ask ourselves: why don't we bother to do stuff like that more often? Afterwards, we had pints and pub food at a nearby Irish bar, and then wandered around Hell's Kitchen until we happened upon a lonely little karaoke bar with only a handful of patrons in attendance.

We sat at the bar and got drunk. A tipsy woman in a low-cut blouse flirted with Natasha while her bored husband kept checking his cellphone. The karaoke line-up rotated through the same three or four singers, one of whom was the flirty woman sitting next to Natasha. Everyone but the bored husband was having a blast. I put my name in. I belted out Bowie's "Changes," sat down, ordered more drinks, and then got up again to go croak out my wretched rendition of "Ziggy Stardust." The bored husband announced he wanted to go home. His wife didn't and they got into a loud argument. She stomped out of the bar in a huff. The husband scooped up his wife's abandoned purse and ran out after her. The bartender announced last call. Natasha and I finished our drinks and wandered out into the cold, clear night, holding hands and laughing, giddy as a pair of tourists.

The next day, on Saturday morning, we woke at a leisurely hour, pleasantly hungover. I shuffled into the kitchen, fed the cat, put the kettle on. Natasha joined me on the couch. As we sipped our mugs of coffee and tea, we discussed what we might like to do with the blank canvas of three obligation-free days that stretched before us. The temperature had dropped precipitously overnight, and the world outside our windows looked windy and cold.

There was something of a holiday feeling in this little bracket of days we had to ourselves, a secret holiday, just for us. This was important to me because we had just emerged from the woodchipper of the actual non-secret Holiday Season. I must confess I am one of those people who does not like Christmas. More accurately: I *loathe* Christmas. I dread its hateful approach, and every year, starting in November, I am seized by fits of Yuletide rage and compulsively subject my poor wife—who loves Christmas, as all decent people do—to spasms of outraged, spittle-flecked invective regarding the Season To Be Fucking Jolly.

I don't like the gift-giving, which requires planning and shopping, two activities I find unenjoyable and anxiety-producing, and then there's the preemptive matter of advising other people what they should give to *me*, which I also don't like, because the things I would actually like to receive are either trivial and utilitarian (a large carton of Home Depot garbage bags, or a new filter for our air purifier) or they are big-ticket technology items (a fancy gazillion-pixel DSLR camera; a faster, sleeker laptop uncrippled by porn viruses) that are too expensive to ask anyone to purchase on my behalf.

I don't care for gingerbread houses, elves, or plastic reindeer, and I can't stand the horrid music, which unpleasantly evokes the polo shirts and missionary positions of the Eisenhower Era, and by Christmas Day I've been forced to endure those two dozen canonical songs in every public space for nearly two months. Santa Claus is vaguely pedophiliac and also just plain stupid. The geographically-disadvantaged toy workshop presents obvious logistical issues, the invasive tracking of naughty-or-nice metrics violates any number of European privacy laws, and a fat old man who insists upon delivering gifts by cramming himself down smoking chimneys sounds like a surefire candidate for the Darwin Awards. I'm sorry, Virginia, but Santa is a slapdash assemblage of codswallop foisted upon gullible children by corporate advertisers, and your friends are right to scorn you. I wish we had a Krampus tradition in this country, a malignant, leering, red-eyed Krampus prancing behind an enormous coal-black phallus, a truly pagan Krampus who would induce brain-exploding seizures of Puritanical outrage in Fox News commentators every December. *That* would be something to be merry about.

I would prefer to spend Christmas as the Jews do. With other Jews. In a Chinese restaurant, followed by a movie. Every year, I devote resentful hours of thought to the liberating possibility of converting to Judaism, but no one would take me seriously—I just want to be *Jewish*, not *a practicing Jew*—and besides, my conversion would saddle me with all sorts of additional social obligations, and the goyim would still make me do Christmas.

Admittedly, I do like Midnight Mass. I'm not much of a church-goer, but I like the warm darkness and the flickering candles, the organ and the choir and the majestic Baroque carols, the big-hearted solemnity of gathering together with strangers in a place that is not sports arena or a bar. I like Christmas trees, too. That's a lovely tradition. The evergreen scent, the lights, the gold and red.

Oh, but the *presents*. The presents ruin everything. They look nice under the tree, all the fancy wrapping and ribbons, but why can't they just be symbolic? One year I came up with the idea that everyone should just give each other figs. You know, those clever little circular packages of dried figs they sell at the supermarket? Everyone likes figs. They are cheap, they are nutritious, and they are vaguely Biblical. You wouldn't have to wrap them because everyone would know that you are giving them figs, but you could wrap them if you felt like it. Re-gifting figs would be a breeze.

Because it wears you down, the sheer ugliness of the frenzied consumerism. Charlie Brown was right to be troubled by it. Christmas is supposed to be a season when you take stock of your shitty selfish nature and think of the less fortunate for a change—*peace on earth and goodwill to men*—but it's just an orgy of thoughtless greed. Gimme gimme gimme. Xbox. iPhone. Roomba. Fifty-five inch flatscreen with five-speaker Surround Sound so you can watch George Bailey sacrifice ambition and opportunity for the sake of community service in high definition OLED. Like, not to shit on anyone's parade, but there's an Australia-sized wad of plastic crap floating in the Pacific, the fish are dying out, the glaciers are melting, and polar bear cubs are floating off into the sea. I don't want to be the tree-hugging sourpuss at the holiday party who whines, Come on, people, think of the planet—but *Come on, people, think of the planet! Why won't you merry-making assholes think of the planet??*

But what I hate most about Christmas, the real underlying nugget of radioactive hatred, is that it is socially obligatory. *You are not allowed to opt out.* Think about it. You can opt out of birthday parties. You can even opt out of your own birthday. (It's delightful.) You can opt out of dinner dates, dentist appointments, and poetry readings. You can opt out of weddings—that's what RSVPs are for. You can opt out of funerals and send flowers instead. But you can't opt out of Christmas. Even if you try—and I have—you will just sit by yourself in an eerily quiet apartment subjected to Dickensian visitations from the Ghost of Christmas Guilt, and you'll wind up spending the whole day feeling resentful and sorry for yourself because you have to spend Christmas Day alone. And so, against my will, I will be be dragged away from all the things I like to do or need to do, forced to lug shopping bags of laboriously wrapped gifts on busses trains airplanes so that I may ritualistically distribute these perfunctory and unnecessary consumer goods to various relatives, and I must in turn receive items I do not want or need which will take up precious space in my apartment, I will overeat pie eggnog nuts fruitcake because I have no self-control, I will gain ten pounds and spend the rest of the year trying to lose five of them, I will have to keep up the exhausting pretense that I am brimming with joy because this is the Happiest Time of The Year and everyone will strain to be painfully nice to one another because no one wants to spoil Christmas because *spoiling Christmas* is the moral equivalent of *kicking a puppy.*

Whew. Okay, okay, deep breath.

All of this is undeniably true, but . . .

Christmas was *over.*

It often takes me all of January to recover from it.

The rage, the shame. The apologies.

And perhaps that's why having no plans for this three day weekend in mid-January made it feel like a *secret holiday,* an anti-Christmas. We had no social obligations, and no one was around anyway, they were all skiing, and anyone who wasn't off skiing would assume that we *were*, even though we don't really ski. The phone wouldn't ring all day with friends and relatives calling to wish us a Merry Martin Luther King, Jr. Day. We didn't have to give each other anything, didn't have to haul the once-a-year boxes of gaudy holiday paraphernalia out of the deep recesses of the closet.

It was too cold and windy to think of going anywhere far, and that made the apartment seem like a cozy refuge. If we'd had a fireplace, we would have lit a fire, it was that kind of a day. Of course, once our maniacal super woke up and cranked the boiler up to Maximum Discomfort, the apartment would grow sweltering and fetid and we'd have to open all the windows, but for the next hour or two it was still possible to maintain the idyllic illusion of a winter holiday for two, our own private Brooklyn.

Natasha offered to make some nice, greasy omelets for breakfast. I wondered aloud whether we should commit to a truly unproductive day by transforming breakfast into brunch with a spicy pitcher of Bloody Marys.

In the midst of this pleasant conversation, our cat Luna sauntered into the room and meowed once, announcing her presence. With the concentration of an Olympic gymnast preparing to execute a vault, Luna positioned herself in the center of the floor, lowered her head, crouched down, and backed up across the room while spewing out a long glistening line of barely digested Fancy Feast.

❄   ❄   ❄

Luna! A graceful, intelligent, and quick-tempered creature whom we'll be hearing a lot more about. We can pick her up and stroke her belly; you can't. Don't fuck with her or you'll wind up in bloody ribbons. Her eyes: luminescent green, and darkly limned, like the eyes of a silent film star. Her coat is as soft and white as a bank of snow, and spattered with random black markings, as if an enraged abstract expressionist had flung a pot of ink at a blank canvas. The first two inches of her tail are white but the rest is charcoal black, as if dipped in it, with a pale watermark ring towards the tip. Her face, like her body, is mostly white, but a thick smudge of black edges the top of her pink nose, as if drawn in marker; her chin is also black; and a puddle of black fur encircles her right ear, cocked over her forehead like a small beret, giving her the overall appearance of a jaunty French mime sporting a greasepaint mustache and goatee.

We'd found Luna on the sidewalk of East 78th Street on a brutally cold February evening almost exactly eight years earlier, a three-month-old stray kitten darting back and forth on the icy concrete, mewling desperately at everyone who passed because she was, literally, freezing to death. With the help of a kind stranger—who ingeniously helped us lure her into his building lobby with a string, and offered us his own cat's carrier—we captured her and brought her home, where we discovered she was covered in motor oil from seeking warmth in car engines. Some hot metal part had singed her whiskers, which were shriveled and bent like tiny pipe cleaners. We cleaned her, fed her, and soon became devoted to her with the ferocious intensity of a married couple with no children to care for.

Luna has been a solace and a friend to each of us when Natasha and I are at odds; she completes the purring circle of domestic harmony when we are at peace. Her antics and waggery never fail to delight; she provides an inexhaustible topic of conversation when we've run out of interesting things to say. She is a nuisance when she wants her breakfast in the early dawn while we are still sleeping: she pounces up and down our sprawled bodies, or wedges herself between our pillowed heads and purrs loudly, or—occasionally, and with unhappy results for all concerned—unsheathes a single razor-sharp claw and inserts it into the bare flesh of my arm.

She is an object of preternatural beauty when she reposes, Sphinx-like, among the houseplants in the mid-morning sun, and the subject of more of our photos than anyone else including each other. We love her and she loves us, but she pukes.

Cat puke is a routine event for anyone who keeps a cat. As with poopy litter boxes, shredded furniture, and fur-drenched clothing, scooping feline vomitus off the floor (or your favorite sweater) is just another contractual obligation built into the longstanding interspecies arrangement between humans and cats. You knew what you signed up for.

But when Luna does it, I get worried. There's a history here. On several past occasions, puking has been the overture to a mysterious ailment that causes her, quite uncharacteristically, to refuse food, sometimes for days.

Cats, with their finicky obligate-carnivore digestive system, do not tolerate even short periods of starvation well. When animals (including *homo sapiens*) go without food for long enough, the body begins breaking down stored fat, sending it to the liver to be converted into lipoproteins, which the body can use as an emergency source of energy. For some reason, domestic cats aren't very good at this. This seems to be particularly true of indoor cats, who are typically overweight with lots of fat available to process. Their livers tend to get overwhelmed and clogged up with all that accumulated fat. Fatty liver disease is not a pleasant experience, and cats won't eat when they feel sick or in pain—another mysterious evolutionary trait of *felis catus*—so once this process starts, the cat will be even more likely to avoid food. It's a feedback loop. The longer the cat goes without food, the less interested she will be in eating food, and the cycle can quickly spiral into permanent liver damage and death.

Luna's occasional and unpredictable bouts of anorexia started when she was about three years old, a year or so after we moved from Manhattan to Brooklyn. Her vet says the underlying cause is pancreatitis, the painful inflammation of the spongy doohickey tucked behind the stomach which secretes insulin and digestive juices. I'm skeptical. My half-assed internet research has left me with the impression that pancreatitis in cats is something of a catch-all condition, mysterious in origin, difficult to diagnose with certainty, and therefore a convenient medical-sounding explanation for why your cat suddenly won't eat.

On two occasions, Luna's anorexia lasted long enough to result in harrowing and expensive visits to the animal hospital, and on both occasions, the vet in attendance raised the possibility of surgically inserting a feeding tube into her esophagus as a last-resort attempt to break the cycle before it was too late. Both times, I opted to take her home and think about it, because the notion of subjecting our fierce little monster—who has been known to ferociously attack veterinarians, cat sitters, and small, terrified children—to a prolonged invasive procedure with only a partial chance of success. It wrenched my soul to think of putting her through that, and so I took her home to miserably contemplate our choices, including dismal possibility that if her condition went on long enough, we might have to have her euthanized.

Twice Luna had skidded to the edge of that precipice and twice opted to exercise the Nine Lives clause in her contract. Both times—after many miserable days of forcing prescribed medicines down her throat and trying to coax her to eat—we lucked into finding some special food that she'd found too tempting to resist. (For convoluted reasons, ordinary kibble did the trick the first time around; on the second occasion, we discovered the lure of rotisserie chicken.)

Those experiences had been awful but they were outliers. Most of the time, Luna's puke is just regular old cat puke, harbinger of nothing worse than a shitty start to the day. She's greedy and gobbles down her breakfast with such alacrity that her overwhelmed stomach sends it back out for reprocessing. In an hour or two she'll register the loss of her breakfast and pester me to serve a replacement.

So I was a little worried about the puke because it is my nature to worry but not very worried because I know that it is my nature to worry.

I tossed a soggy wad of paper towels containing the warm contents of Luna's stomach into the trash, and concluded that the pitcher of Bloody Marys was no longer optional but obligatory. Natasha got out the eggs and cheese. After this decadent repast, a nap was negotiated and agreed upon. We'd planned to devote the afternoon to requisite weekend chores but by afternoon we punted all that to Sunday in favor of more puttering and lounging. We had ambitious notions of heading back into Manhattan for dinner, but it was cold and we'd already been ambitious the night before, so we fell back on the local option of pizza and beer at a neighborhood pub.

When we got back, I saw the food in Luna's dinner bowl had remained mostly uneaten and had grown crusty and hard. She gets a snack of dry kibble in the evening, and I was happy when she came running to get it, but she only ate a few pieces before walking away. Was this something to worry about? Yeah, maybe. But there was nothing I could do about it at this hour.

☼ ☼ ☼

Natasha retired, sensibly, around midnight, but feeling like I ought to properly let loose on this three-day weekend, I took the party into my study, by which I mean I grabbed a Corona from the fridge and parked myself in front of a glowing computer screen—*woohoo!*—and let myself get swept out into the vast internet sea of Netflix and YouTube and clickbait listicles ("14 Reasons Why Trump Will Drop Out of the Race Before the Primaries"). When I ran out of beer, I began drinking rum. I don't like rum but I was out of beer and it was just as well because by the time I found myself drifting towards the bottomless vortex of pornography that endlessly threatens these virtual waters, I realized I was too drunk to navigate another click, and shut it all down. I performed my evening ablutions and staggered off to bed at three in the morning.

By then, I didn't feel so good, but what did I expect? Rum is a terrible thing.

Lying in bed next to my wife, I tossed and turned. I do that most nights because I am an insomniac but on this particular night a disagreeable gurgling in my bowels had come to my attention. Fluids, shifting about restlessly.

I didn't want to wake Natasha with my thrashing and gurgling, so I got up and went to lie on the couch, but the couch kept wanting to spin. I got up. I sat down. Something wasn't right. A pushy insistence at one end of me suggested that immediate action needed to be taken. I jumped up, grabbed a magazine, and rushed to the bathroom. I shucked off my sweatpants and underwear in one fluid motion and slammed my ass down on the toilet.

Nothing happened. I sat for a long time. As in the time it takes to read every paragraph of one of those long *New Yorker* articles about the fascinating history of the thumbtack or whatever, plus all the Talk of the Towns. It was hard to concentrate. My bowels seemed to have acquired sentience and were writhing like snakes. Willful, selfish, unproductive snakes.

Wind did not break.

No loaves were pinched.

The kids? Not dropped off at the pool.

The trains, they did not run.

Nothing, in fact, saw the light at the end of the tunnel.

Regular scheduled service has been interrupted. Due to an obstruction ahead we are momentarily holding this train until service resumes.

Deep in the tunnels some major catastrophe had occurred. A sewer main had collapsed. Orange-vested night-shift workers in heavy boots rushing down stairs into the darkness, frantically waving lanterns and lighting emergency flares, desperately pulling track switches, screaming into walkie-talkies. Explosions, smoke, a distant rumble as unseen tunnels disintegrated into rubble. Angry, frightened passengers pounded at the doors, but no one was going anywhere.

This train is out of service. We apologize for the inconvenience. Thank you for riding with us today.

During the next few hours, while making many pointless, brokenhearted journeys between the couch and the toilet, I had the opportunity to think about many things. But the thing my mind kept circling back to was my friend Valerie's stump.

Around five-thirty in the morning, Natasha came out of our bedroom, rubbing her eyes.

"Why are you sleeping on the couch?" she asked.

"I'm not sleeping," I said. "Can you please get your phone and look up *appendicitis* on Wikipedia?"

She got her phone. "How do you spell it?"

II. Natural Selection

> We now live, as Earth always has, in an Age of Bacteria. These simplest organisms will dominate our planet (if conditions remain hospitable for life at all) until the sun explodes. During our current, and undoubtedly brief, geological moment, they watch with appropriate amusement as we strut and fret our hour upon the stage. For we are, to them, only transient and delectable islands ripe for potential exploitation.
>
> —Stephen Jay Gould
> *Leonardo's Mountain of Clams and the Diet of Worms*

S O SAY YOU FIND YOURSELF in New York City and you're planning a trip to the emergency room. The obvious thing to do is to call 911. Please don't do that. What you want to do is call a local car service. You know, the ones who, on a daily basis, carpet bomb your doorstep with dozens of urgent-looking business cards, advertising *CHEAP!!* and *CONVENIENT!!* private transport to *JFK!! LA GUARDIA!!* and even *NEWARK!!* Even if you are just visiting and staying in a hotel room, a few of these have undoubtedly found their way to your door. Go fish one of those cards out of the wastepaper basket and dial the number. If you are under thirty, and lack a conceptual framework for procuring goods or services without downloading an app, just use Lyft or Uber or whatever faddish Silicon Valley start-up is currently destroying the local economy. In either case, your car will arrive in under ten minutes and get you to the hospital quickly and affordably, probably for under twenty dollars. You will avoid all the alarums and shenanigans of First Responders muddily stomping through your apartment and their clumsy attempts to carry you in a stretcher down two flights of narrow tenement stairs. You will also save an ambulance fee of roughly $15,000.*

No one who enters an emergency room for any reason will leave in less than twenty-four hours. You know this. So before you call the car service, have your wife pack a small bag of things that you would like to have handy for a hospital visit of unknown duration: laptop, toiletries, phone charger, extra underwear, all that e-cigarette paraphernalia you have to drag around everywhere since you quit smoking. You will be doing a lot of sitting around and waiting, so ask your wife to grab a handful of those unread *New Yorkers* from the overflowing stack next to the couch.

Oh, and remind her to leave a bowl of food out for the cat.

Is that a honk outside? Great. Your wife has the bag, so walk down the stairs under your own steam. Take your time—savor these last precious moments of bipedal mobility and the under-appreciated dignity of wearing pants.

Local New York City politics are byzantine and inscrutable. When Bill de Blasio, New York's current mayor, had first run for office a few years earlier, he'd won mainly on the strength of two campaign promises of questionable significance to most New Yorkers.

The first was that he would abolish the carriage horses of Central Park on his very first day in office. That didn't happen. The mayor was now in his second term and the unhappy carriage horses, in all their Gilded Age frippery, were still trotting bored tourists around the park.

De Blasio's second campaign promise was that he would keep LICH open. Though it sounds like the name of a Gotham City crime syndicate, LICH is—or rather was—the unfortunate acronym of the Long Island College Hospital, located in the Cobble Hill neighborhood of Brooklyn. Like many urban hospitals, it was steadily going

Source: I made it up.

broke. Its owner, the State University of New York, wanted to shut it down and sell off the property, which was worth a fortune. Angry local residents and hospital employees staged protests. De Blasio, sensing a brilliant campaign opportunity, got himself arrested at one and made all the papers. Man of the People, Defender of the Little Guy, etc. After he won the election, the usual NYC shenanigans followed. LICH was of course shut down (as everyone knew it would be) and sold off to a real estate developer who'd contributed heavily to de Blasio's campaign, and who promptly disclosed plans to build a monstrous complex of expensive condos and office space. As a sop to the public interest, the developer agreed that a nominal portion of this real estate windfall would be occupied by healthcare facilities of some sort. And so NYU—whose own vast real estate empire has spread, cancer-like, throughout much of lower and mid-Manhattan—seized the chance to establish a new colony in Brooklyn, and opened an emergency care clinic on the first floor of the former hospital.

Few people seem to know about this NYU clinic, which is why it is such a great place to go if you are hankering after some emergency medical care. It is a clean, well-lit place. With a nod to the sleepy security guard, you can stroll right in, saunter through the empty waiting room and proceed directly into the triage office. You'll find two staff members waiting for you, who will ask you a few sensible questions before a kind of medical concierge arrives to escort you to your hospital bed, all in a matter of minutes.

❀   ❀   ❀

We knew about this obscure emergency facility because we'd been there twice before almost exactly a year earlier. The first time was in early January when, after a recent workout at the gym, Natasha suffered intense back pain and shortness of breath for two days in a row. Was it a heart attack? A pulmonary embolism? She panicked and made an emergency appointment to see her doctor. The doctor assured her that she'd just pulled a muscle, and prescribed some pain-killers and a muscle relaxant. That evening, Natasha sat on the couch for hours in a rigid, upright position, frozen in agony, breathing shallowly. The drugs hadn't done much for her. She kept complaining that her back pain was way too intense for a mere pulled muscle.

I Googled stuff, and reported that the internet offered many personal anecdotes of painful back spasms. "Give it couple of days," I told her. I made her some tea, which she didn't drink, and heated up a compress, which she wouldn't use because the slightest pressure on her back increased the pain dramatically.

I didn't see what more I could do for her, so I left her on the couch, and retreated into my office to waste time on the internet. Suddenly I heard her cry out my name. She stood in the living room, staring at me in horror. She held out a crumpled ball of tissue paper spattered with thick, dark wads of blood.

I wanted to consult Google for a reassuring explanation, but Natasha insisted on calling her doctor. By then, the doctor had gone home for the night and the grumpy nurse who'd answered the phone didn't want to page her. "The doctor already diagnosed you," she said. "She said it's a pulled back muscle."

"I'm coughing up *blood!*"

"So what?" the nurse snapped. "She already told you what's wrong. If you're worried, call 911."

Natasha was stunned. "You should be fired," she told her and hung up.

Natasha's conviction that her doctor's nurse should lose her job was informed by professional expertise. I may not have mentioned this yet, but Natasha is a hospital administrator, with decades of experience in hiring and firing medical personnel. She is in charge of two large departments at a local hospital, where she has worked for many years.

So her next step was to call the emergency room at her own hospital. She asked to speak to the attending physician, who was friend of hers, and told him that she was in a tremendous amount of pain and she'd just coughed up blood. He agreed that she needed hospital care right away, but warned her that the emergency room was crowded and short-staffed that night. "We're totally swamped," he said. But, he continued, he'd heard good things about a new emergency facility that NYU had opened on the former grounds of LICH.

"Why don't you go there?" he said. "No one seems to know about it."

And so we packed a bag and called for car service.

As much as you can ever have a good experience going to the emergency room, we had a good experience at the NYU clinic in Cobble Hill. *Great service, 4 stars, A++++.*

I'd been skeptical of Natasha's conviction that she'd had a pulmonary embolism, but with a blood test and a CT scan, the clinic confirmed that she was right. A nasty blood clot had dislodged from some vein, broken into shards, and those shards had gotten lodged in the capillaries of her lungs, which explained why she was in such pain and short of breath. They shot her up with blood thinners, loaded her into an ambulance, and shipped her off to the main NYU hospital in Manhattan. The doctors there determined that she'd been lucky, the damage probably wasn't permanent, but she'd have to be on blood thinners for six months, with weekly doctor visits to check her blood levels and lung capacity.

They also suggested that she might like to talk to a therapist, since, after all, she had almost died. She made an appointment.

The therapist said she seemed to be coping pretty well, and prescribed Xanax.

About a week later, we went back to that emergency room. During MLK weekend, actually.*

During the week, Natasha had gone back to her regular doctor to get her blood levels checked, because with the kind of anticoagulants she was on, you have to constantly make sure that you haven't over-thinned your blood or you can bleed to death. The tech in her doctor's office fucked up the blood test. She'd had trouble finding a vein, and kept poking around until she finally collapsed a vessel, and

---

*While writing this account, I've been struck by how often memorable events in my life seem to occur over MLK weekends. I've developed an obsession with odd, recurring coincidences like this, which I'll explore later in the section that concerns Natasha's second embarrassing phone call to Dr. K.

even then—as the lab later informed us—had failed to draw enough blood for the test.

Natasha's left arm turned black-and-blue from the tech's clumsy handiwork and over the weekend it grew cold and numb. Was it another blood clot? She called one of her many relatives who practice medicine. "Go to an emergency room," he urged her. We knew which one to go to this time. Diagnosis: she hadn't had another PE, but her blood had become dangerously thin. Another ambulance ride over the Brooklyn Bridge. They kept her overnight to make sure her blood levels had stabilized and sent her home in the morning.

Later that day, she called her doctor to terminate their relationship.

"I'm sure you can understand why," Natasha said.

"Yes," her doctor said, sadly. "I do."

The medical concierge, or whatever his actual title was, had been the same person during our two previous visits last year, and here he was again: a short, slender young man with a well-groomed appearance and an immaculately professional demeanor. He was perfectly assigned to his role. Perhaps that was why he was always there. He escorted me to my bed, in a curtained berth directly across from the nurses' station. I felt certain this was the same bed Natasha had occupied when we'd last been here. Brandishing an iPad, the concierge verified all the information—name, social security number, insurance carrier—that established my mortal existence in the NYU data universe. He secured one of those plastic hospital bracelets to my wrist. "Someone will be here to talk with you shortly," he said, and glided away with his tablet. I wondered what he did when not doing this. It was easy to imagine him standing in a closet until summoned.

An orderly procession of medical personnel filed past my bed. Vital signs measured and recorded. A nurse came to divest me of my clothing and my dignity, and issued me a billowing hospital gown. I was hooked up to the machine that goes *ping.*

Strange to be the one in a hospital bed, with Natasha sitting in a chair by my side.

"I guess it's finally my turn," I said to her.

"You can't let me have anything for myself," she replied.

The physician's assistant came to interview me. When Natasha was here the year before, the PA had been a chubby, tattooed Korean-American sporting pink sneakers and a punkrock hairdo, who looked as though she might've been good at volleyball. (I know what I'm talking about, I've been playing in a recreational league for two decades.) She'd been awesome, a calm and careful listener who'd explained all the diagnostic steps with succinct clarity. Because nearly every aspect of this place seemed unchanged from the year before, I had expected to see her again, but she was not on shift.

My PA was a tall, slim woman of South Asian ancestry in her early thirties. She was heart-breakingly beautiful, I glumly observed, with smooth brown skin, long black hair tied back in a ponytail, and large expressive eyes. *I love you,* I thought. She was kind and sober and reassuring, and it was not at all nice to meet her while costumed like a mental patient and attached to beeping machinery.

She took notes and left, and someone brought me the nasty drink they make you drink before a CT scan, which tastes like a gin and tonic made for diabetics, a cocktail with all the nice things that make cocktails nice painstakingly extracted, leaving behind only the bitterness and regret.

Clutching my giant styrofoam cup like a three-year-old, I sat up in my bed with nothing to do but watch the doings of the emergency room, that weird intersection of two very different populations.

The people who worked there were people at work: *same shit different day*, wishing they'd gotten more sleep, hovering bleary-eyed over computer screens, transferring papers from one location to another, pushing carts back and forth, and relieving their boredom with jokes and mild flirtations and gossip. You could spot the doctors and PAs among them, because they were the only people who looked like they actually *wanted* to be there, that they were perfectly happy to spend their three-day weekend mucking about with broken tibias and scabies.

And there were the people who didn't work there. Patients wearing the glazed, vacant expressions of caged animals in a laboratory. Loved ones shifting back and forth between helpless anxiety and excruciating boredom.

I thought then of the painter George Tooker's haunting portrait of modern alienation, *The Waiting Room*. Kafka wanted to write books that could be "the axe for the frozen sea inside us." *The Waiting Room* depicts that frozen sea.

If you've never seen it, go ahead and Google it—I won't be going anywhere for a while.

I'd finished my drink some time ago. The beautiful physician's assistant returned, pulled the curtains shut, and asked me to remove my underwear. I had a good idea of what came next. I told my wife to go away.

As the PA snapped on a pair of blue nitrile gloves, I studied her face and wondered who she was when she wasn't here. What shows did she follow on Netflix? Did she have a dog, or enjoy reading manga? Did she rent a beach house with her old college friends for a week every summer? I wondered if she liked to rollerblade. It was pleasant to imagine her rollerblading in the summer, sunglasses and knee pads, her dark ponytail swinging behind her helmet as she bobbed and weaved through crowded city streets.

She slathered some goop over her fingers and told me to turn over.

I took a breath, my mouth set grim, and then something occurred to me. "I'm sorry," I stammered. "I . . . I didn't have a chance to take a shower."

A very human expression came across her face, a strangely familiar look of embarrassment and tenderness. I then realized what

I was reminded of—the awkward reassurances extended by romantic partners on those youthful occasions when alcohol had compromised my ability to fulfill the evening's plans.

"Oh . . ." she said, looking away. "That's all right. Don't worry about that."

I rolled on my side, and she inserted her lubricated finger into my asshole.

After she left, I realized I'd forgotten to ask if this procedure had yielded any diagnostic information.

❀   ❀   ❀

How long had we been here? There's no time in these places. We'd arrived early in the morning, just before dawn, but it felt like it was late at night, and perhaps it was. There were no windows here. The world could have ended outside, the sun could have snuffed itself out, leaving nothing behind but the headache-glare of fluorescent tubes and the lingering scent of Pine-Sol. Here you saw the shape of eternity, the minutes falling away, each as discrete and meaningless as drops of water leaking from a faucet, and at last you understood why the Chinese Water Torture discussed so much as a child might truly live up to its reputation. You knew you were in trouble, but that was everyone else's problem now. There was no course of action you could take, and nowhere you could go, and the tendrils of your attention retreated from the ordinary world of concerns that nourished and vexed your soul. You lost interest in the violent Armageddon brewing inside your bowels, didn't bother with the laptop or the magazines. Your wife, sitting beside you, preoccupied herself with texting various family members (her family, not yours) with updates on your status, but your own smartphone, with all its endless distractions, lay inert in your hand. Sure, it might be fun to post a selfie in your hospital gown, or play a round of Angry Birds, but the remorseless presence of your surroundings—the white tile and stainless steel, the respiratory susurrus of humming machines, the steady syncopation of pings punctuated by occasional cries of pain—laid bare the empty vanities of the digital universe. This entire place was a refutation of everything Silicon Valley had to offer. We live in our bodies, stuck with the same model for the duration of our brief lives.

✾ ✾ ✾

I was getting thirsty, too, but by then I had crossed over into a dry country and was no longer allowed to have any water.

✾ ✾ ✾

At last the physician's assistant returned with the results of my CT scan and blood tests. "So yeah, it's what we thought," she said. Sympathetic expression: *sucks to be you.*

So, appendicitis. *Told you so.* Natasha was upset, she'd insisted that there was no way that was what I had, exactly as I had insisted, a year earlier, that there was no way she'd had a pulmonary embolism. But I wasn't surprised by my diagnosis, just as a year ago, she hadn't been. Sometimes your body really does know.

At least Stuff Was Happening.

In theory, anyway. We were informed that an ambulance had been summoned.

As a mere colonial outpost in the vast NYU medical empire, the emergency clinic in Cobble Hill is really just a frontier way-station, where captured bodies can be subjected to preliminary interrogation before shipping them off to headquarters in Manhattan.

Apparently the time-bomb of the appendix ticks very slowly. Everything that could be done here had already been done. Plans had been made, orders dispatched, but nothing happened for a long, long time. It felt like being in a sleepy diner where no one will bring you your check. In the meantime, I'd rallied a bit, enough to experience, side by side, both terrible pain and terrible boredom. I passed the time by making unnecessary trips to the tiny private bathroom by the nurses' station, ostensibly to urinate, but really to surreptitiously puff on my e-cigarette. Tendrils of white vapor, redolent of pancakes and artificial maple syrup, wafted out every time I exited. No one seemed to care.

At last the Ambulance People arrived, wheeling in the stretcher they planned to strap me to. Hooray. It was a sequence of events all unnervingly familiar from the year before. They parked themselves near my berth—and waited.

Those EMS guys stand out in the hospital setting. The hospital pays their salaries, but this is not their natural environment. Not for them the dull white rooms ticking down the moments of eternity. With their bomber jackets, and bored, impatient expressions, they always remind me of fighter pilots at a debriefing, restlessly tapping their feet while awaiting assignments for their next daredevil mission.

I say "guys" in the non-gender-specific plural vernacular sense, common to my native patois of Northern New Jersey. One of my EMS guys was female. I have no idea if she was of Irish descent but if I'd been forced to randomly guess her full name, I would've gone with Colleen Anne McMartin. No, really, she *had* to be Irish-American, I totally pegged her as a variation of a type endlessly iterated in the Catholic-inflected suburb I'd grown up in. Young, short, a little pudgy, a round face with rosy cheeks and pale freckles, and a fiery defiant stare that cast a perpetual warning to the world: *If you value your kneecaps, don't fuck with me.* She would have been well-cast in *Battlestar Galactica* as scrappy squadron leader with an unsurpassed Cylon kill count.

The other guy was a guy. Swarthy Mediterranean white dude, jet-black hair, his brooding handsomeness emphasized by the kind of action-star five o'clock shadow that requires daily maintenance in order to look like you just forgot to shave for a couple of days. He had the hooded eyes of a contract killer. He would've been well-cast as a Cylon.

I don't know what we were all waiting for, some kind of go-ahead from the main hospital lining up a surgeon, or perhaps some crucial form designed to prevent me from suing NYU if the ambulance crashed. Whatever it was, it finally came through. Everyone snapped into life. I quickly signed a bunch of forms without reading them, my wife gathered our belongings, and the EMS guys strapped me in and wheeled me out.

"Good luck!" the PA called after me as we slid through the double doors. I weakly raised my hand in farewell. *Yep, thanks, beautiful PA, have fun with the rollerblades.*

Huzzah, at last released into the grey January day. It was overcast and gloomy, but there was light, and the sound of traffic, and the sharp, invigorating scent of motor oil, and the novel experience of being loaded into the back of a vehicle like a pallet of Budweiser.

I can't deny that there's a certain thrill to rattling over the Brooklyn Bridge in an ambulance, lights blazing, sirens screaming, the sense that you are in some exciting narrative, like the kind you watch on TV, instead of your ordinary, non-narrative life, which is mostly plotless tedium relieved by watching TV. But I'd already checked ambulance-ride-over-the-Brooklyn-Bridge off my bucket list the year before. Twice. This was my third time, and being the one in the stretcher didn't much alter the basic experience. But it was still fun. Someone ought to open a concession where you can pay to ride around New York in the back of a speeding ambulance while in perfect health, so you can enjoy the experience without the distraction of being injured or dying.

Last year we'd taken selfies in the ambulance, and Natasha suggested we do it this time too. Sure, why not? She crouched down next to me and aimed her phone. I gave a goofy thumbs-up and we smiled for the camera.

As we were doing this, I caught the eye of Colleen Anne Mc-Martin. A slight smirk twitched at the corner of her lips. She'd been staring at me the whole ride, and her expression was difficult to read. She didn't smile—I had a feeling that she was parsimonious with her smiles—but there was something of a smile in her eyes. I couldn't tell whether it was an expression of contempt, amusement, or curiosity but it felt uncomfortably charged, as if we had an old connection that I'd somehow forgotten. Unnerved, I tried to focus my attention elsewhere, stared out the window at the fractured jumble of Manhattan flowing past and tried to deduce our current location and probable trajectory. But I felt the pressure of her gaze on my face and every now and then I involuntarily flicked my eyes back towards her and was met each time by the blunt challenge of those inscrutable eyes.

This whole ambulance thing was weirding me out on all sorts of levels. Natasha was on the phone with her sister in Trinidad, excitedly reporting on our current mode of transportation. I felt lightheaded, overpowered by a sense of déjà vu. I had the eerie feeling that I'd fallen into some kind of eternal return, that I was looping through the timelines of the multiverse and would eventually experience this ambulance ride in every possible permutation and from every possible viewpoint. Perhaps in the next iteration I'd be the ambulance driver. Or Colleen. I turned to look at her again, and this time I met her gaze straight on and gave her a friendly we're-all-in-this-together smile. Her expression did not change. Our prolonged eye contact did not rattle her in the slightest. It was like having a staring contest with a cat. The hint of that ironic smirk passed across her lips again. She gave a slight nod of the head—a gesture which seemed to encompass both acknowledgment and dismissal—and turned away towards the window.

We'd been dumped in the bowels of the NYU mothership, a place dreadfully familiar to me because, yes, Natasha and I had been here the year before. That had been in the middle of the night, and, now, I was reasonably sure, it was around mid-morning. Not that it mattered in this underground place. It was a kind of depot, like a parking garage, but for human beings on stretchers. A vast, crowded place of low ceilings and flickering lights.

I lay on my stretcher with little to do but observe the other people on stretchers and glumly note our categorical similarity. *There's some profound difference*, I thought, *between human beings and human beings on stretchers, and we ought to have a word to distinguish the latter, the way we have the word "corpse" for human beings who are dead.*

I speculated—as one tends to do—that the Germans probably have a precise term for this state, something that would encompass not only the degrading physical situation but also the exact flavor of demoralization that accompanies it. *Gemittenschäftengörenblitzen* or whatever. Something packed with umlauts and despair.

And then I thought, why make it complicated? There's probably already some obvious and simple hospital slang in use, like . . . *rollie.*

A non-employee in a hospital setting: *patient.*

A cot on extendable wheels: *stretcher.*

The living and the mechanical joined in unhappy union: *rollie.*

The boss says we have to get all those rollies out of the 8th floor corridor, it's a fire hazard and they're blocking access to the break room.

Jesus, someone left a rollie in the Sabbath elevator. It's been stopping at every floor for hours. Wasn't that dude scheduled for heart surgery?

Ah, for once to be on the right side of triage! I was processed out of rollie purgatory with startling speed (*woohoo—suck it, gunshot victims!*) and wheeled backwards into an elevator by an unseen man whose sole comment was to warn me to tuck in my feet. He then proceeded, from behind, to chat with the middle-aged elevator operator sitting in front of me on a stool. *Christ, what a job*, I thought.

I guess the upside would be that you'd eventually know every single employee in the hospital by name, and you'd be privy to all sorts of secrets. People would probably do nice things for you, like buy you lunch or give you an Xbox for your grandkids, because they'd remember last year's annual holiday party and what they did in the elevator with drunk Steve from Endocrinology, and they'd know that you remembered too. The downside, of course, was that you had to spend forty hours a week sitting in a windowless metal box pressing the same 27 plastic buttons. I wondered if he ever pined for the old skilled-labor days, with the rattling gates and the brass lever. He never bothered to address me at all. I suppose, for him, it would be like talking to the packages of the UPS man.

The year before, when Natasha was a rollie—and, if I'm being honest, in considerably more pain than I was now—we'd arrived after midnight and there were no rooms available, so they parked her in a narrow corridor right in front of the nurses' station. In a gesture both touching and absurd, the staff tried to conjure up the illusion of an actual room by surrounding her stretcher with these ridiculous curtained screens on wheels, which of course made everything worse because people kept bumping into them, and the screens would roll into the hallway or into Natasha, and whoever had done it would apologize and attempt to roll them back into place, which usually took a few tries before they got it right, and that's how Natasha spent her entire night, bumped and jostled and enduring hour after hour of graveyard-shift work banter until she'd finally passed out from sheer exhaustion only to be woken by the boisterous arrival of the morning crew, all perky with coffee and danishes.

Which is why you should never schedule your emergencies for the evening.

It was different for me. I got rolled right into a semi-private room with real walls and a sliding curtain, where I was promptly hooked back up to the machine that goes *ping* and an IV bag brimming with opioids.

Things get blurry here, like driving through a heavy rain at night, the window of memory smeared and refracted through the oily sheen of narcotics. Stationary and drugged, I'd slid back into lab animal mode. Object, not subject. It, not Thou. No point in getting involved in whatever was happening even though it was happening to me. They were going to do what they were going to do. Various hospital personnel came in to palpate my abdomen, and I had no idea if they were doctors or nurses or just curious janitors.

I do remember Hanna, the young Polish nurse who'd been assigned to me. I don't remember how I knew she was from Poland because events no longer occurred in their customary order, or in any order at all. But her name was Hanna—it was written right there on a whiteboard hanging on the wall, in case I forgot, which sometimes I did—and she was from Poland. She seemed so wholesome and cheerful as to belong to another century. Long flaxen hair, parted down the middle, tied neatly behind her head. Peaches-and-cream complexion, her eyes the sky-blue of a warm midsummer day, and she habitually wore an expression of pleasant surprise, as though she hadn't expected you but was glad that it turned out to be you. You'd cast her as the winsome farmer's daughter in some pastoral period movie. Easy to picture her in one of those universal European peasant dresses, puffy blue sleeves and embroidered white apron cinched around the waist, her freckled arms clasping a pitcher of milk.

Hanna had the face of a good listener, attentive and charitable, and you wanted to tell her things, to confide in her with reckless abandonment. I remember chatting up a storm with her, but can't recall a word of what I said. Of those vanished dialogues, I would later feel an indeterminate sense of shame, the kind I often feel when waking up hungover after a night of heavy drinking with friends. I suspect I blathered indiscriminately, said things I should not have said. Did I talk about my chronic depression, my fits of rage at certain uncooperative inanimate objects, my nightly struggles with alcohol and Netflix, my discomfort with any situation involving horses, my co-dependent relationship with my cat?

Whatever I talked about, Hanna gave me her full attention, as if I were her best friend confessing to an extra-marital affair.

I think.

I mean, does that make any sense at all? How could Hanna, in the middle of her busy nursing shift, possibly have time for long conversations of any sort?

On the other hand, I knew things about Hanna. I knew about Poland. I knew that she now lived in Bay Ridge, which she liked okay because she lived near a supermarket and she liked the way the Verrazzano Bridge curved across the skyline, but she thought a lot about moving to Queens because the commute to work sucked.

Actually, maybe Hanna shared these details of her personal life with Natasha, not me. The two of them had more in common, after all. They were both immigrants, they both worked in hospitals. Both of them were standing on their feet, and neither of them was on pain meds.

Or maybe I just manufactured the whole dialogue in my head, knitting together an imaginary conversation out of the random chatter of people passing through the halls. My narcotic haze and horizontal orientation made it difficult to distinguish the boundaries between me and all the stuff in the world that was not me.

❃ ❃ ❃

I slept, but you never really sleep on drugs like those. You *descend*, Jacques Cousteau in a dim-lit bathysphere, sucked down into the twilight depths of semi-consciousness, pulled along by Freudian undercurrents, a dispassionate observer drifting through the alien ecosystem that churns just below the shimmering surface of your everyday mind. Random memories float by: the faces of ugly strangers momentarily encountered in fast-food restaurants, misconstrued childhood theories of human reproduction, a disastrous marijuana-and-whiskey incident that had taken place either on a rooftop or a boat, the sad spectacle of a much-loved Raggedy Andy doll abandoned on a rainy playground and mourned over for days.

The outer world permeated my druggy reveries like weak sunlight filtering down to the ocean floor. My hospital roommate, as yet unseen behind the semi-privacy curtain, was watching a football game on the overhead TV at an ear-piercing volume and my half-dreams echoed with the staccato announcements of sports commentators, punctuated by the impassioned cheers and jeers of my semi-private companion. Based purely on the gravelly cadences of his shouts and mutters and sighs, I pictured him as an African-American a decade or so older than me, a lifelong New Yorker, a big man grown paunchy in late middle-age, slightly hard of hearing, with a badly trimmed mustache and thinning scalp, and dressed—I felt with uncanny certainty—in a tattered blue bathrobe that he'd brought from home because goddamn if he was going to walk around all day with his black ass hanging out for the world to see.

This vision came with such precise clarity that I wondered if I'd tapped into some extra-sensory faculty. They say that we only use 10% of our brains, although I've often wondered who first asserted this statistic with any kind of empirical confidence and how that pioneering scientist happened to arrive at such a specific percentage. But perhaps it was true, and perhaps the sweet flow of opioids had released my brain from certain constraints, freeing up dormant psychic powers that had been repressed by childhood socialization. Because later, when I finally met my roommate, every one of my speculations turned out to be right on the money, down to the exact color of his tattered bathrobe.

Of course, the more likely explanation is that I'd already seen him on one of his trips to the bathroom, which was on my side of the room, and I'd forgotten about it because one of the main constraints I had been liberated from was the ridiculous insistence that causality had to flow in any particular direction.

His name was Fred, and we would soon spend a rather harrowing night together.

But that came later.

At some point, I became aware of a lot of conversation happening near the vicinity of my feet—familiar voices chatting amiably, as if I'd been drinking heavily at a dinner party and wound up passed out under the table. I opened my eyes. Or they were already open and I just hadn't noticed.

Over the blare of my roommate's television, my brother-in-law Sean and his wife Sylvia were talking with Natasha, all three standing wedged in around the foot of my bed. A jumbled pile of my discarded clothing, toiletries, and magazines had been shoveled into the single available chair, so the narrow gap between the end of my bed and the wall was the only space left for human beings to inhabit.

The three of them were talking about Donald Trump, because that's all anyone talked about in 2016, and they were laughing, because it was early in the year and Trump's candidacy was still hilarious, juicy fodder for late show monologues and Twitter memes, and the whole country was still all LOL ROFLMAO ¯_(ツ)_/¯ at this narcissistic publicity-seeking buffoon because we hadn't yet understood that the joke was on *us*, that the not-so-funny punchline was that we'd never again talk about anything else, that in the months and years ahead the bloated, obscene topic of Donald J. Trump would soon come to engulf all public discourse, all private conversation, all human thought, in much the same way as the rancid stew of half-digested food, backed-up turds, and infectious bacteria had wholly engulfed my gurgling bowels.

❀　❀　❀

I'm a social person and I felt the need to entertain my visitors. I had never entertained guests from a hospital bed, and I found it awkward. I didn't know what was expected, socially, in my situation, but I did my best to be charming under the circumstances. I thanked everyone for coming to my operation. Some lame attempts at gallows humor: *I'd like you to know that none of you are currently mentioned in my will, but that could change . . .* Ugh. It was hard to be a good host in bed while my guests towered over me in customary adult verticality, and exhausting to generate a stream of witty banter while slipping in and out of consciousness mid-sentence like a junkie on the nod, later waking up to realize that the clever remark I'd formulated was for a conversation that had moved on without me some time ago.

An additional challenge was that Natasha kept interrupting my urbane monologues to point out that I had once again kicked off my sheets and my junk was hanging out of my gown on full display.

"I don't care," I said defiantly. This was true.

"I know," she said, pulling up the sheet. "But have some consideration for other people. No one wants to see that."

Within minutes, I'd twist and squirm and kick the sheet off again. My brain may have been numbed by pharmaceuticals, but my body knew that I was actually in agonizing pain and thrashed about accordingly. All I knew was that it felt *good* to squirm, and I didn't care if everyone got an eyeful of my floppy bits because I had discovered a secret long-known to heroin addicts throughout the world. Narcotics don't just remove *pain*, they remove *shame*. At last I understood why junkies were capable of such astonishing things. Liberated from a sense of shame, you were free to do as you pleased. You could take a nap on the floor of a Toys R Us, or take a shit on the sidewalk. The world was your oyster.

In retrospect, my overall impression is that in spite of my compromised circumstances I was nonetheless very charming indeed. That impression is, of course, dubious. The record of my memory has numerous lapses, but also inexplicable artifacts. For example, I have a distinct memory of the three of them—Natasha, Sean, Sylvia—sitting on the end of my bed eating noodles out of Chinese take-out containers. You don't forget something like that. I even remember feeling sorry for them; it seemed so dreadfully unappetizing to have to eat dinner right next to my unwashed feet and in full view of my exposed nethers.

"That never happened," Natasha said when I mentioned it later.

But I know it did.

I distinctly recall Sylvia dropping one of her chopsticks on the floor and saying, "Ah, shit."

And then I said, "Oh, just wipe it off. I mean, what could possibly be cleaner than *a hospital floor?*"

Now that's a pretty good line. You don't just make something like that up out of thin air—you have to have *actually witnessed someone eating noodles on the end of your hospital bed and dropping a chopstick on the floor.*

Natasha disputes this. "We absolutely did not eat noodles on your hospital bed! That's disgusting, why would we do that?"

And it's true, why would they? They could've gone outside to the waiting room to eat their noodles. And I can't think of why Natasha would lie about this, unless she's simply ashamed. I mean, I certainly would be.

But if they didn't eat Chinese noodles on the end of my bed, *then who did?*

Everyone had finished their noodles by the time Natasha prodded me awake again. I had another visitor. I lifted my head and saw a clean-cut, sober-looking fifteen-year-old boy wearing a lab coat, a stethoscope, and other I-Am-A-Doctor signifiers. He kept his thick blond hair swept back into an impressive pompadour, emphasizing his high, intelligent forehead. He wore thick square-rimmed glasses, undoubtedly chosen to add gravity to his boyish face, thereby reducing the possibility of being subjected to Doogie Howser jokes by aging Gen-Xers like me. And, in fact, that's exactly the kind of joke I was about to make when I caught a glimpse of the cold blue eyes behind the ridiculous frames, and the words died in my throat. Even opiated, some hind-brain sense of self-preservation remained intact and alert, and it warned me not to fuck with this guy.

The young doctor introduced himself as a member of my "surgical team." Gah, the language of the hospital. Who comes up with this stuff? It sounded like a Monty Python skit. *Go Team Surgery!*

I missed his name. He became, in my mind, and in this narrative, Dr. Boy.

Dr. Boy was not fifteen, of course. He was the Chief Resident of Surgery. I suppose he must have been in his late twenties, maybe even mid-thirties. It was distressing to realize that I had lost the ability to determine how old anyone was. This wasn't the drugs, it was just middle age. Everyone younger than me—which was most people, apparently—looked astonishingly, implausibly young, even Chief Residents.

When did I get so fucking old?

It's a question you ask yourself a lot once you are that fucking old.

Lying there with my junk hanging out while feeling old and unattractive bothered me more than the fact that all these attractive young people would soon be cutting me open and fishing out my goopy vestigials.

❖ ❖ ❖

Dr. Boy did some light palpating and other doctor busywork, checking the oil, gapping the sparkplugs, and then he raised the back of my bed so that I could sit up facing him. He launched into a lengthy explanation of my condition and prognosis. *Blah blah blah lower right quadrant, pouch-like structure, calcified feces, bacteria, mucus, sepsis, intestinal gas, laparoscopic.* I knew all this. I'd read the Wikipedia entry that morning, and the basics had been elaborated upon by the various medical personnel I'd encountered since. And I was familiar with the concept of laparoscopic surgery, since Natasha had already had two for her endometriosis. My understanding was they basically poked a few tiny holes in you and inflated your belly with gas. A camera went in one hole, and some kind of robotic Swiss Army knife in another. They sliced, diced, and pureed, and then vacuumed out the leftovers. But I didn't tell Dr. Boy any of this. I was the guest of honor at this party and I wanted to be polite, so I adopted that look of intense fascination I like to deploy when I've completely lost interest in a conversation.

But then Dr. Boy said something that was interesting indeed.

"It's important to understand all your options," he said. "Surgery is the obvious option but it's *possible* to delay surgery and instead treat you with high doses of intravenous antibiotics."

I pulled myself up with difficulty. "Oh *really*?" I said, trying, and failing, to sound only mildly interested. "No one mentioned that option."

Dr. Boy grimaced. He had been expecting this reaction. "Okay, but hold on a second." He actually held up a hand to blunt my enthusiasm. *Whoa there, pardner—not so fast.*

Now came the list of caveats, the numerous reasons why substituting antibiotics for surgery was *possible* but *not advised.* Blah blah blah. The only one that caught my attention: that antibiotics might clear up the infection this time around—*might*—but once you'd had appendicitis, it tended to come back, and then I'd have to go through all this again, and next time around I might not be so lucky. *However*—and here Dr. Boy's voice dropped into a soothing and reassuring register—if I signed off and let them cut out my appendix (that less-than-useless vestigial worm swelling up inside me), I'd never have to worry about it again for the rest of my life. Because, after all, you can't get your appendix removed twice!

I sank back into my cot. *Dr. Boy wants me to have the surgery*, I thought, disappointed. *Well of course he does, he's a surgeon. So why bother telling me about the antibiotics?*

"But just to be clear," Dr. Boy concluded, "*you're* in charge of your treatment. I can't tell you what to do. It's ultimately *your* choice whether you want to risk the antibiotic treatment"—a not-so-subtle wince crossed his face, as though the very *idea* pained him—"or just have the surgery today and be done with it." He smiled. "It's a very routine procedure—we do them all the time."

Now I understood why he'd offered a choice. This was one of those Joseph Campbell things. Whatchamacallit, the Hero's Journey, familiar to me from *The Wizard of Oz*, and every *Star Wars* movie ever made, and the gazillion screenwriting manuals gathering dust on my shelves at home. Before you *crossed the threshold* into the under-world, you had to freely make the choice to do so. In short: it's a plot point, the first major one that opens up the premise of the story.

Dr. Boy was like Morpheus in *The Matrix*, forcing Neo to choose between the red pill or the blue. Would you like to know an aston-ishing but horrid secret concerning the illusory nature of human existence—*cough* *life is a dream and we're all really just batteries for su-perintelligent robotic squids *cough*—or do you want to just go back to bed and forget all this weird shit ever happened?*

---

*Oh, yes, I'm aware that in recent years the Red Pill metaphor from *The Ma-trix*—which symbolizes facing an unpleasant reality in place of a comfortable delusion—has been co-opted by a host of hateful online communities. The toxic version seems to originated with *incels* (short for "involuntary celibates"), a misogynistic subculture of basement-dwelling young men who blame their col-lective failure to get laid on a feminized society which unfairly grants women the right to refuse sexual congress with misogynistic, basement-dwelling young men. After mutating in that fetid swamp of chans and subreddits, the phrase "red pilled" came to mean something like "waking up to the reality that all women are evil, conniving vixen who oughta be having sex with us," a worldview which also proved popular with bitter divorced men owing child-support and from there memed its way into all the adjacent mouth-breathing r/subcultures: wingnuts, wifebeaters, gaybashers, Q-anonymites, Oathkeepers, Proud Boys, neo-Nazis, and of course, TheDonald.

I say it's time to take the Red Pill back. I'm tired of everyone letting the But-thurt Brigade smear shit over all our cool stuff—*The Matrix*, *V for Vendetta*, the King James Bible, the Gadsden flag, Tiki torches, the OK hand gesture, and poor old Pepe the Frog. Enough is enough. Dig that neglected Hawaiian shirt out of the closet and wear it with pride, as God intended: in the loving Aloha spirit of sun-shine, chillaxitude and abiding Dude-itudiness.

Of course, there's really only one correct choice—the shitty one—but you had to choose for yourself, that was the rule.

So Dr. Boy stood at the gate, offering me access to the painful road that might free me from the burden of my malfunctioning appendix, but I had to *own the journey*, otherwise my trials and tribulations would be meaningless, and . . . I don't know, I'd turn into Darth Vader or Jar Jar Binks or . . .? In spite of all those screenwriting manuals, I was fuzzy on the consequences of choosing to walk away from an important plot point.

Dr. Boy looked at me expectantly.

"I guess . . . I might as well have the surgery?"

"Great! I think that's the smart choice," he said in a congratulatory tone that filled me with despair and regret. I felt as if I had just been talked into buying a timeshare.

He briskly produced a clipboard of papers for me to sign and initial, indicating my next of kin, my explicit reluctance to sue anyone, and my level of interest in pursuing drastic and costly measures to keep my body alive if I should somehow wind up brain-dead.

I signed and initialed, and as I slumped back into bed, someone gently removed the pen from my hand.

What time is it?

Time to be sitting in a wheelchair, apparently.

We were all going off to surgery now. I had an entourage as we left the room, and a kind of cheerless festivity hung in the air, everyone straining for a jaunty effervescence, making lighthearted jokes and speaking to me in the bright, chipper tones that one might use with an incontinent dog before taking him to the vet to be euthanized.

Witnessing things from the point of view of the wheelchair was not unlike the point of view of a small child: a world of legs all around, talking about you and making decisions for you, and you had to make an effort to look up if you wanted to see who the decision-making legs belonged to. Natasha was there, of course, and as I tilted my head to look around, I discovered all the others were there, too—Sean, Sylvia, and a couple of other friends I haven't mentioned because this narrative is already ridiculously long as it is.* Who else? A nurse or two, an orderly, and oh, look, here's Dr. Boy in front, escorting us down the halls like a bored tour guide leading schoolchildren through a museum. As we progressed through the halls, he explained, with forced jocularity, all the stuff that would happen next, where I'd be going *(an operating room!)* and what they'd be doing with me once I got there *(slicing up my appendix with the aid of modern technology!)*. Apparently Dr. Boy gave these speeches all the time. His monologue had a rehearsed, paint-by-numbers quality to it; he even threw in a few groan-worthy jokes that everyone laughed at politely.

At a juncture between two connecting halls, he stopped and asked if we had any questions.

"Will I get to keep my appendix after you take it out?" I quipped. *Har har.*

Everyone laughed, but Dr. Boy did not laugh.

"Absolutely not. There are very strict policies concerning the disposal of human tissue."

Everyone stopped laughing, in the awkward way people might at a social gathering when you've made a dumb joke about some outlandish sexual fetish that someone present evidently pursues with passionate devotion.

Sylvia cleared her throat. "So . . . do you get a lot of requests to take body parts home?"

"You'd be surprised," Dr. Boy said grimly. He seemed genuinely furious about it.

---

*Sorry, Penny and Pat! Thanks for coming to see me in the hospital. You were in earlier drafts, I swear!

We had arrived at an elevator. Natasha stepped in with various medical personnel, one of whom pulled in my chair from behind, a maneuver I found unsettling. It felt like being dragged into a cave.

Our friends had to stay behind, framed by the rectangle of the closing elevator doors. I waved to them. *Goodbye, Scarecrow! Goodbye, Tin Man! I hope you find what you are looking for!*

Here we were, then, at the next stage of the Hero's Journey. We were descending to the underworld, and I was losing my companions. Only Natasha was allowed to remain.

I was deposited in the grey cinderblock hallway of some sub-sub-basement, placed directly in front of large metal swinging doors that said DO NOT ENTER. The medical personnel who had accompanied us scurried away, and we were alone. It was suddenly very quiet. Natasha took my hand.

Someone in scrubs and a surgical mask popped out of a door to the right, and launched into a sprint down the hall, but then he noticed us and skidded to a stop. "Oh!" he said from behind the mask. "You're here!" As if I were a dinner guest who'd arrived too early.

He politely introduced himself as a technician of some sort, and then rushed off into DO NOT ENTER. From the hall behind us, a woman approached, similarly masked. She was as small and slight as a ten-year-old girl.

"Tyler Gore?" she asked in a wavering voice, terrified and awkward, as though I were an employer about to interview her for a position. "I'm your anesthesiologist? I'll see you inside?" That was all she could manage. She darted away through the double doors. We began to hear a muffled flurry of activity from behind those doors. Thumps, metallic clangs, scattered shouts, like a restaurant kitchen being prepped for the lunch rush.

Another woman in scrubs and a mask appeared. Totally different vibe. You knew right away she was in a position of authority, she radiated confidence. She warmly introduced herself to Natasha and me. Even with her mask on, I could tell from her eyes that she was smiling and that she was probably very pretty. Weren't they all? She was my head surgeon. "Don't worry," she told Natasha. "We'll take good care of him."

She winked at me. "See you inside," she said, and briskly strode off through the double doors.

Now Dr. Boy showed up, wearing a mask and carrying a clipboard. It was a checklist of questions. He ran through the preliminaries: full name, age, sex, social security number. Then he asked, "What kind of surgery are you expecting to have today?"

Was it a trick question?

I snorted. "Well, isn't it . . . *an appendectomy?*"

Dr. Boy glared at me through his thick frames. "We always have to check. You wouldn't want us to give you the wrong kind of surgery, would you?"

"No," I said in a small voice.

He went through my list of medications, mostly the outrageous pharmacopoeia of vitamins and health supplements I take to soothe my chronic hypochondria, plus the Schedule II stimulants I am prescribed by a shrink for my ADD, and then he spotted Rogaine on the list and decided to make *a bald joke*. Little smirk behind the glasses, some quip about *bald or not* I'd still have to wear a hair net during surgery anyway ha ha ha.

I dredged up an ingratiating smile.

Fucking Dr. Boy, I thought. I had been trying to think of a metaphor that would capture his personality, and now I knew what it was. *He's like the dorm roommate you get assigned on the first day of college, and the next day you go straight to the housing office to request a different room.*

❀ ❀ ❀

Someone came to fetch Natasha. It was time. She squeezed my hand, kissed me on the lips, and we exchanged the words that we customarily exchange whenever one of us is about to embark on an adventure with an uncertain outcome.

She left.

For an odd minute or two, I sat alone in the empty hallway, staring straight ahead at the words DO NOT ENTER.

The operating room, tiny and cramped, looked as if it had been hastily converted from a storage closet and was so crammed with medical equipment there was barely room for the operating table. Rolling metal carts stacked with boxy, Sputnik-era electronics had been shoved into corners, and everywhere coils of thick black cable snaked across the floors and up the walls, seeking electricity. Scattered around the room, a constellation of machines and monitors blinked contentedly in cathode ray green. Six or seven young people in green scrubs and masks lounged about in whatever remaining spaces they could find, leaning against cinderblock walls, sitting on cabinets and counters, swinging their feet. It felt as if I'd stumbled into the A/V Club at a suburban high school. On my arrival, they sprang to life, strapping me to the narrow table, hooking me to machines, and the tiny girl from the hallway fitted a plastic mask over my face and told me to breathe.

I thought of Marilyn Monroe. She'd had appendicitis, too. Those were the days before minimally invasive surgery, when you emerged from an appendectomy with a long, ugly scar, leaving you looking like you'd been gutted like a fish. As Marilyn lay unconscious on the operating table, the doctors lifted her gown and discovered something strange. She had taped a note to her belly. It turned out to be a poignant letter to her surgeon.

She begged him, in heavily underlined words, to _cut as little as possible._

I know it seems vain, she wrote, _but that doesn't enter into it. The fact that I'm a woman is important and means much to me._ She asked her surgeon to think of how much his own children meant to him, and pleaded for him to leave her fertility intact. _For God's sakes Dear Doctor no ovaries removed—please again do whatever you can to prevent large scars._*

---

* _Source:_ "Letters of Note" at https://www.lettersofnote.com/2012/03/no-ovaries-removed.html. Excerpted from _MM—Personal: From the Private Archive of Marilyn Monroe_ by Lois Banner and Mark Anderson (Harry N. Abrams, 2011)

I hadn't thought to tape a note to my belly, but if I had, Dr. Boy surely would've removed it. But remembering Marilyn's letter, I decided to take advantage of my last conscious moments to address all the bright young people standing around me.

I cleared my throat.

"Well, everyone," I said. "I hope you'll all do a good job on me!"

They replied in unison, like a chorus of good schoolchildren. *We will!*

☼ ☼ ☼

The mystery of anesthesia. It's not like narcotics. It's not like sleep. There's no sensation of the ego's slow dissolution in the ocean of the subconscious, no hallucinatory swim through the coral palace of dreams, no gasping sense of surfacing into the bright waking world. No fade in, no fade out. It's instantaneous in both directions, hours of your life simply snipped out and left on the cutting room floor.

Our existence is predicated on the passage of time. So where does one go during those vanished hours?

Wherever it is, it is a dry place.

I was very, very thirsty. I can't remember ever having been that thirsty. It felt like my throat had been packed with sawdust.

"I'm thirsty," I croaked.

"You'll get something to drink in a little while," someone said.

"No," I said. "I'm thirsty. I need water right now."

"I know. You'll get some in a little while."

Like, WTF? That was a totally unacceptable answer to a desperate request for water. I craned my head in the direction of the voice, and saw a pregnant woman with long, heavy African braids, dressed entirely in white, sitting at a desk in an otherwise empty and featureless room, mulling over some paperwork. She had high cheekbones and stern, chiseled features, and the shadows cast across her face made it impossible to determine whether or not she was looking at me.

The rich metaphorical suggestiveness of this tableau did not escape me. An ominous suspicion began to form. I half-expected to see her weighing my heart on a set of golden scales.

But fuck it. This was the person denying me water, and for that very reason also the person who might give me water.

"How about ice chips?" I said coyly, knowing how they loved ice chips, these hospital people. It seemed like a good strategy on any plane of existence.

"She can't give you water," my wife said. "You're in the recovery room. They'll give you water when they bring you out."

I lifted my head slightly, and realized the room was bigger than I'd thought. At the back of the room, a row of chairs stretched along the wall, empty except for Natasha. It had the vague feel of a funeral parlor, a sad service for someone mostly unloved.

"I'm thirsty," I said, bitterly.

❀   ❀   ❀

Oh, I was happy when they rolled me back to my old room, where I drank and slept, slept and drank. No amount of water could quench that thirst, but I could only drink for so long before I needed to sleep again. Back to the murky half-sleep of narcotics. From time to time, my roommate in his bathrobe shuffled past the foot of my bed on his way to the bathroom, and chatted with my wife a bit about his own surgery. A day or two ago, he'd had some important body part tinkered with—I can no longer remember what it was, but it wasn't *vestigial.*

Doctors came in, inquired about my pain, took turns admiring the three tiny incisions on my lower abdomen, which had swollen like the belly of a dead fish rotting in the sun. Carbon dioxide, they told me. They had pumped my abdominal cavity full of gas so that there was plenty of space between my organs while they were digging around in there. When they are explaining the wonders of laparoscopic surgery—which is indeed a modern medical miracle, don't get me wrong—they gloss over the effect of the gas, which is inaccurately described as "uncomfortable." The correct term is "extremely painful." I looked and felt as though they had inserted and inflated a beach ball in my belly, which, come to think of it, is more or less what actually happened.

In the late afternoon, my cheerful Polish nurse announced a desire to return to Bay Ridge, and introduced us to the night nurse.

You are probably rolling your eyes and wondering if I am going to describe the night nurse as "young and attractive." Why are you so concerned with what she looked like? She was a trained, experienced RN working the grueling night shift. Her job was to provide care and comfort to human beings who were ill and in pain, and often frightened. She had undoubtedly saved many lives just in the course of her regular duties, but she also offered reassurance and kindness to people going through the worst time in their lives, even while changing their bedpans and wiping up their vomit. That's what we should be concerned with, not her physical appearance.

But yes, she was attractive. Gorgeous, frankly. And young, like maybe around thirty. Oh God, it dismays me too. Actually, the night nurse bore a strong resemblance to the young-and-attractive physician's assistant who had fingered my ass in Brooklyn. This woman, too, was ethnically South Asian, with coffee-brown skin, dark eyes, and long, glossy black hair, but it was more than that. She had a similar shape of face, large eyes, strong jawline, long neck, and a wiry, athletic build that, yes, did make it easy to imagine her rollerblading. A somewhat different vibe in personality than the Brooklyn PA, though. There was a hint of physical toughness about the night nurse. Like, I could imagine that when she wasn't rollerblading, she spent weekends rock climbing in New Paltz. That she liked outdoor adventures, and her vacations were spent doing things like hiking the Appalachian Trail, or riding dirt bikes through the hilly backroads of the Thai countryside. You couldn't possibly imagine the physician's assistant in Brooklyn doing any of that, they were totally different that way.

I hope you don't think that I'm stereotyping, that I somehow think all attractive South Asian women look the same or that I assume they all enjoy rollerblading. I mean, Natasha is also a woman of South Asian ancestry,* and although I can be expected to sing the praises of my wife's physical beauty, it is a simple fact that she is an attractive woman. But Natasha's a totally different type. Her hair is also black and glossy, but she keeps it just slightly too short for a ponytail. Different shape of face than the other two, a little softer, less angular. Also: I can't possibly picture Natasha rollerblading through the streets of New York. And she hates outdoor adventures, unless we're talking about sipping margaritas on a tropical beach. She likes stuff like *Star Trek* and *Game of Thrones*, Victorian novels, comic books, trips to European cities, casual dinner parties with friends. (Works for me—I, too, dislike mosquitoes and broken ankles.) Natasha's real passion is pottery, a pastime which she refers to as *clay*—she belongs to a local studio and our apartment is overflowing with the stuff.

In this brief round-up of South Asian women I have met and/or married, I can imagine the Brooklyn PA liking *Game of Thrones*, but not the night nurse. She had a practical, down-to-earth manner that suggested to me a disinclination towards entertainments involving dragons. It's hard to guess whether or not the night nurse was into pottery—that's always a tough one to suss out. They don't all wear overalls and drive pickup trucks.

I have to refer to the night nurse as *the night nurse* because I can't remember her name and don't feel like making one up. It must've been written on the whiteboard, but it was late now, and they had dimmed the lights, and when I wasn't drinking water, I was sleeping. It had been a long day.

---

*That's right. Natasha is both West Indian and East Indian. Like the novelist V.S. Naipaul—and roughly half the current population of Trinidad—Natasha's ancestry can be traced to South Asia. In the 19th century, after slavery had been abolished in England, tens of thousands of Indians were shipped to the British colony of Trinidad (and other colonies in the Caribbean) to work as indentured laborers. Their presence in the New World played an essential role in shaping the unique, multifaceted culture of modern-day Trinidad and Tobago. Indian Arrival Day—a national holiday observed every May 30th—celebrates this history, commemorating the arrival of the first laborers from India in May 1845.

My wife was tired, too. After the Polish nurse left, Natasha announced that she, too, would like to return to Brooklyn for the night. "Are you okay with that?" she asked.

I waved her off. I didn't need her. I had water and narcotics and the young, pretty night nurse.

Doctors used to regularly perform surgery on babies without anesthesia under the then-prevalent, gobsmacking notion that babies don't feel pain. I'm not talking about medieval barbers with jars of leeches, I'm talking 20th-century doctors of the Marcus Welby era. It is still fairly common to hear the claim, dressed up in scientific puffery, that animals don't feel pain. That this claim is most forcefully asserted by lab researchers and slaughterhouse owners should be cause for some skepticism. But it's an attractive supposition, one that enjoys wide currency even among ordinary people who are not professional sadists, just your average kindhearted folk who hook fish through the mouth or toss a living lobster into a vat of boiling water and then explain to their horrified children that these primitive creatures don't feel pain.

It's total crap, of course. Pain is an evolutionary feedback system, and to assert that it is somehow the exclusive domain of adult *homo sapiens* flies in the face of both empirical evidence and plain commonsense.* What lobsters and babies have in common is not that they don't feel pain, but that they can't tell you when they do. They can't beg you to stop hurting them, any more than they can file a lawsuit or talk to a news reporter. Living bodies are fragile constructions and require vigilant upkeep and safeguarding. Evolution designed bodies to experience pain so that the inhabitants of those

---

*And, of course, until quite recently (in the West, anyway) the subset of *homo sapiens* deemed capable of experiencing pain—at least for the purpose of medical experiments and forced labor—was largely limited to white, male human beings, with the definitions of all three terms subject to fluctuating historical and cultural interpretation. I guess you have to draw the line somewhere.

bodies know when something has gone very wrong and needs immediate attention. To be alive is, necessarily, to suffer.

When I was a teenager and found myself suffering from some annoying, persistent pain—a sore throat, a cut in my mouth from my poorly maintained orthodontics, a swollen pimple that I'd screwed around with until it had gone radioactive—I often fantasized about some future technological development that would allow you to turn off physical pain in much the same way as you can turn off a smoke alarm that's gone off while you're frying onions in oil. I imagined an actual knob marked PAIN, like the volume knob on a stereo, which you could turn down or switch off altogether. Okay, body—got the message, those wisdom teeth need to come out. I'll take care of it, so shut up already. *Click*.

Of course, there really is such a knob, and that knob is labeled NARCOTICS.

If you like to fry onions a lot and you're tired of running into the hallway with a broomstick to poke at the OFF button on the smoke alarm, you might be tempted to yank out the batteries, a practice that is rightfully discouraged because you will definitely forget to put them back in, and then you won't wake up when your house is on fire—which it will be, because that's the kind of universe we live in, a universe that bends inexorably towards irony. And it is for very similar reasons that God did not supply us with a built-in OFF switch for pain.

Which is why it's a strange, disorienting experience to slip out of the neurological muffle of a narcotic sleep and gradually realize that the persistent nagging feeling of discomfort you are struggling to identify is actually tremendous, blinding, *oh my fucking god*
sweet-jesus-motherfucking-christ
oh god oh god oh god
pain!
pain! painpainpainpain pain!
PAIN!!!!

I lay on my back in a darkened room paralyzed with pain. Making the slightest movement sent searing bolts of agony through every nerve in my body. Even breathing hurt. Blindly, I fumbled around with my left hand until I found what I was looking for—that little red button on the end of a plastic cord. I couldn't remember whether it increased my narcotic dosage or summoned medical attention, but I banged on that motherfucker like I was transmitting *War and Peace* by Morse code.

This had exactly the effect I desired. The night nurse rushed into the room.

"What's wrong, what's wrong?"

It hurt to speak. "I'm in . . . *incredible . . . PAIN,*" I croaked.

"Where? Where's the pain?"

"Mmnnngggh . . . *EVERYWHERE,*" I gasped.

"Okay okay," the nurse said. Her words echoed in the darkness, a distant report from the world outside of the body I was locked in. "Just hang tight, I'll be right back."

I lay in the dark as motionless as possible, trembling like a water balloon in a child's hand. I don't know how long I lay there like that. There was no way to measure time. I heard a lot of agonized moaning which grew louder and louder because it was coming from inside my own head.

"Hey buddy? Are you okay?" The baritone voice came from far, far away, across the curtain that divided us.

Noooooooooo, I moaned.

"She's coming back, they're gonna take care of you," Fred told me. "I'm right here, buddy—you're not alone."

Ahh ahhh Aaaahhhhhhh, I responded, which was intended to serve as a grateful acknowledgment.

The sound of footsteps echoed in the hall, growing louder as they approached. Then all sorts of things happened at once. Blinding white lights flooded the room. I was being grasped, pulled upward, pain surging through me like an eighteen-wheeler hurtling through a brick wall, and there were way too many arms for one nurse.

The extra arms, roughly jerking me up by the armpits, belonged to Dr. Boy—where the hell did *he* come from?—who stared down at me from a great distance above in dreamlike clarity. No nerdy, intellect-signifying glasses adorned his face, which I could now see was handsome with an attractive edge of genuine brutality. His enviably thick blond hair, no longer swept back, tumbled over his forehead in a cascade so flattering that it implied the handiwork of a skilled blowdrying professional. No white lab coat, no stethoscope. Instead, emphasizing the broad expanse of his chest, a thick sweater of bright 1980s Cosby Show era patches which would have looked ridiculous on nearly anyone, but which on him signified the confident cockiness of elite prep schools and four years on the Harvard crew team.

Dr. Boy no longer resembled Doogie Howser at all, that had been a disguise. In his natural state, Dr. Boy bore an uncanny resemblance to the asshole rich kid played by James Spader in *Pretty In Pink*. He had that exact aura of cruelty, privilege, and plummy douchebaggery. With surreal insight, I suddenly knew two things. The first was that Dr. Boy had just been summoned away from a date at some nearby restaurant or bar. The second was that I was terrified of him.

Dr. Boy must have been asking me to characterize the precise degree of pain I was experiencing, because I heard myself suddenly blurt out with articulate fury, "You know that fucking one-to-ten thing you keep asking? It's *ELEVEN!* Eleven like the guitarist's amp in *Spinal Tap!*" And then some part of my brain calculated the extreme unlikelihood that this recent Harvard graduate would grasp an allusion to a thirty-year-old cult comedy. *"It's the worst pain I've ever experienced in my life!"* I shouted.

Dr. Boy's response was bewildering and unexpected. He violently seized my shoulders and shook me like a rag doll. I lost all sense of where I was or what was happening. All I knew was that Dr. Boy was trying to kill me.

I screamed.

He pushed his smooth handsome face close to my ear and whispered, "You know what I think, Tyler? I think you didn't tell us the whole truth. I think you take painkillers pretty regularly, don't you?"

"What?" I cried. He thought I was a junkie!

He shook me again, hard. "Come on, now!" Dr. Boy shouted. "We can't help you unless you tell us, Tyler! What is it, OxyContin? Percoset? Heroin?"

"*Gahhh!* No no no, I swear!" I cried. "Just Advil and stuff like that! And, like, hardly ever! I swear!"

At the same exact time, the nurse had somehow pulled my torso over her lap so that I was draped over her like one of those Renaissance crucifixion scenes. I was dimly aware that she was injecting me with something.

When I try to make sense of this memory, to visualize this scene, I find that I can't. How could the nurse pull me across her lap while Dr. Boy was thrashing me like a thug in an alley? It seemed as if I had more torsos than normal. My all-encompassing agony had obliterated all internal sense of my body's configuration. Head, torso, limbs, it was all a confusing jumble. I was like that Borges definition of the universe, a sphere of infinite circumference whose center is everywhere, and that ubiquitous center was an endlessly exploding supernova of pain.

"I'm going to have to catheterize you," the nurse told me. I nodded emphatically, *yes yes please do that,* unsure exactly what *that* entailed except that it involved something disagreeable being done to my weenie. That I so eagerly embraced this proposal is a testament to my state of extreme desperation.

With the forefinger and thumb of one hand, the nurse grasped my frightened penis, which had shrunk to size of a garden snail trying to pull itself back into its shell. With her other hand, she threaded a plastic tube into my urethra.

Under the right circumstances, the hissing gurgle of a powerful stream of urine hitting the surface of a metal bedpan is a sound of unspeakable delight. I was the Hoover Dam, collapsing. A fire hose dousing a burning building. A tapped keg bursting with foamy goodness. On and on it went, at first a raging river, and then a happy summer brook. All the pain drained out of me, swept away on a torrent of piss. The sound of my own voice screaming had faded away some time ago, and as the last golden drops trickled into the pan, I sank into the welcome embrace of black oblivion, not caring in the slightest whether it was sleep or death.

III. The Ice Age

> This reminds me of the ludicrous account which he gave
> Mr. Langton, of the despicable state of a young Gentleman
> of good family. "Sir, when I heard of him last, he was run-
> ning about town shooting cats." And then in a sort of kindly
> reverie, he bethought himself of his own favourite cat, and
> said, "But Hodge shan't be shot; no, no, Hodge shall not be
> shot."
>
> —James Boswell
> *The Life of Samuel Johnson*

"OH MY GOD," my wife said, after she had returned the next day and had been given a basic summary of my night of terror. Late morning sunlight flooded the room. The chatter in the hallways and the blare of my roommate's television restored a sense of comforting normality to the world. "I wish I could've been here for you!"

I thought of the humiliations I'd endured in the night, of Dr. Boy in his prep-school fury, shaking me down as if for lunch money, of the night nurse assaulting my shrunken manhood. Would I have wanted my wife by my side, witnessing all of that?

"It's okay," I said. "There wouldn't have been anything you could've done."

The Polish day nurse was back, chipper as ever. "I heard you had a bad night," she said. "That's okay, some people are just more sensitive to pain."

This sounded critical to me, the subtext being: *Man up, Nancy.* Her Slavic accent somehow made it worse. I could picture her telling an illustrative anecdote about the Polish farm she grew up on: *My father had appendicitis and my brother had to dig it out with a rusty pocketknife and my father laughed the whole time and then went off to milk the cows.*

Fuck you, I thought. She was pretty and sweet and wholesome, but still, *fuck you*.

After Hanna left, and my wife had gone off to the cafeteria, Fred spoke from behind the curtain. "They don't know the pain you were in," he said in his deep gravelly voice. "But I do. That was some real bad shit."

"Thank you," I said, my eyes growing moist.

❋ ❋ ❋

Foodstuffs of an unappetizing nature were piled up on the tiny surface of the rolling table positioned over my bed. I ate some dry Cheerios with my fingers, feeling like a fussy toddler.

"Would you like some coffee or tea?" Hanna asked.

"Oh God, yes," I said. "I would love a cup of black tea with milk."

While Hanna went off to get the tea, Natasha stood near the edge of my bed, making phonecalls. Her evening at home had not been restful. In our one-day absence, our building's heat had stopped working.

Natasha had been trying to get hold of our landlords and our super all morning, and now she was calling our friend Valerie, who she'd asked to check in on the status of our apartment and, more importantly, our cat.

In the early morning, before returning to the hospital, Natasha had managed to coax Luna into eating a half a spoonful of Fancy Feast and a few morsels of dry food but that was it. She hadn't eaten much of anything since Saturday. Natasha said she seemed increasingly listless. I was desperate to go home to her. Now that it was a new day, and I was no longer drugged out of my mind, no longer in agonizing pain, all I could think about was Luna, alone and sick and slowly starving herself to death in our freezing apartment.

❋ ❋ ❋

Having no heat in the middle of January is not an unusual event in our apartment. By the brutal standards of New York City, the apartment itself is Not Bad. We're near the subway. There's a crappy laundromat nearby and also a crappy supermarket. High ceilings, lots of windows, plenty of light and air in the summer, and a narrow but majestic sunset view of the Gowanus Bay and the Statue of Liberty, and—if you crane your neck a little—a glimpse of the Manhattan skyline, with the World Trade Center* and Empire State Building glittering just beyond the blighted industrial landscape of auto shops, asphalt plants, and waste processing facilities.

But the building is a dump. Our pathologically cheap landlords are indifferent to the most basic requirements of maintaining a legally habitable building. They leave repairs up to the discretion of our super, who lives in the basement. I'll call him Godot. He is Cuban and can do remarkable things like fix your broken faucet with a paper clip. The problem is that a paper clip is not the best way to fix a broken faucet. But with no budget from our landlords, Godot resorts to salvaging construction dumpsters for potential materials, adapting whatever he happens to have lying around to whatever needs fixing. All fixes are temporary fixes, but you're lucky to get them at all, because Godot works several jobs and is rarely available. You can call for weeks, making and confirming appointments, but it's useless. You're waiting for Godot. Months later, he'll bang on your door in the middle of the night, toolbox in hand. He'll futz around with paper clips for half an hour, swearing in Spanish, and shake his head. It's no good; he needs parts from the hardware store. Which is closed at that hour. He swears he'll return in the morning, but the second you close the door he'll have forgotten all about it.

Sometimes it's just as well. Godot doesn't always leave things better than when he arrived. He measures once, twice, writes it down, loses the paper and then just wings it. He gets angry if you're critical. He once installed a panel of above-counter cabinets in our kitchen flush against the ceiling, so high that you would need a ladder every time you wanted to fetch a can of beans. I have no idea why; I suspect it was just easier to make sure the unit was level by pushing

---

*Yes, I'm referring to awkward, blocky structure which replaced the equally awkward, blocky Twin Towers destroyed in the terrorist attacks of 9/11. I just can't bring myself to call it the Freedom Tower, a title which preserves the Orwellian propaganda of the Bush years. (Lest we forget: "Freedom Fries.") It is technically One World Trade Center, so my usage here is not incorrect.

it against the ceiling, and he hadn't devoted much thought to what people actually do with kitchen cabinets. When Natasha pointed the inconvenience of the arrangement, he tried to justify his mistake by arguing that the best place for your cabinets was several feet above your head where they wouldn't get in your way. It took a while for Natasha to coax him into reinstalling it properly. Later, he custom-built a clothes closet for us that turned out to be so shallow that you couldn't fit the hangers on the rod. We never did get him to reinstall that. We just learned to hang our clothes at an angle.

You have to keep your eye on Godot. If he's in a good mood, he can get creative, constructing elaborate things out of scrap that you didn't ask for and do not want and which do not actually address the problem you summoned him for. One time, I went to check on him while he was supposed to be repairing a leaking steam riser in our bathroom, and found him happily slapping yellow paint all over the walls. He'd found an old can in the cellar and decided to surprise us.

Godot controls the boiler, too. Steam heat. It is the source of his crippling power over all of our lives, and he uses it to punish and reward, but mostly he just treats it like his personal thermostat. It's cold in the basement and he cranks it up high while he's getting dressed in the morning and then forgets to turn it back down before he leaves for work. One afternoon, the entire apartment filled with so much steam from the overworked radiators that it melted the drywall tape holding together our ceiling, huge wet strips of the stuff dangling down like streamers at a party.

Another time, the boiler exploded. The entire building shook. I happened to be taking a bath at the time, when—*BOOM!*—a tremendous force from below launched my naked ass six inches into the air. I landed with a thump, water sloshing all around me. In that bewildered state, I thought someone in the apartment below had just swung a sledgehammer at the underside of the tub—everyone in this building does a lot of their own repairs—when Natasha burst in and announced, "I think the boiler just exploded." Which turned out to be the correct hypothesis.

Godot's ex-wife lives in the apartment above us. She's pleasant and neighborly, but she's also the most absent-minded person I've ever known. I'm always finding her keys, wallet or cellphone on our stoop. She is a practicing Catholic, and I have lost sleep thinking about her fondness for votive candles.

She lives with a revolving cast of their adult children, grandchildren, visiting relatives, and various significant others. They are all friendly people, and so are we, and so we enjoy mostly cordial relations with our upstairs neighbors—but we'd like them a lot more if they didn't live right above us. Collectively, they are a grievous vexation to the spirit and a significant source of our maintenance needs. Broken windows in the hall. Ripped garbage bags dragged down three flights of stairs, spewing coffee grounds and eggshells every step of the way. Cigarettes stamped out on the hallway floors, discarded chewing gum stuck to the walls. Unpleasant things involving toilets and sewage lines because those flushable wipes are not actually flushable but they keep flushing them anyway.*

But mainly, they *leak*. So many leaks over the years! Broken pipes, dripping radiators, unsupervised children playing with the faucets, meat left to defrost in an overflowing sink. It isn't always their fault, but it is so often that it's just safer to assume that it is. In every room of our apartment, sections of ceiling have collapsed at some point. Even in deep sleep, the faintest sound of dripping water can jerk me out of bed in a panic.

Once, I came home to find a pool of blood coagulating in the middle of our living room floor. A drop fell from above, splashing into the puddle. In horror, I gazed upward at our ceiling fan. Between the rotating blades, a crimson droplet oozed out of the switchbox and detached itself. *Plink.* I couldn't quite process what I was seeing; there was no narrative I could construct to account for blood dripping out of my ceiling fan. With the logic of a dream, I bent down, dipped the tip of my index finger in the sticky red pool and touched it to my tongue.† It was cranberry juice. Cranberry juice!

---

*Godot claims that it's actually the family who lives *below* us who are responsible for flushing the unflushable wipes. In fairness, he's probably right. We tend not to blame our downstairs neighbors for problems around the building because they don't leak on us all the time. Occasionally, in fact, we've leaked on *them*.

†Natasha: "Ewww! I still can't believe you did that!"

They have set their apartment on fire at least once. A serious fire, accompanied by fire engines and firefighters.

This is why I don't like going away for the weekend. I worry about Luna.

I know we should move. Natasha says we should move.

But you really can't beat that view of the Statue of Liberty.

I never get sick of it.

❁ ❁ ❁

Natasha finished her call and turned to me. "So, get this—Valerie says that there's still no heat, and guess what?"

Just then, Hanna came in to set down a styrofoam cup of hot water and a tea bag on my little table. "Oh," she said, raising a finger to her cheek. "I forgot your milk."

Hanna went off to fetch it, and Natasha continued. "She says there's no *water*, either. As in *none*."

At that moment, I started screaming.

Natasha, confused, stared at me in horror.

I screamed directly in her face. "*Ahhhh! Ahhhh! Ahhhh!*"

I myself had no idea why I was screaming. It just seemed to be a thing that was happening. A commotion ensued out in the hall, as nurses and orderlies gathered around the door to my room, mouths agape.

Hanna pushed her way through the crowd, holding a small carton of milk.

By then I had become aware of intense but fading pain, which had localized to a burning sensation in my left foot. I stared at it. Steam—actual steam!—rose from my sock, which was damp, as if . . . *as if an uncovered styrofoam cup of boiling water on an unlocked rolling table had been jostled by someone, dumping the scalding contents directly over my foot.*

I stopped screaming and glared at my wife, who stood in suspicious proximity to the rolling table and upended cup.

"I'm okay! I'm okay!" I shouted at the crowd at the door, fending off the possibility of being catheterized again.

"They thought you might have fallen," Hanna said, as the crowd dispersed.

"No," I said. "My wife dumped boiling water on my foot."

Hanna shrugged. "Falls are the worst."

Subtext: *Once, when I was mad at my brother, I hurled a pot of boiling water in his face. He just laughed, and continued to butcher my favorite pig, Princess. But you know? We had her for Easter dinner, and she was delicious.*

Natasha unpeeled the steaming sock. My foot, once exposed, was bright cherry-red, but otherwise disappointingly undamaged. No blisters. Some people are just more sensitive to pain.

I was furious at my wife with the special kind of fury—rich with historical significance and accumulated bitterness—that you reserve for a beloved spouse. Like, fucking *typical*. Natasha was always doing stuff like pouring boiling water on me. I mean, she hadn't specifically done that *exact* thing before, but it was the *type* of thing she did. Like that time thirteen years ago, when she kept leaving sharp knives at the bottom of a soapy kitchen sink full of dishes, and I kept asking her not to do that, and then one day when I was washing dishes, I reached in and sliced my hand pretty badly, and so I started screaming at her, waving the bloody hand in her face, and then she started crying, and then I felt even more angry because *I* was the one who got cut, but it was hard to yell at her while she was crying, so I just filed the whole thing away in the bristling mental file cabinet labeled RESENTMENT.

I was mad at Natasha about my scalded but unblistered foot, and also for adding yet another humiliation to this whole humiliating shitshow, but I couldn't express the full extent of my fury under the current conditions. We don't like to fight in public.

And besides, I couldn't really afford to alienate her. She was doing a lot of useful things for me, getting our local pharmacy to fill my scrips, checking in with Valerie, and making all the bureaucratic arrangements necessary for us to get the fuck out of this place. They were ready to send me home; all that remained was paperwork, which inexplicably took hours to produce.

❂ ❂ ❂

But of course, when it was time to go home, we couldn't go home. We had no heat and we had no running water. We took a taxi to Valerie's apartment instead. She was sympathetic to my situation—after all, we'd had the same organ removed—and offered to put us up until our own place was restored to a semi-habitable condition.

Valerie had a fold-out sofa in her living room. This wasn't one of those horrors from your childhood, the kind with the wafer-thin mattress stretched over tight metal springs with a back-breaking support rod running across the middle. It was much worse. It had an inflatable mattress that for unknown reasons could not be fully inflated. This meant that when Natasha and I got into bed, the collective weight of our bodies created a giant pocket of air which unpredictably shifted around the mattress with the slightest movement.

Valerie's two cats were delighted by this novel development in their circumscribed lives. We couldn't keep them out of the bed, which meant that there were now four living creatures attempting to find equilibrium on the seismically shifting topology of a half-filled air mattress. From time to time, we'd all settle down—two humans, two cats, one giant air bubble—and the complex physics of our sleeping arrangement would seem to have arrived at a stable configuration. But every time I drifted into sleep, some cat or human would shift position, setting the whole undulating surface back in motion. An hour earlier, I'd taken the Oxycontin I'd been prescribed for pain, but it made no difference. It was like trying to sleep at the bottom of a rubber dinghy caught in a typhoon.

I was more than partially inflated myself, and desperately felt the desire to pass some of that excess gas out of me, but I was afraid to try. Call me old-fashioned, but I didn't want to fart loudly in the presence of Valerie or my wife—although, *ahem*, one of those parties does not always extend the same courtesy to me—and I was also uncertain whether my farts would just be farts, and this wasn't *my* crummy air mattress to despoil with the as-yet-unknown contents of my newly streamlined bowels.

❅ ❅ ❅

One night of that was enough. On Tuesday morning, Natasha made some angry phone calls to our landlords, threatening to withhold rent and notify various city agencies. Natasha is very good at yelling at people. She doesn't yell often, but when she does, she does it with a cold, righteous fury, like a judge handing down a sentence to a pedophile.

We returned home late that afternoon, after Natasha had confirmed that our heat had been restored and our plumbing repaired. At last I had the opportunity for some much-needed privacy. I was eager to determine the status of my own plumbing. I waited until Natasha left to run some errands, because I was certain that once I took the throne, mighty trumpets would sound, the gates would creak open, and an unholy Apocalypse of Shit would manifest within the tiny chamber of our lavatory.

I spent an uneventful hour reading magazines.

I squirmed, I squatted, I pushed—I even poked—but the valve was sealed tight.

I gave up. Abdicated the throne, quite literally washed my hands of the whole business. At the sink, I popped open my prescription bottle and shook out an Oxy tablet.

❅ ❅ ❅

I went to check on Luna. She remained curled up in her bed in the hall. Uncharacteristically, she hadn't shown much interest in our return to the apartment after a few days absence. I'd hoped our arrival—and the restoration of the heat—might lift her spirits and excite her enough to eat something, but the bowl of Fancy Feast we'd set out when we'd gotten home had begun to crust over, untouched. It had been—what? Three days since she'd last eaten?

Yes, now it was time to worry.

Much to my chagrin, we've arrived at a point in this story requiring a cursory account of my cat's history with dry food. Kibble is not a subject I ever expected to write about. Then again, I never expected to write about the state of my bowels. And yet here we are.

After we'd rescued Luna from the streets eight years earlier, we fed her both dry food and wet food because that was my understanding of recommended feline dietary needs, derived from a childhood spent in a house swarming with cats. But Google hadn't existed in my childhood. In 2008, it did, and what Google told conscientious new cat-owners like me was that kibble might not be so good for them after all. The stuff is high in carbs, low in moisture, and is suspected to be a factor in obesity, diabetes, and kidney disease. So I resolved that our newfound cat, who'd only been with us for a few months, would be henceforth on a wet-food only diet.

One day, a few years later, Luna stopped eating for no discernible reason. This was our first encounter with Luna's anorexia, and it was frightening. She stopped eating for eight days. Vet visits, medicines, despairing internet research. A trip to the animal hospital where she'd mauled her first vet. Nothing worked, not even canned tuna. Running out of options, I went out and picked up an assortment of cat treats, and on impulse, grabbed a box of the kind of dry food she'd eaten during her first months with us. I poured some out in a bowl, and Luna came running into the kitchen, meowing frantically. She gobbled up every last morsel.

That one bowl of kibble broke the cycle of anorexia, restoring Luna to a glorious life of gluttony. The wise course of action would've been to continue feeding her an exclusive diet of wet food, and reserve the magic kibble as an emergency appetite restorative. But I felt strangely moved that Luna had remembered kibble from her earliest days with us, and that she adored it above all other foods. She'd had no way of telling me that during the years I'd withheld it from her diet, but now I knew. As a prisoner in a cramped New York City apartment, Luna's pleasures are necessarily curtailed. She is deprived of solo adventures and outdoor explorations, of sunning herself in the grass under an open sky, of chasing butterflies and hunting small creatures in the underbrush. So fuck it. Life is short. If she loved kibble so much that she'd wolf down a bowl of it when she felt otherwise too sick to eat at all, then I could at least offer her this measure of daily joy. So now, in addition to her daily allotment of two cans of Fancy Feast, she got an evening snack: a small scoop of kibble.

I didn't regret my decision. Luna loves food with piggish abandon, but that late night serving of kibble is the most exciting event of her day. Even accidentally jostling the plastic kibble container while reaching into the cabinet can send Luna into the kind of deranged frenzy one might elicit at an electronic dance music festival by tossing bags of molly into the crowd.

Luna's keen attunement to the gravelly sound of kibble yielded a useful side effect when we discovered that shaking the container could instantly summon Luna from her secret hiding spots, not all of which are known to us. One rattle, and within seconds she'll skid into the kitchen, her sleep-rimmed eyes bright with anticipation. This can be useful if, for example, I need to give her medicine, or if we are planning to evacuate the building because we suspect our upstairs neighbors have set their apartment on fire again.

You know where this is going. Time for some good old Pavlovian stimulation. I marched into the kitchen, pulled the plastic container from the shelf and shook it like a pair of maracas.

Ta da! As if I'd rubbed a magic lamp, there she was, meowing and butting her head against my leg. *I'm a bloody genius!*

I poured some into a bowl. *Ooof.* Not so easy to set it down on the floor. With all the unexpressed gas and poop bloating up my middle, I had the flexibility of an overstuffed bratwurst. Halfway down, I felt the seams straining to burst. I tried squatting instead, my left hand gripping the counter for support as I lowered myself down far enough to extend my arm to the ground.

Luna shoved my hand out of the way to get at the bowl.

She bent her head. Sniffed.

She took a step back and cocked her ear, as if puzzled.

And then, with an air of disappointment, she slunk back to her bed.

Shit.

Not a genius. She didn't know why she didn't want to eat and neither did I.

I heaved myself up. I dug a few morsels out of the plastic container and carried them to her. With coaxing and patience, I got her to nibble a couple from my hand. In the evening, she showed up in the kitchen when I cracked open a can of Fancy Feast, but when I set down the bowl, she walked away without even sniffing it. Natasha managed to hand-feed her a few more crunchies, and that was it for the day.

❊   ❊   ❊

Lying in bed that night, I struggled to fall asleep, in spite of the painkillers I'd taken. I normally sleep on my side, but my beachball belly made this impossible, so I lay on my back in the dark, listening to Natasha breathe.

Luna had not eaten since Saturday morning, and it occurred to me that this was the same duration of time since I'd last taken a shit. Did our alimentary synchronicity hold some deeper significance, indicate some hidden biological correspondence, akin to the mysterious way women's menstrual cycles are said to align themselves in a shared household?

This did not seem like something I would be able to Google.

I thought about the category of *Things Easily Googled*. All sorts of things, for sure, but the most obvious topic suggests itself. From the dawn of the web in the early 90s, advances in internet technology have been fueled by two widespread, enduring interests. The first of these: Cute kittens doing cute things. Flushing toilets, hopping in and out of cardboard boxes, asking if they can *has cheezburger*. In a world that so often feels brutal and cold-hearted, people can't seem to get enough of the kittens, and who can blame them?

But LOLcats are not what I was thinking of. I was thinking of that other hugely popular internet diversion—the one which deserves more credit for driving the development of compressed image technology, streaming video, and online payment services. Pornography. People can't get enough of that, either.

Homo sapiens are obsessed with sex, the green force that drives evolution. Every fairy tale begins with a childless couple, every comedy ends with a wedding, but the biological imperative to find a mate and reproduce is the least of it. Like an invasive vine, the perfumed tendrils of libido creep over the works and days of our clever species, and nothing we think, do, or make can push free from that lush entanglement.

Freud was right. Once you start thinking about it, it's hard to escape the conclusion that sex colors everything, supplies meaning and nuance to a broad spectrum of human activity. If you look for it, you'll find it. Poetry and politics, fashion and philosophy, Instagram and Twitter. It's not just about the *content* of these endeavors—which, of course, can be quite removed from anything remotely sexual or romantic—it's about the *underlying motivation*, the reason why we endeavor at all. Achievement in any sphere, no matter how minor or personal, is perhaps its own reward, but c'mon—the reward everyone really wants is *recognition*. Standing ovation, Best In Show, hip hip hooray. It's not much of a stretch to link the quest for public admiration—racking up those Likes—with some instinctive drive related to sexual selection, a display of evolutionary fitness. Sex appeal, in other words—of which physical appearance is only one component, Darwin's vexing peacock feathers notwithstanding—and perhaps a lesser one at that. Ambition is framed by the ungratified lineaments of desire. We want and we want to be wanted: the two-stroke engine that propels the human race. Deny it all you like, but as any purveyor of toothpaste or automobiles can tell you, we think about sex even when we're not thinking about sex. In our fecund imaginations, a cigar is never just a cigar.

Meh. Laying it on a bit thick, aren't you? I thought. I shifted around under the blankets, struggling to adjust the pillow I'd placed under my knees.

It's the trouble with grand unifying theories that try to pack away the messy attic of human experience into a single Goodwill box. It's not that they don't have anything true to say; it's that what they have to say is not true for everything. To a hammer, everything looks like a nail; to a Freudian, everything looks like an unresolved anal fixation.

There's a funny moment in *The Sandman*, Neil Gaiman's magnificent graphic novel series, in which a sleeping mortal woman encounters Morpheus, the King of Dreams. "Do you know what Freud said about dreams of flying?" she asks him as they soar through the air. "It means you're really dreaming about having sex."

"Indeed?" Morpheus responds. "Tell me, then, what does it mean when you dream about having sex?"*

Freud—like Darwin, Marx, or Picasso—was one of the great post-Enlightenment revolutionaries, setting a torch to all the musty old proprieties of the Victorian era, blazing a path to the liberating possibilities of twentieth-century modernism. Freud shaped the future, but he was shaped by the past. That human beings, men and women both, have sexual appetites of a wide-ranging nature, is now old news and no longer needs to be hidden from one's superego in the brown-paper wrapper of subconscious sublimation.

These days, you don't have to dream about flying when what you want to dream about is sex. Oh brave new world! Pornography has become something of a taken-for-granted utility, like indoor plumbing, and is now available on tap from the comfort of your home, although no one is quite sure of the underlying economics, how such an infinite supply of the stuff gets produced when no one has to pay for it anymore. If you want to buy a butt plug or a ball-gag, you no longer have to wear a raincoat and sneak into a triple-X store in the shitty part of town; you can stroll right into a clean, well-organized establishment run by professional sex educators who will guide you to the instrument best-suited to your particular physiology and proclivities.† Many of the longstanding taboos of the past have been obliterated. The love that once dared not speak its name now shouts it proudly in the streets, often with corporate sponsorship. Oh, true, the promises of the sexual revolution are hardly fulfilled—the war against the holier-than-thou prigs and puritans rages on—but we no longer need Freud to liberate us from our antiquated shame.

* *The Sandman, vol. 2: The Doll's House* (DC Comics, 1990). I own a signed first edition.
† Well, you can in the state I reside in.

In such an era, you'd think we'd grow bored with sex, but, nope, we're still obsessed with it, and our libidos still get us in all sorts of trouble. The rationalist approach—to demystify sex, to treat erotic satisfaction as a personal health issue, akin to a sensible diet and regular exercise; or legalistically, as an itemized contract negotiated between mutually interested parties—has severe limitations. Because Freud. Because the sexual drive *isn't* rational. (Otherwise, as the old joke has it, we'd never bother putting ourselves through all those ridiculous motions.) Lust is a compulsion built into the operating system, deep-rooted, systemic. No matter how enlightened or liberated we think we've become, people still do terrible things for sex, feel terrible when they get it, feel terrible when they don't. Plenty of shame to go around. The difference between Freud's era and our own is that we can now openly talk about our wanton urges—and we do, all the time, breathlessly, on Snapchat and Twitter and TikTok, on talk shows and TED Talks, in blockbuster movies and bestselling books, and in oh-so-many Parental Advisory pop songs.

But you can live without sex. Unhappily, perhaps, but no one has ever died from lack of sex. Joan of Arc died a virgin. Okay, she was only nineteen when she got burned at the stake, so not the best example. But she's hardly alone. Popular listicles of "Famous People Who Died as Virgins"—easily Googled!—also include such luminaries as Elizabeth I, Isaac Newton, Nicolas Tesla, Andy Warhol, Lewis Carroll, and Mother Teresa.* *Extraordinary lives—lived without sex!*

Know what you can't live without?

Eating and shitting.

The body is a factory that manufactures itself. If you want to keep living, you have to keep supplying the factory with raw material on a daily basis, cramming stuff into one end and squeezing it out the other. For the individual of the species, making sure this happens is way more critical than anything related to sex or repro-

---

*There are dozens of these virgin listicles festooned across the interwebs, all of dubious provenance, and they all seem to be cribbed from one another. Interestingly, I've yet to see Jesus Christ listed on any of them. (Or the Virgin Mary (!)—but that's probably because she had other kids after the famous one.) Immanuel Kant appears with surprising regularity.

duction. It's true for birds; it's true for bees. It's true for cats, bats, armadillos and crabs. Eating and shitting, day after day after day. Mother Teresa had to do it, and so do you.

Sex is overrated. But eating and shitting? Reliably satisfying, universally pleasurable.

I closed my eyes and folded my hands over the bloated swell of my belly. *Yes, that's it,* I thought, drifting into sleep at last. *There lies the real meaning of life.*

❁ ❁ ❁

The next day, I began exploring the world of stool softeners.

My post-op instructions permitted the use of Colace, which so far was literally not doing shit. I turned on my computer. Search term: *constipation.* Soon I had compiled a long list of popular remedies, various powders, pills, and applications. In loose sweatpants and an overcoat, I waddled out of my apartment to the pharmacy across the street and stocked up. On the way back, I stopped at the corner store to purchase a bottle of prune juice. *Oh, you also sell actual prunes? Yeah, lemme get some of those, too.*

Natasha and I have a longstanding, mutually agreed-upon policy of avoiding discussion pertaining to the state of our bowels, so I did not disclose the nature of my purchases. I stashed everything away in my office, and waited. In the late morning, Natasha announced that if I didn't need anything, she planned to spend a few hours at her pottery studio, since she'd already taken the day off work to look after me. At last! Time to deploy my arsenal of laxatives—there's a pun here, but I can't quite work it out—in a full-scale attack against the shuttered gates of the citadel.

Bottles uncapped, solutions mixed, prune juice glugged, and then I headed into the bathroom to launch my shock-and-awe offensive against the rear flank. Trousers dropped, Vaseline applied, and (with some difficulty) position assumed. I'd bought a box of four enema bottles, and two seemed sufficient for now. After waiting the prescribed amount of time, I stood up, and for good measure executed a vigorous little belly dance, rapidly wiggling my tummy as best I could, side to side, back and forth, hips in, hips out, like a spastic Hokey Pokey. *Oh, yes! That's the way! Shake it all about!* I could feel a watery chowder of mixed fluids jostling around in my GI tract, rousing the coiled snake of my colon into action. I was ready. I sat down and opened a *New Yorker*.

Nothing.

Nothing!

Total #enemafail. How was this biologically possible? I wished I had a personal CT scanner so I could see what the hell was going on in there. Maybe I'd been so dehydrated that I'd soaked everything up at, like, the cellular level. But no, I could still feel it all gurgling around. It all went in easily enough but it didn't want to come back out. That couldn't be good.

After a half hour or so, I abandoned camp and sloshed back to my computer to Google a diagnosis. Consultations with the internet were not reassuring. They never are. By the time you've exhausted the deliberately uninformative official literature (TL;DR—*Seek the advice of your health practitioner*) and you've had the disagreeable experience of looking up medical questions on Wikipedia—whose basement-dwelling editors, as a matter of policy, favor clinically explicit photographs of the most stomach-churning variety—you're left with the user forums, Reddit, Yahoo Answers, Quora and all the wretched Eco-Mommy blogs, a hypertextual codex of conflicting and alarming personal experiences, instructive primarily as a case study confirming the utter worthlessness of anecdotal evidence.

I learned nothing. Either something was deeply abnormal and horribly wrong, or everything was peachy-keen, and I just had to be patient with the healing process.

Natasha returned, carrying several bags of groceries.

During my unproductive half hour on the toilet, I'd had the opportunity to note the tattered state of my bandages. I didn't know how I'd gotten them so dirty in such a short span of time. I was afraid that if I removed them my insides might ooze out. I asked Natasha if she knew whether I was allowed to change them yet.

She did not.

I then broke protocol and confessed that my drainpipes were still hopelessly clogged in spite of all the pills, liquids, and nonsoluble fiber I'd dumped and squirted into both ends of myself.

Natasha stopped unpacking groceries and frowned. "Are you sure you should be taking all that stuff at the same time? That sounds dangerous."

I shrugged. It wasn't working, so how dangerous could it be?

In our marital division of labor, medical stuff—doctor appointments, bills, insurance—tends to fall under Natasha's purview, just as I, in turn, take care of all matters related to garbage, electronics, and cat shit. So Natasha volunteered to call Dr. K—my surgeon—to inquire about my filthy bandages and immoderate use of laxatives, and I did not object.

"Just see what they say," I said. "I don't want to make an appointment yet."

The thing about handing off your responsibilities to someone else is that it's easy to forget that it's still *your* problem, and you'll still suffer the consequences of the final outcome. It's like when someone offers to drive you somewhere, and instead of paying attention to where they are taking you, you daydream and gaze at the scenery and complain about the driver's taste in music, and then after you get out of the car and wave goodbye, you look around and realize you have no idea how you got there, how you'll get back, or even if this is where you thought you were going in the first place.

And so when Natasha called the surgeon's office on my behalf—although I was perfectly capable of calling them myself—I hadn't really considered the implications of letting her speak as my proxy. As a rule of thumb, whenever you call a doctor to discuss any unexpected health issue, the doctor will automatically tell you to come in to the office. This is especially true after you've recently had surgery. Medical malpractice isn't cheap. Why risk giving advice over the phone?

I was making a cup of tea in the kitchen when I heard Natasha say, "Three o'clock this afternoon? Yes, that works. Thanks for fitting us in."

I rushed into the living room to stop her, but she'd already hung up.

"Hey, did you just make an *appointment* for me?" I was furious. "I *specifically* asked you not to do that!"

She couldn't understand why I was angry. "But she wants you to come in," she said in a puzzled tone of voice that suggested she was struggling to determine if I was as irrational as I sounded, or if she had just misheard me.

"Weren't you listening? I told you that *I did not want to go in!*"

"But today's the only day she has office hours! They had to rearrange her schedule! She's expecting you!"

You can see what happened here. Because she'd made the call on my behalf, she now felt responsible for the outcome. Natasha is a Good Patient. She takes drugs exactly as prescribed, and does not flush half of them down the toilet, or offer them to uninsured friends, or hoard them for future recreational use. She follows medical advice scrupulously, and does not consult Reddit for second opinions. And if she calls the doctor's office with concerns and they ask her to please come in, then she *comes in.*

I had known this aspect of Natasha's character from her many medical adventures over the years, but because this was the first time in our marriage that I'd played the role of patient, I lacked experience in guarding myself against oversolicitous caregiving. It was one thing to let Natasha handle my medical *paperwork,* but quite another to let her handle my medical *decisions.* We really were very different people in this regard. I took medical advice as *advice*—and advice is *optional.*

"You know," Natasha warned me, "if you don't go in to see her and something happens later, you'll have to go to the emergency room instead."

"I don't care," I told her. "I am not going. No fucking way."

Natasha looked very unhappy. Because we have been married for a long time, I knew there were exactly three reasons for her unhappiness. First among them: she could not wrap her head around the idea that anyone who had *concerns related to recent surgery* would refuse to go see their doctor, especially when this was the only available appointment for a week. I could tell by her horrified expression that Natasha thought my decision here was shockingly irrational, and possibly even insane. Secondly, as a hospital administrator, Natasha dreaded the professionally embarrassing prospect of having to cancel an appointment she had just made because her husband was irrational and insane. She didn't want to be the spokeswoman for a *non-compliant patient*. And finally, she was worried about me, because she loves me, and she didn't want me to die from some easily preventable intestinal mishap out of my own stubborn stupidity. Because, after all, NYU had screwed up our friend Valerie's surgery, so maybe they'd screwed up mine, too. Maybe I had a *stump*.

But I had good reasons for being so adamant. I began enumerating them.

For starters, I'd been home for only one evening, and I didn't want to go back to the city. It was a miserable January day—looking out the window, I could see pedestrians huddled in parkas and scarves, fighting the icy wind. Crackles of white frost rimed the streets and overhead, a heavy gray sky threatened to crap buckets of snow over the whole city. Also, in case anyone had forgotten, our cat was still sick, and I wanted to stay home to be with her. And finally—and this was crucial—within the last two hours I'd washed down a handful of laxatives with a gooey glass of prune juice, swallowed several spoonfuls of olive oil, slurped down a porridgey cup of Metamucil, eaten half a dozen prunes, and administered not one, but two enemas. Although thus far my regime had failed to produce any effects, I was not going to risk getting stuck on the Brooklyn Bridge in a snowstorm while my bowels erupted like a fecal geyser all over the backseat of a taxi.

There was something else, too, that I didn't tell Natasha. Even if we'd happened to live next door to the hospital, I would've refused to go. I was terrified that if Dr. K had even the slightest concern about my recovery, she would want to re-admit me, and I would once again have to surrender my autonomy to the inexorable machinery of the hospital, to catheters and rectal exams, to Dr. Boy and his midnight hazing, to the sweet Polish nurse and her cups of boiling water.

It had been a mistake to let Natasha speak for me. She didn't understand my healthcare priorities, the most important of which was *to stay the fuck out of the hospital*. Really, what I needed to do was to get back in the captain's chair and take control of my own goddamn destiny.

But that could wait.

I had an appointment that needed to be canceled, and, with a little coaxing, Natasha seemed willing to do it.

I hovered nearby while she made the call, and I was not happy with what I heard. She quickly got derailed from the main priority, which was to cancel the appointment, and instead, began reiterating all the symptoms she had described the first time around. And then—oh God—she mentioned that I had experienced *some pain*. Fuck! That was a red flag for sure!

I waved my hands frantically at her, which had no effect, so I shouted instead. "No! No! Not pain!" I bellowed. "It's just the gas! It's not pain, it's *mild discomfort!*"

She glared at me and covered the mouthpiece. "It's your surgeon, I'm trying to hear what she says!" she hissed.

Natasha proceeded to give a detailed catalog of every complaint I'd had for the last twenty-four hours. I'd had a lot of them because I habitually complain even when I haven't had surgery. Shouting interjections from the sidelines, I countered every description she gave of my condition with a less urgent version, and Natasha did her best to ignore me, even going so far as to put a finger in her ear.

"Tell her about the taxi!" I shouted. "Tell her that *I don't want to shit all over the taxi!*"

There could be no doubt that my surgeon on the other end could surely hear me screaming like a lunatic in the background, and I could tell by Natasha's apologetic tone that she was mortified with embarrassment, both personal and professional. I stopped shouting when I heard Natasha promise that I would come in next week instead, since I was obviously in an uncooperative mood today.

Natasha hung up the phone and gave me a baleful look. "She sounded *pissed.*"

I was pissed, too, but Natasha already looked quite upset and I didn't want to antagonize her any more than I already had. This was a *teachable moment* and I had important things to say about what had just happened. I took a deep breath so that I could share my observations in a calm and measured tone.

"Look, I *truly* appreciate everything you've been doing for me through this whole thing," I began.

I already sounded furious.

I tried again, aiming for a more conciliatory tone. "I probably should've called the office myself instead of having you do it for me."

Natasha nodded in emphatic agreement, which I found profoundly irritating. To calm myself, I began pacing, but our tiny living room is not amenable to pacing. There is only a narrow conduit of floor space, three or four feet long, between the coffee table and the bookshelves, and by the time you've paced two paces it's time to turn around and pace back. There's no room to pontificate or make interesting hand gestures, or puff meditatively on a pipe, or thoughtfully stroke your chin before suddenly stopping in your tracks as if arrested by a profound insight. You can never establish a proper pacing *cadence* in this place, it's all just back-and-forth, back-and-forth, like a duck in a shooting gallery.

I stopped pacing, now twice as irritated. I turned to face her and took a breath.

"Natasha, you need to understand something," I told her. "If I am ever in a terrible car accident, or have an aneurysm, or somehow become otherwise incapacitated, I do *not* want heroic measures. *No heroic measures!*"

It wasn't clear what this had to do with anything at all, but I felt it needed to be said, and I figured that if I kept on going I'd somehow bridge the connection.

"I want to be in control of my *own* medical decisions," I continued. "Not the doctor. Not you."

Of course, if I ever actually wound up incapacitated by an aneurysm, I would be, by definition, explicitly *not* in control of my own decisions . . . ugh, the line of thinking was getting a bit muddled here. Better wrap it up. Drive it all home.

"And so I want you to know," I concluded grandly, "that I don't *care* if the doctor is pissed, or thinks I'm, whatever, non-compliant, a so-called *bad patient*. You know what? Maybe I *am* a bad patient!"

Natasha took a moment to process all this, and then burst out laughing.

"You are *definitely* a bad patient!"

I tried hard not to laugh because you can't laugh and be self-righteous at the same time, and also because in my current condition, I'd discovered that it really hurt to laugh. But the musculature involved in *suppressing* a laugh is similarly abdominal—you often don't realize how something works until it hurts—and the effort shifted something inside of me.

"We'll talk about this later," I blurted, and ran for the bathroom.

☼ ☼ ☼

False alarm. Nothing. But I remain certain that if I had been seated in a taxi, or in any public place, things would've gone quite differently.

In the evening, I helped Natasha change the untouched bowls of food we'd scattered around the apartment. While she'd been out, she'd bought all sorts of delicacies to seduce Luna into eating—canned tuna, rotisserie chicken, and a wide variety of commercial cat foods and treats. On my mother's advice, I'd had Natasha buy jars of Gerber Baby Food, which she'd had trouble sourcing because who the hell still feeds their baby gloopy pink spoonfuls of beef slurry?

Luna didn't want any of it. Now and then, she'd oblige us by eating a few crunchies if we hand-fed them to her, but that was it.

In the back of my skull, I felt a dull throb of despair. I didn't want to think about what would happen if she didn't pull through this time, if we couldn't get her to eat. I hadn't yet consulted our veterinarian, but if this continued another day, I'd have to make an appointment before the weekend kicked in.

Luna spent much of her time curled up in her little bed that sat on the floor just outside the door to my office. From my desk, I could turn in my chair to look at her. I knew I should let her rest—in fact, I kept telling Natasha to stop fussing over her and leave her in peace—but I couldn't resist getting up to go stroke her head and scratch her under the chin.

"You'll be okay," I whispered, trying to reassure myself.

❀　❀　❀

On Thursday morning, Natasha called me from work and told me that she'd made arrangements at her hospital for me to come in on Friday to see a doctor who could change my bandages and make sure my incisions weren't infected.

I kept up my regime of painkillers, prunes, and enemas, and in the afternoon, I managed to push something through. I hovered over the toilet staring at what I'd produced. It wasn't very impressive. A sad little turd that I thought of as *an old lady shit*. I have no idea why that particular phrase occurred to me. It just seemed right. I imagined a wealthy society matron with white hair and pearls positioning herself in front of the commode and lifting up the hem of her skirt. She lowers herself down, pursing her lips in distaste. *Ka-chunk.* She leaps up and hastily pulls up her knickers. Adjusting her pince-nez, she leans over the bowl to inspect the tiny fruit of her labors. With an air of grim satisfaction, she depresses the chrome handle, making sure that all evidence of the unhappy transaction has vanished without a trace. And then, I suppose, she powders her nose and rushes back to the charity luncheon.

I wondered where it had all gone, the prunes, the Metamucil, the Colace, the enemas. Was it all backed up in the tubes? Or had these substances somehow been transubstantiated into bits of me? The phrase *immaculate digestion* came to mind. I made a mental note to Google it, although I had a hunch that the search term *old lady shit* would yield far more results. Not that I was going to test that hypothesis. There are some phrases you should never enter into a search engine.

✿　✿　✿

By mid-afternoon, Luna had not improved. If anything, she seemed worse: listless, and, I suspected, depressed. Her days are organized around meals: the hour-long anticipation beforehand, the sharp little chirps she barks out while rubbing against my leg so that it's impossible to ignore her presence; rushing hopefully towards the kitchen every time I rise from my desk to go take a piss; parking herself in front of her empty food bowl and staring at me with fixed, unwavering intention, as if trying to psychically compel me to get off my lazy ass and use those opposable thumbs to dish out some grub; the electric thrill of the moment when I finally crack open the lid of the can and she rises on her hind legs like a dancing poodle, unable to contain her prandial elation; and, when it's all over, the leisurely, contented ritual of washing up. With the loss of her appetite, all of that was gone, the very structure of her daily life.

It was time to take her in. I made an appointment with our vet for late Friday afternoon, a couple of hours after my own medical appointment. Natasha promised she'd come back with me from my visit to her hospital so that she could carry Luna to the vet's office, since I wasn't supposed to lift anything for the next week.

✿　✿　✿

Although I still had pain—sitting, standing, picking things up, putting them down—it was bearable, and I decided that I should start phasing out the painkillers.

I used to think I liked OxyContin. Like, if someone mentioned OxyContin in a conversation, a little part of my brain would murmur to itself, *Ooh, yeah, OxyContin, I like that*, in much the same way it did if someone mentioned *baklava* or *Venice*. Not a lustful craving, just a quiet inner affirmation: *Good stuff*. When Natasha had her surgeries, she was prescribed OxyContin pills. She never took them. She has a bad reaction to opioids. She gets dizzy and nauseated, and these side effects are so unpleasant that she'd rather just deal with the pain. So I took them instead. This wasn't exactly recreational. Lying around on the couch in a stupor isn't my thing and I've always preferred the brisk embrace of uppers if I'm planning a chemically-enhanced night on the town. But I am a horrible insomniac. So every now and then, when I was up late and wanted to pull the plug on my consciousness, I'd dig out that little bottle from the back of the medicine cabinet, wash an Oxy down with a cold beer, and enjoy a smooth, anxiety-free descent into dreamland. I figured I couldn't get hooked because it wasn't my scrip, and the existing supply would run out quickly enough, which it did. But now that I had my own scrip, I wanted OxyContin out of my life as soon as possible. I didn't like the way it made me feel disconnected from my body and indifferent to the world around me, as if I had died and just hadn't realized it yet. Nor did I want to pick up a new addiction. You hear about ordinary people who undergo surgery and acquire an Oxy habit in just a few weeks, and when they can no longer get their scrip refilled, they turn to heroin. That sounded *exactly* like something I would do. I've made all sorts of forays into the gritty and glamorous world of substance abuse—cigarettes, booze, cocaine, Netflix—but I've always avoided heroin, which may be the one single thing I've ever done right in my life.

So no more Oxy during the day. I'd allow myself half a pill at night—okay, maybe a whole one, at first—so I could sleep, and I hoped I'd soon be able to phase that out too.

Since I was cutting back on the opioids, I figured it was probably fine to start drinking again because I felt very depressed that evening. This is normal for me, particularly in the winter, but the subpar state of my bowels and Luna's illness had pushed me to the border of despair. I opened a bottle of wine to take the edge off and spent the evening listening to sad music and writing long, morbid emails to distant friends.

❀ ❀ ❀

On Friday morning, an hour or so before noon, I changed out of my greasy sweatpants and t-shirt into clean clothes and called a taxi to bring me to Natasha's hospital.* As I stepped into the foyer, I was annoyed to see that, yet again, the lock on the building door had broken and wouldn't close properly.

This isn't some sort of Chekhov's Gun thing. I'm not bringing this up because my observation of the broken door foreshadows some major event later in this story. Actually, now that I'm thinking about it, the broken door does in fact get mentioned later, but only as a minor detail of little significance. You don't need to worry about it. No, I'm mentioning the door only because it's really fucking annoying and there's no good reason for it. It's got a slam latch, the kind where the main locking mechanism is bolted to the inner side of the door. The door is misaligned with the frame—which jolts the lock every time it's shut—so the original bolts fell out long ago and have since been replaced by a succession of inappropriate fasteners which constantly drop out or get stripped so that the door will no longer latch shut, and then I have to badger Godot for months to fix it, and when he finally does, it's always with some half-assed random screw he's found under his couch, so it will break again within a few days.

Being broken is the normal state of our front door. So much so that even during those rare interludes when the lock has been fixed and will latch properly, no one in the building bothers to actually pull the door shut when they enter and leave, because they are accustomed to the door being broken and *think of it as broken even when it's not.* As a result, flies and mice get in, and so do Jehovah's Witnesses. Given the high population of junkies roaming our neighborhood, I'm always expecting to come home and find our apartment

---

*Yes, I sure was taking a lot of taxis that January, which might give you a distorted impression of how I get around the city. In my ordinary life, like all real New Yorkers, I ride the trains (or, when absolutely necessary, the goddamn bus). Taxis are for special occasions: international flights, bulky Home Depot purchases, late night trips back to Brooklyn with drunk friends, and recent appendectomies.

ransacked, which causes me endless worry because Luna's there and what if the junkies burglarizing our home let her escape, or even deliberately hurt her? There's no telling what these people will do, they're *junkies.*

And so I can't even leave my building for a doctor's appointment that I'd rather not go to without this additional small, shitty anxiety added to all the other small, shitty anxieties of the day. I want to scream at them all—the inconsiderate neighbors, the distractible super, the cheap-ass landlords—for letting things slide like this, for thinking that these little things don't matter, for failing to recognize that *entropy is our natural enemy*, and we must band together to fight it with all our strength, every day of our lives.

If there's a point to this long aside about the broken door, well, that's the point, reader. Rust never sleeps. Things fall apart. In the heat of our daily battles with one another, how easy it is to forget the real war being waged against us. The goddamn Second Law of Thermodynamics. Entropy creeps through every unpatched crevice in the ceiling, sneaks past every broken door, stealthily gnawing away at the foundations of the world, tearing apart all the fine things we have labored to build in our short tenure on earth. Tireless, inexorable, unrelenting, the long fingers of entropy will one day snuff out the very stars in the sky. Be ever vigilant, friends! Set straight the crooked picture on the wall! Retrieve thy underwear from the bathroom floor! Clean up after your dog, recycle your plastic, and don't forget to floss. Our collective failure to tighten the loose screws holding the world together is why it becomes a shittier place with every passing year.

Stepping outside, I saw that someone had, once again, strewn chicken bones all over the stoop. I kicked them onto the sidewalk, suppressing my rage as I walked to the corner where my taxi was waiting, already honking impatiently because I was late.

The hospital where Natasha works dates back to the mid-19th century, and since the days of crippled Union soldiers and Irish shanties, it has historically served the underprivileged from every quarter of Brooklyn. It's located in what had been, for many decades, a working-class black neighborhood known for its large community of West Indian immigrants and their descendants. Over the last twenty years, the frenzied Brooklyn real estate market has dramatically shifted the demographics of the surrounding area. Wealthy "creatives"* now inhabit the rehabilitated brownstones and once-crumbling old Victorians, and stylish new high-rises seem to pop up from the concrete on a daily basis, accompanied by cranes and jackhammers. But the hospital still largely serves the same clientele, who struggle even more in these years of high rents and displacement. The hospital has also served as a local employer, so it's not surprising that a significant proportion of the hospital's faculty and staff—my wife among them—are also West Indian.

As it happens, I am neither black nor West Indian. I am a white dude who grew up in suburban New Jersey.

So here's the thing that happens whenever Natasha manages to insert me into someone's busy schedule at her hospital. I'll mosey by in the afternoon, and text Natasha to let her know I'm here so she can alert the front desk of whatever department I'm going to. She comes out to fetch me, guides me through a maze of elevators and halls, and then we'll open a door and step into a waiting room crammed with glassy-eyed patients in the hopeless, vegetative repose induced by waiting rooms, draped over chairs, wilting like neglected houseplants, staring vacantly at the dreary daytime television shows broadcast on the wall-mounted screens, checking and rechecking their phones for signs that the world outside still exists.

At the front desk, Natasha quietly introduces me as her husband, murmurs a few friendly words to the supervisor and then says goodbye and heads back to her office.

As I glance around for an empty seat, it's difficult not to notice that I am—often enough, anyway—the sole white person in the waiting room. I sit down, pull out something to read. I've barely

---

*Don't get me started.

opened my magazine when a nurse pops out and calls my name, and then I'll feel my face flush with embarrassment because I know how it must look to everyone else, all those People of Color who've been waiting around so long they've forgotten why they came. *The optics are not good.* It's like that old *Saturday Night Live* sketch where Eddie Murphy disguises himself as a white man and discovers that white folks not only ride the city bus for free, but also receive *complimentary champagne.*

And so, as I'm being escorted away to the examining room for my non-scheduled appointment, I'll self-consciously picture the entire waiting room glaring resentfully at my back. I often have the urge to stop, turn around, explain to everyone the peculiar circumstances of my advantage. *I know! I know what it looks like!* I want to say. *But I swear to you, this isn't #whiteprivilege! It's my wife with the privilege—and she's brown!*

But no one ever objects. No one rushes up to the front desk, demanding to see the sign-in sheet. Indignant old men do not rise out of their chairs to shake their canes at me. There's not even an agitated shuffle, a murmur of discontent. It's doubtful that anyone in those waiting rooms ever notices me one way or the other, not for the color of my skin, or my stained canvas bag full of *New Yorkers*, or for the fact that I'm called in just moments after arriving in the company of my brown-complected hospital administrator wife. By definition, people sitting in a hospital waiting room have more important things to worry about. And besides, no one anywhere notices anything anymore because every person in every public place is staring fixedly at the glassy rectangular screen of a smartphone, their attention sequestered in a solipsistic bubble of distraction, which allows small but cumulative injustices like a middle-aged white man skipping the line in a hospital waiting room to take place in plain view. But such is the way of the wicked world we live in, and I should just stop indulging my self-serving guilt and enjoy the fact that in this one local, underfunded hospital, I am a low-level VIP.

The doctor Natasha had arranged for me to see was a short chubby woman in her early thirties. She kept her long black hair loose around her shoulders, and wore emerald-green pumps that seemed far too big for her. I liked her right away. Over the last few weeks, interrupted only by my malfunctioning appendix, I had been binge-watching my way through all nine seasons of *The Office*, and this doctor reminded me of the actress Mindy Kaling. It was more than the superficial physical resemblance. She had a bouncy, impish quality about her, restlessly shifting her weight from one leg to the other as she spoke, twisting around on the heels of her pumps, as if she had acquired them recently and was still delighted by the purchase.

Dr. Mindy was in the company of a mournful young man in a white coat, whom she introduced as an intern. He looked like an intern: bored and disengaged.

The intern raised his hand tentatively, as if to greet me, and then changed his mind and let it drop to his side. Why bother? His role was entirely superfluous.

"He's tagging along for the day," Dr. Mindy said. "You don't mind if he watches, do you?" I shook my head. I didn't think any ass-fingering would be on the agenda today, so the more the merrier.

Dr. Mindy asked me some perfunctory questions about my surgery and then told me to take off my sweater and lie back on the examining table.

She removed my bandages. "Wow," she said, her eyes widening. "These are some great stitches!"

She called the intern over to take a look. "See what I mean?" she said. He dutifully peered at my incisions and nodded.

I craned my neck to stare down my abdomen. I had three tiny incisions: razor-thin, bright-red lines etched into my flesh, each no more than a centimeter or two in length. The longest line extended down from my navel; just below it, a tiny horizontal cut traversed the stubble of my recovering pubic hair; to the right, in the region of my excised appendix, an equally small cut slanted at a 45-degree diagonal. The cuts were so straight and precise that they looked as if they had been drawn with a ruler; the stitches so tight and minuscule that they were nearly invisible from my awkward angle. Taken together, the three incisions—two perpendicular, one diagonal—had a mathematical quality, a geometry proof inscribed in living tissue, as if intended to demonstrate some Euclidean principle governing the arrangement of the organs just a few centimeters beneath the surface of my skin.

Dr. Mindy palpated my belly a bit, wiped my incisions with antiseptic, put on fresh bandages.

The constipation, she assured me, was nothing to worry about. "Just drink more water or whatever. Gatorade's good, if you like it."

She twirled a bit on one heel.

"And the opioids can, you know—clog up the pipes."

Huh. I hadn't thought to factor the pain meds into my Google searches on constipation.

I told her that, since yesterday, I'd been restricting myself to Advil during the day, and only using the Oxy at night so I could sleep.

"Really? Why stop so soon? You just had surgery!"

"Yeah, I know," I replied. "I just don't want to get . . . *addicted.*"

She raised her eyebrows in astonishment. "*You?* Oh God, you don't need to—I mean, we see all sorts of addicts in here, but—*you?*" She looked at the intern and shook her head: *totally not the type.*

I felt absurdly pleased. *Take that, Dr. Boy!*

❀　❀　❀

Natasha met me on the sidewalk outside the entrance of the hospital.

"How did it go?" she asked.

I wanted to tell her about Dr. Mindy's new shoes, and brag that I didn't look like a junkie. But we had no time for that. We had to stop off at the apartment before heading off to the second medical appointment we'd scheduled for that Friday afternoon, the one I felt truly anxious about: Luna's vet.

That's just how it is, most of the time. When it's not the same thing over and over, it's one thing after the next.

I stepped off the curb to flag a taxi.

✿　✿　✿

I'm going to call my cat's vet Dr. Katski. I know it's dumb, and kind of lazy, but it's hard coming up with these stupid names for doctors, and I'm beginning to regret I ever started it. To be honest, though, Dr. Katski kind of looks like she *could* be a Dr. Katski.

At that time, Dr. Katski had been Luna's vet for over five years, and she never seemed to age at all. She's blonde, slim, and she looks young, but I suspect she isn't quite as young as she seems. Her casual references to bygone cultural artifacts of the 80s and 90s—Guns & Roses, *Miami Vice*, Ginsu knives—lead me to believe that she's not much younger than me, a decade at most. Dr. Katski has a nasal, drawling Bay Ridge accent—awash in lush glottal stops and sumptuous diphthongs—which I find absurdly erotic, probably because it's a sociolinguistic cousin to the North Jersey accent favored by certain female classmates I admired during the years of my sweaty adolescence.* Dr. Katski has manicured nails, heavily lidded eyes, and a laid-back, blasé demeanor that drives me nuts when the topic of conversation is my sick cat. I used to take her languid manner for either indifference or sleep deprivation, but apparently that's just her baseline personality. I am convinced that in high school Dr. Katski was one of those hot girls who inexplicably hung out with the stoner kids: all feathered hair and faded denim, getting wasted with Tricia Lucci in the park on Friday nights, passing around a syrupy bottle of blackberry brandy while Skeet O'Connor and Greg

---

* Can I really distinguish a Bay Ridge accent from, say, a Canarsie accent, or even a White Plains accent? No. There are many New York City accents, and if you live here long enough, you learn to recognize them as such, but they tend to fall into broad categories defined more by ethnicity and economic class than by neighborhood. But they all build on a substrate of the stereotypical—and enduring—New York accent familiar from films and television, the legacy of the immigrant populations who came through Ellis Island in the early 20th century, as well as the African-Americans who fled north in the earliest wave of the Great Migration. The New Yorkese manner of tawkin' diffused out, in watered-down variations, to the commuter suburbs and small cities of Long Island, northern New Jersey, and southern Connecticut—not coincidentally, all places where you can also find decent bagels and pizza.

Papadopolous slogged through yet another dopey argument over the guitar-shredding gnarlitude of their hair-metal idols—*Dude, did I just hear you compare Slash to Eddie Fucking Van Halen? Are you, like, mentally retarded??*—and meanwhile, of course, quietly maintaining a GPA high enough to earn a scholarship to Tufts. She wasn't going to hang around those losers forever.

Dr. Katski's clinic sits on a corner just a few blocks from our building. We live on a noisy, heavily-trafficked avenue, and for the entire five minute duration of our walk, Luna yowled and moaned inside her carrier as if she'd been tossed out of an airplane.

Once we had been buzzed into the tiny waiting room, indoors and secluded from the terror and chaos of Brooklyn traffic, Luna settled down, as she always does, crouched in the back of her carrier, staring through the bars of the front hatch with watchful green eyes.

Luna's calm is a deceptive calm. When Dr. Katski's burly, tattooed tech called us into the examination room, and Natasha set Luna's carrier on the steel table, he took a step back.

"Oh, yeah," he said. "I remember this cat."

I may be a bad patient, but Luna is a worse one.

I've sometimes had trouble getting vets who haven't encountered her to take my warnings seriously. As long as one of us—usually me—stays with her in the examination room, she remains wary but compliant. This is because Luna loves us, and her faith in us is unconditional and absolute. If we're close by, stroking her fur, gripping the nape of her neck and murmuring reassurances, she will permit the staff to poke and prod her. For our sake, she will suppress her terror and rage, and endure these hateful violations at the hands of strangers. But if they take her away from us to some room in the back, she'll turn vicious. People will get hurt. As I alluded to earlier, on the two separate occasions when Luna had been hospitalized for her eating disorder, the attending veterinarian returned to the waiting room shaken and pale, with bandaged hands and a blood-streaked lab coat, and apologized for not listening to me in the first place.

But they know Luna at Dr. Katski's. The tech kept his distance as Natasha lifted her onto the scale, and waited for me to wrap my arms around Luna's upper body before delicately pushing a cold thermometer into her butthole. He took some notes and went to fetch Dr. Katski.

Natasha took a seat on the small bench by the wall. I released Luna from my grip, and she jumped off the table and began exploring, searching for potential exits and hiding spots, sniffing the cabinets and walls as she systematically worked her way around the perimeter of the small room.

"You wouldn't even know she's sick," Natasha observed.

It was true. Luna looked alert and healthy.

"I guess it's adrenaline," I said.

The bench was only place she could find to hide. She slid between Natasha's feet and crammed herself under as best she could. Natasha reached down to pet her.

The lab door opened and Dr. Katski walked in.

She greeted us, and some small talk ensued. I felt obliged to disclose that I'd recently had my appendix removed.

"Oh, wow! How are you feeling?"

"Bloated." I shrugged. I was here to talk about Luna, not me. "But fine otherwise," I lied. "It was laparoscopic."

She nodded. *Routine surgery.*

She glanced at Luna's chart on the computer and peered under the bench.

"So, Luna, I hear you're not eating again," she drawled. "All right, Miss Kitty, let's get a look at you."

Natasha dragged Luna out and plunked her on the table. I held her by the scruff of the neck so Dr. Katski could examine her. She poked that pokey ear-thing into her ears, lifted her tail, squeezed her belly, pried open her jaw.

"Teeth look good, no infections, but those gums are still slightly inflamed."

This was something Dr. Katski mentioned every time we came in.

"I bought a toothbrush kit for her," I volunteered.

"Fantastic!" She'd been urging me to do this for the last few years.

But my moment of virtue ended as soon as it began. I confessed that this was the *second* kit I'd bought, because I'd never even opened the first one and the toothpaste eventually expired.

"The new one's probably expired by now, too," I admitted. "I only used it for about a week and that was months ago."

Brushing a cat's teeth sounds like the answer to a Zen koan. The phrase conjures up an image that is both intriguing and grotesque. Vets recommend it, but I doubt many cat owners follow through. I can tell you from experience that it is not an exercise to undertake lightly. The cat won't like it and neither will you. You're supposed to gradually accustom the cat to the idea by rubbing the chicken-flavored toothpaste on her teeth every day. The cat enjoys this about as much as you would enjoy someone attempting to smear a hamburger patty over your lips. Supposedly, the cat will learn to tolerate and even look forward to this revolting interaction, and then you can introduce the toothbrush. I value my fingers and never made it to that stage.

"It's just such a hassle," I told Dr. Katski. "I can't keep it up. I have a hard enough time remembering to brush my own teeth."

This was meant to be a joke, but to my surprise Dr. Katski nodded enthusiastically.

"Oh, I *know!*" she said. "Like, after dinner? When you're all cozy watching TV in bed? It's just, like, too much *trouble* to get up and schlep all the way to the bathroom sink." She rolled her eyes. "Half the time I don't even bother."

This little window into Dr. Katski's private life startled me. She wears lip gloss and has expertly blended highlights. I'm pretty sure she hits a tanning salon in the winter. She does not look like a person who regularly neglects her dental hygiene. It seemed like something she must've picked up from those dirtbag stoners in high school. My appreciation of Dr. Katski's aesthetic qualities dropped a notch. I knew that from that point forward, every time I encountered Dr. Katski I would involuntarily imagine her curling up on her pillow with unclean teeth.

I released Luna. She leapt to the floor and crawled back under Natasha's bench.

Dr. Katski moved on to the more urgent matter of Luna's week-long anorexia. We'd been through this harrowing experience twice before, and Dr. Katski said the things I expected her to say. That she suspected the underlying cause was pancreatitis, which was painful and made Luna reluctant to eat, thus initiating the starvation spiral, because the pain would get worse the longer she went without food. If Luna went long enough without eating, she'd start to sustain liver damage, and that could quickly turn fatal.

"I'll give you some oral syringes of Buprenex," she continued. "It's an opioid that will help with the pain."

I nodded again, but Dr. Katski saw the hesitation on my face. After the last time Luna had recovered from this strange illness, I'd confessed to Dr. Katski that I'd never administered the painkillers she'd been prescribed. I'd been afraid of an accidental overdose.

"It's safe," Dr. Katski assured me. "And she may not show it, but she really is in pain."

"I'll give it a try this time," I said. I sounded as unconvinced as I felt.

"Trust me, it'll make her feel better. She doesn't have all the options we have"—Dr. Katski raised her thumb and forefinger to her lips, as if puffing a joint—"if you know what I mean."

I smiled. Dr. Katski may take lousy care of her teeth, but she has her charms.

"Luna has diarrhea," Natasha said, suddenly remembering. "Tyler brought you a stool sample."

I dug around in my bag and produced a plastic yogurt carton. I'd chosen one with a clear lid, so you could easily determine that it didn't contain yogurt: it contained a wet lump of cat shit encrusted with grains of kitty litter.

"Oh . . . thanks." She glanced at it with distaste. "You can just put that on the counter over there."

I knew it would be tossed in the garbage the moment we left.

"I'm also going to prescribe Flagyl, an antibiotic that should help with the diarrhea," she said. "And Cerenia, for the nausea."

I had expected all this—Dr. Katski had prescribed exactly the same medications the last time.

"But here's the problem: right now, we're out of both of them. And the pharmacy closed early today and won't open until Monday."

Shit. The whole point of dragging Luna here was to get those fucking medicines. Luna's sudden recovery during the last two episodes had been as mysterious as the illness itself. But since I had never given her the painkillers, it stood to reason that antibiotics and the anti-nausea meds had played a crucial role.

I now remembered an annoying little blue bottle in the refrigerator that tumbled out of the butter bin every time we opened it.

"I think I might have some antibiotics left over from last time—could we use that?"

She pulled up Luna's chart on the computer to check the prescription date. "Yep. If you kept it cold, you could get her started with that until we can get more on Monday."

We were basically done here, but I had to ask—even though I already knew the answer—what the next steps would be if none of this stuff worked.

Dr. Katski shrugged in her blasé way. "If we can't get her to eat, she'll have to go to the hospital again. They can keep her hydrated, and give her IV antibiotics. But if that doesn't work—well, you know. They'll probably want to try a feeding tube to stop the liver damage. But a lot of times that can kick-start their appetite and end the cycle."

I looked down. Luna peered out from under the inadequate bench, hiding behind Natasha's feet. I thought of her sitting in a hospital cage with a plastic tube inserted through her neck, unable to understand why we would let someone do this terrible thing to her.

My throat grew dry, and I had trouble responding. "I don't know if I can put her through that," I finally said.

"I know," Dr. Katski said sympathetically. "Let's see what happens over the next few days."

At home, I put out some dry food for Luna as soon as Natasha let her out of the carrier. I always feed her a little compensatory snack whenever I bring her back from the vet—it's my way of apologizing—and I hoped, once again, that a customary ritual might trigger a Pavlovian response.

It didn't. She slunk right past the bowl without even sniffing it and proceeded directly to her bed.

I opened the refrigerator. The butter bin contained nothing but butter. No antibiotics. I couldn't bend down easily, so Natasha got on her knees and rummaged around until she found it on the bottom shelf, tucked between some rotting produce and an ancient jar of capers. The little blue bottle was empty. I don't know if the medicine had leaked out or if, over the course of a year, it had somehow evaporated, or if I'd used it all during the course of Luna's earlier illness and had then decided—for reasons unknown to my present self—that this useless container should enjoy permanent residence in our refrigerator, much like our impressive collection of empty salad-dressing bottles.

I called Dr. Katski, but her office had already closed, apparently right after we'd left.

Well, of course it had. Everybody was closing shop early that Friday afternoon.

A storm was coming in.

❄ ❄ ❄

While our household had been preoccupied with two malfunctioning digestive systems, the approaching snowstorm was all anyone else talked about that week.

By all accounts, it was going to be a big one.

Winter Storm Jonas—a swirling mass of nasty weather smeared across a thousand miles of sky—was churning towards the coast and expected to blanket the entire Eastern seaboard with feet of snow, affecting over 50 million people in some of the most densely populated regions of the country.

All Friday afternoon, gleeful weather forecasters had gone into full-blown apocalyptic mode, using words like *white-out* and *crippling* and *storm of the century*, grimly predicting 50 mile-per-hour winds, up to three feet of snow, widespread power outages, canceled flights, stranded passengers, supermarket panics, fires, floods, and the wrathful vengeance of an angry God.

In New York, Governor Cuomo, following state and city officials up and down the coast, declared a state of emergency. In response, Mayor de Blasio summoned the National Guard, deployed plows, salt trucks, and emergency workers. He pleaded for all New Yorkers to make their panicky bread-and-milk runs before the storm hit—because imagine the horror of facing *an entire weekend* without bread or milk!—and then hurry home and stay put. Broadway theaters canceled performances, sporting events were called off, museums shut their doors. Travel bans had already been issued in other major cities, and it was expected that New York would soon follow suit.

The big question was whether they would shut down the subway.

Because that was the remarkable, unprecedented thing Cuomo and de Blasio had done just a year earlier—in January of 2015—when a powerful storm moving up the coast was predicted to drop two feet of snow on the city.

❀ ❀ ❀

Snowstorms can make or break a New York City mayor. Aside from crime and subway service, it's pretty much the only metric that counts. (To this day, New Yorkers speak with acid contempt of Mayor John Lindsay's disastrous failure to prepare for the Great Blizzard of 1969—which stranded thousands, caused the deaths of 42 people, and left the entire borough of Queens snowbound for days.)* So in

---

*Lindsay, in a misguided attempt to show solidarity with his stranded working-class constituents, ventured out to Queens and his limousine got stuck in the

the winter of 2015, Bill de Blasio—whose own tenure as mayor had been particularly vexed by weather*—had seized the opportunity of an approaching snowstorm to redeem his flagging reputation. At a presser staged inside a Sanitation Department garage, reporters were treated to the absurd spectacle of the mayor waving around a printout of the city's top-ten worst historic snowstorms like an ill-prepared sixth-grader trying to wing it through a class presentation.

The occasion seemed to inspire in the mayor a flare for zero-hour theatrics. "My message to New Yorkers is to prepare for something worse than we've ever seen before," de Blasio declared, with the clenched-jaw demeanor of a Gotham City mayor planning to fire up the Bat Signal. "This could be the biggest storm in the history of New York."

But a bizarre aspect of New York State's notoriously dysfunctional government is that the state, not the city, controls the Metropolitan Transit Authority. Andrew Cuomo, the Machiavellian governor, had no intention of letting the mayor crown himself King of the Storm, and one-upped him at the last minute by announcing that—*for the first time in its 110-year history*—the entire subway system would be shut down.

If you're not familiar with NYC, it's hard to convey what a Big Deal this was. It's the equivalent of putting the city into a medical coma. We have the largest rapid transit system on the planet, carrying over 5 million passengers a day, seven days a week, along hundreds of miles of tracks connecting 472 subway stations. You think it's a joke to shut all that down, even for a single day?

---

snow. Angry residents jeered him in the streets. This was an election year, and a rival candidate, Mario Procaccino, coined the enduring epithet, "Limousine Liberal." The "Lindsay Snowstorm" cost the him the Republican primary. By running on a third-party ticket, the once-popular Lindsay (barely) managed to get re-elected, but his political career was ruined. His case has served as a cautionary example for NYC mayors ever since.

* Indeed, as newly-elected mayor in 2014, de Blasio fucked up his first major snowstorm. Inadequate preparation left much of Manhattan—especially the Upper East Side—unplowed, causing traffic jams and school cancellations. Al Roker, jolly *Today* show weatherman and irate Upper East Sider, used his airtime to deliver a pissed-off rant, closing with a warning. "Two words, Mr. Mayor: John Lindsay!"

That evening, the entire city held its breath as the mighty blizzard hurtled up the Atlantic coast . . . and veered sharply out towards Long Island, fifty miles to the east. A few measly inches of snow fell on New York City.

Whoops.

☼   ☼   ☼

So now, in 2016, almost exactly a year later, here we were again. Same mayor, same governor, new blizzard. And this one really did seem like a sure thing. The National Weather Service had been unmistakably blunt. If public officials didn't take serious precautions, a lot of people were going to die.

Washington had already shut down the DC Metro system. If there had ever been a time to pull the plug on the subway, this was it. And if nothing else, the 2015 shutdown had at least served as proof-of-concept—*it could be done*. Sure, it cost the city a ton of money and overtime. Lost productivity and wages, stranded workers, angry tourists, etc. People got pissed when it was all for nothing. All those fucking cartons of milk and loaves of bread. For a week or so, the tabloids had jeered, and unflattering memes percolated through the Twittersphere. But you know what happened after that? Nothing. The churning cycle of public outrage moved on to something else. People got over it.

But both Cuomo and de Blasio have always had a tenuous grip on popularity, in spite of checking all the right ideological boxes for New York's mostly liberal demographics. They are not particularly likeable men—the mayor is peevish and the governor is dour—and they also famously dislike one another. So, with the humiliation of last year's winter debacle still fresh in public memory, these two unhappy bedfellows waffled on the issue of closing down the trains. They'd wait to see how bad it got during the night and make announcements on Saturday morning. Embattled by bad press and unloved by the public they served, the governor and mayor were hedging their bets.

❁ ❁ ❁

After dinner that evening, I wrapped Luna in a bath towel—so she wouldn't be able to maul me—and brought her to the couch to administer the painkiller Dr. Katski had given me. It was the only medicine I had. The narrow syringes held just a few milliliters of clear liquid. No needles. I wiggled the end of the syringe into the corner of her mouth until she reflexively opened her jaw and shot the stuff down her gullet. Over in half a second. She leaped off the couch, washed herself indignantly, and then retreated to her bed in the hall.

Natasha retired to the bedroom with her laptop to watch whatever show she was currently binge-watching. I poured myself a glass of wine, and plopped myself into my office chair. Skimmed through the frenzied weather coverage, poured another glass, loaded up whatever season of *The Office* I'd gotten up to. Two or three episodes in, I glanced at the window and saw snowflakes blowing past.

I stood up to look outside. Although the flurries were light, a thin layer of powder already blanketed the empty streets and sidewalks. I leaned against the windowsill, watching the flakes swirl by. Over the plumbing garage across the street, an American flag fluttered and strained against the pole, snapping in the wind.

I turned from the window and went to check on Luna. She was exactly as I'd seen her last, curled up, motionless. For a moment I got scared. But no, she was still breathing, I could see the slight rise and fall of her belly.

I went back to my desk and loaded up the next episode.

❁ ❁ ❁

On Saturday morning, I awoke to the sound of howling wind. Outside the frosted windowpanes of our bedroom, a writhing vortex of snow lashed through the streets. Violent bursts of wind rattled the streetlamps and sent the traffic lights swinging above the abandoned sidewalks and streets. Way up the avenue I could make out two heavily-wrapped figures struggling against the icy wind, trudging through what must've been a foot of snow. I felt oddly dislocated, as if I'd been transported to a cabin on the edge of the Yukon frontier. The familiar act of putting the kettle up on the stove only amplified that Laura Ingalls feeling. I felt I ought to be doing something with chopped wood.

I brewed some coffee, brought Natasha a cup of tea. The order of things seemed out of joint. Customarily, my first obligation of the day (even before coffee!) is to crack open a can of Fancy Feast. It felt strange to get out of bed without Luna badgering me for breakfast, racing down the hall ahead of my sleepy footsteps to cut me off from any destination that is not the kitchen. Under normal circumstances, if I have the audacity to take a detour into the bathroom, Luna rushes in to headbutt my ankle while I'm standing over the toilet, throwing off my aim so that one or both of us gets spattered with piss. A morning devoid of these shenanigans felt as cheerless as a funeral parlor.

Luna hadn't come into our bed that morning. She remained where she'd been the night before, curled in her bed in the hall. I let her sleep, and set about collecting the bowls of food we'd scattered around the apartment so I could wash and replenish them. No indication she'd eaten any of it. But I did spot some tell-tale clumps of fur floating on the surface of two of the water bowls we'd laid out. I'd noticed that the day before: she'd been drinking an unusual amount of water. I didn't know if that was a good sign or a bad one. Domestic cats are descended from desert wildcats in North Africa, and I've read they are supposed to have a poor sense of thirst, although I don't know how anyone who is not a cat can assert that with any level of authority. But it's true that I rarely see Luna drinking any water at all. She does enjoy sitting in the kitchen sink to drink from the faucet if I turn it on for her, but that seems to be a purely recreational pastime, unrelated to biological need. I have speculated that she deliberately conceals her intake of water, waiting until we're asleep or out of the house to slake her thirst, just to fuck with us, the same way she'll suddenly jerk her head and stare, wide-eyed and alert, at some invisible movement just above my head, knowing that I'll fall for it—*made you look!*—every time. Even so, she's not as clever as she thinks. Every morning I see white strands of fur floating in her water bowl.

I cleaned out her litter box and discovered she'd had diarrhea again. I wondered, as I had before, if the underlying cause of these scary episodes of anorexia might not be pancreatitis (although I remained confused as to what that actually was) but rather some kind of ordinary intestinal bug. It didn't seem far-fetched. Luna does not observe the five-second rule. She eats all sorts of crap she finds on the floor. She washes her ass with her tongue. Supporting this hypothesis: the fact that the vets had prescribed antibiotics every time she'd gotten sick, and eventually she'd recovered. Maybe antibiotics were all that mattered. But I didn't have any antibiotics, and I wouldn't be able to get them until Monday, assuming the city had recovered from the blizzard by then.

Natasha emerged from the bedroom with her tea and headed straight for Luna's bed. She sat on her knees and threw her arms around Luna's curled form, pressing her face against her fur. Natasha has no restraint in these matters. She grew up with dogs.

"Good morning, Luna-belle!" Natasha has many nicknames for Luna. *Belle-belle. Pumpkin. Monkey-Munk.* "Did you know it's snowing outside?"

Luna opened her eyes, raised her head and then it drop. A weak flick of the tail to indicate her obligatory annoyance. I didn't like how she looked. If anything, she seemed worse than the day before.

Natasha stroked Luna's fur. "Did she eat last night?"

I shook my head.

Natasha went into the kitchen and returned with a small handful of crunchies.

"Don't force her," I said.

"I know."

She held her cupped hand under Luna's nose and coaxed her into eating two of them. It was something, at least.

❁ ❁ ❁

While Natasha was preoccupied with making breakfast, I took my cellphone into the bathroom and glumly lowered myself onto the seat. Dr. Mindy's assurances had diminished my enthusiasm for squirting stuff up my ass, but I'd continued taking the Colace and the prunes—washed down with Gatorade and coconut water—which I hoped might be sufficient to grease whatever rusty gear was holding up the production line. While I waited, I scrolled through the weather news.

As expected, a travel ban had been declared. Starting at 2:30pm, all non-emergency vehicles—including delivery bikes, commercial trucks, and taxis—were barred from public streets throughout the city, western Long Island, and most of southern New York State.

The situation with public transport was murkier. One point of clarity: bus service stopped at noon. Boldly stated, hard to misinterpret. But, Christ, the trains . . .

The MTA had lumped all the rail systems under their authority—Metro North, the Long Island Railroad, and the NYC subway system—into a single entity (which they most assuredly are not) and issued a set of directives so convoluted that you wondered when they'd get to the missionaries and cannibals:

— All lines that ran *above ground* would close by 4:00pm—"or earlier";
— However, *some* above-ground lines would offer only "limited service";
— This was also true of some lines that ran *below ground*;
— But certain *other* lines, *regardless* of whether they ran above or below ground, would not offer any service at all.

The term *above ground* was left undefined. The commuter lines run mostly above ground, but occasionally travel underground; the situation is exactly reversed for subways. Did the binary designation of *above* or *below ground* apply to an entire line, or just to stations along relevant stretches of it? You wished they had provided a Venn diagram, or at least a decoder ring.

What the MTA *had* provided was a tiny online map, which looked to be wonderfully inscrutable in the classic tradition of NYC subway maps, riddled with arcane symbols that augmented and negated one another, but it was hard to tell since the image could not be enlarged into any kind of legibility.

Even for New York, this was an impressive piece of bureaucratic chicanery. They must have worked on the plan all night, ramming a short list of commonsense guidelines through the sphincters of a dozen committees until it had been digested into this feculent heap of obfuscating gibberish, under which was buried a simple truth that the mayor and governor were too chickenshit to state plainly: they were shutting down the whole train system.

Deep inside me, the rusty gear turned. *Kerchunk!*

Well! It looked like a line of my own had limited service.

I put my phone on the floor and reached for the toilet paper.

❀ ❀ ❀

Natasha had made us oatmeal. We ate breakfast on the couch, watching the snow rush past the windows. You could hear the wind whistle through the walls of the building.

❀ ❀ ❀

After breakfast, I gave Luna another dose of the opioids. I had my doubts—to me, by definition, painkillers were palliative rather than curative—but I needed to do *something*, and Dr. Katski had said it might help. A couple of hours later, I tried to offer her more crunchies, but she turned her head away.

❀ ❀ ❀

That afternoon, after trying and failing to take a nap, I shuffled into my office and eased myself into the chair in front of my computer. I had projects I was supposed to be working on, bills to pay, an avalanche of unanswered email, but all of those things felt ashen and pointless. I tried to distract myself with the news but I couldn't concentrate.

I kept glancing at Luna in the hall. She was awake, but she looked even worse than she had in the morning. She sat on her haunches, motionless, paws tucked under her chest, staring into the distance with glazed eyes. My chest tightened. I grew up with cats. I'd seen that puzzled, faraway look on animals preparing themselves to die.

I don't know why, but I got my phone and took a picture of her.

A little while later, Natasha found me standing in the living room, leaning against the windowsill.

"Are you okay?"

I shook my head.

"I'm not ready," I said, choking on the words, "to say goodbye to her."

Natasha's eyes widened and she put her hand against my chest, as if to stop me in my tracks. "No!" she gasped. "No, no, no, we're not there yet, that's not what this is."

She started crying too, and buried her head against my shoulder.

For a moment, neither of us could speak.

When we'd both regained a measure of control, Natasha took my hands, looked me in the eyes, and said, "You have to believe me. I just know. This isn't her time."

I nodded, but I didn't believe her.

"We have to be prepared for the worst," I said quietly. "She might not make it to Monday."

"I want some tea," Natasha said. "Okay? Some tea, then we'll figure it out."

For once I wasn't snarky about it, this enduring legacy of the British empire: the conviction that there is no hardship in life so awful that it can't be improved by a nice cup of tea.

I asked her to make me one, too.

❉ ❉ ❉

We became fixated on the antibiotics we didn't have. Natasha thought I should call Dr. Katski, but I didn't see the point. We knew she didn't have the drugs, and besides, she was closed.

What about other vets? Natasha wondered. Our neighborhood is adjacent to dog-loving Park Slope, where there are more veterinarians than laundromats. Even in a blizzard, one might be open and have the drugs we were looking for. And then the obvious solution occurred to both of us at once: the animal hospital near Atlantic Avenue. Luna had been there twice before for this very condition.

I reached for my phone.

A woman answered.

"Oh, thank God," I blurted. "You're open!"

Breathlessly, I summarized our situation. Luna's seven days without food, our visit to Dr. Katski, the empty blue bottle, Luna's past visits to the hospital. All we needed was two or three days of Flagyl, and also maybe that anti-nausea stuff, Cerenia—

"Okay, then bring her in," the woman said.

"Well, no," I said. "We can't do that." I explained that we were two miles away. There were no taxis, and the trains weren't running, and we couldn't carry our sick cat there and back in this weather.

"We can't prescribe medication without seeing the patient," she said, in the unsympathetic, annoyed tone of a weekend receptionist who has been forced to come to work in the middle of a record-breaking blizzard.

I felt that I had not made myself clear. I ran through it again. My cat was very sick, as in life-or-death sick. My vet—who referred patients to this hospital *all the time*—had run out of antibiotics. The very same drugs that had been prescribed by this hospital twice before. I could even name the vets because Luna had mauled both of them!

All we needed was a few pills to get her through the weekend—just a sample's worth! And we'd walk there, in person, to get them, we just couldn't—*obviously!*—make that freezing trek with a sick cat. If it was a matter of the consulting fee—

"We can't prescribe medication without seeing the patient."

But the trains! The blizzard! She's really sick!

"You can make an appointment for next week if you like."

"Are you fucking kidding me?" I shouted. "My cat will *die* without this medicine. You're going to let her die because of some stupid bureaucratic policy? You think I'm not going to get on Yelp and write that *you guys killed my fucking cat?"*

She hung up on me.

"Give me the phone," Natasha said, furious.

"My husband just called . . . Uh-huh. Sorry he got so emotional, our cat's really sick and . . . yes, that's right. Flagyl and Cerenia. What? No! We can't possibly . . . *Just look out the window, that's why!* Yes, I do understand but *we already have a prescription.* That's right, but *so what?* Let me speak to your supervisor. Oh God, *fine*—then let me speak to *a doctor.* Why not? You know what? Give me your name, I'm going to report—"

"She hung up," Natasha said.

"We're fucked," I said bleakly. "We're fucked, Luna's fucked."

"Call Dr. Katski," Natasha said.

"It's just an answering machine."

"Call anyway."

I did, and left a plaintive and rambling message. The empty bottle, the diarrhea, Luna's thousand-yard death stare, the hospital's refusal to help us. *Please call us if you get this. Luna looks like she wants to die.*

Jesus, this really was a lot of snow. Hour after hour, the air was thick with it, like the static on an old TV tuned to nothing. *White-out conditions.* It just kept coming.

In the early years of our marriage, when we still lived on the Upper East Side, Natasha and I might've gotten bundled up and—despite all the end-of-the-world official warnings—trekked out to Central Park for a winter adventure. We had two of these old snow-slider things we'd picked up in some dollar store, basically the most rudimentary form of sled you could have: a stiff, rolled-up sheet of blue plastic with rectangular cut-outs in the front to grip with your hands. You couldn't steer it at all—the best you could do was *aim* it, like a missile. But in terms of sheer speed, those things would totally blow away any of your fancy-ass Rosebud sleds. If you got a running start and dove onto one, you'd shoot down the hill like a greased toddler in a laundry chute, every underlying bump and rock pounding your ribs as you rocketed towards the bottom, praying the whole way that you wouldn't knock out the brains of some small unattended child. One year, during a snowstorm, we took those sleds to the park at midnight—abandoned and silent at that hour—and walked into the hushed landscape of a gothic fairy tale, following a winding path through dark colonnades of trees until we suddenly stepped out onto a vast lawn of untrammeled white, all alone under the silver sky, like two mysterious figures in a Rousseau painting.

We hadn't done anything like that for years. We certainly weren't going to go now, not a week after I'd had abdominal surgery. And anyway, I wasn't sure we even had those plastic sleds anymore; we might have tossed them when we'd last moved.

Still, the blizzard might've offered us a cozy, hot chocolate pretend-we-have-a-fireplace kind of day—the kind we'd tried to have last weekend, right before all of this started—but you can't have that kind of day without your cat purring in front of the non-existent fire, and Luna was in no state for that. Last weekend! The Picasso exhibit, the drunk woman at the karaoke bar . . . God, it seemed so long ago!

Sick with worry for Luna but unable to do anything more for her, Natasha and I retreated to our separate domains, she to our bedroom, me to my office, each of us seeking the empty, mind-numbing solace of the internet, the stupid circle jerk of Facebook posts where curated family vacation selfies pop-up between frenzied declarations of political outrage, the dispiriting scroll of news headlines, the infinite, all-you-can-eat episodes of fictional television characters and their captivating fictional lives which supplanted more and more hours of our own very finite non-fictional lives. Outside my window, the world filled with snow.

In the late evening, an hour or so after I'd washed down a melatonin tablet and half an Oxy with several glasses of wine, I found I could no longer maintain an interest in the zany antics of the Dunder Mifflin Paper Company and took a break from Netflix. I opened a tab and pulled up YouTube.

There's a perverse kind of person who, when feeling sad, wants to hear sad songs. Double down on the feels. Wallow in it.

I am that kind of person.

So that's what I was intending to do with YouTube, use it as a Jukebox of Sadness.*

All that winter, I had been listening to a lot of Regina Spektor, the Russian-born, Bronx-raised singer/songwriter. I had become obsessed after hearing one of her songs used to great effect in an episode of *The Leftovers*.† That song is "Laughing With"—a clever

---

*You're about to find out why I'm not allowed to control the music when guests come over.

†*The Leftovers* (2014–2017), created by Damon Lindelof (of *Lost* fame) and Tom Perrotta (who wrote the novel on which the first season was based) is, simply put, the greatest television series ever produced, a major artistic achievement. I have re-watched all three seasons at least five times. The premise: that at a specific moment on October 14, 2011, 140 million people—2% of the world's population—mysteriously vanished without a trace. The story begins three years after that devastating event—the Sudden Departure—following the trajectories of several characters in a small town in upstate New York. Critics loved it, but

and moving take on the old wartime cliché *There are no atheists in foxholes.* It's a great introduction to Spektor's quirky, poignant approach to songwriting, with lyrics that shift from images of loss and suffering—sickness, war, car accidents, infidelity—to lighthearted whimsy with transcendental ease. The official video is gorgeous—I was delighted to find out that it was directed by Adria Petty, the daughter of Tom Petty—opening with Spektor's luminous eyes peering through the multifaceted mask of an optometrist's phoropter, which part like the wings of a butterfly as she sings the opening line: *No one laughs at God in a hospital.* Echoing the song's themes of suffering and divine intervention, the video depicts Spektor as a kind of otherworldly avatar, strolling casually in a black cocktail dress through a surreal landscape of Escherian stairwells, animated pen-and-ink drawings, a Magritte-inspired room filled with enormous golden apples, a vast field crowded with kneeling worshipers, their heads pressed to the ground in prayer.

After happening upon that miracle of a song, I began exploring Spektor's catalogue. She is a trained classical pianist, but began writing songs as a teenager, and her prolific output varies wildly in both style and subject matter, drawing from literature, history, and religion. Mortality, illness and sorrow are themes she returns to often, but with her bilingual background, she also has a nerdy fondness for wordplay, and she can be very funny, even downright silly. (Her odd takes on the ordinary trappings of everyday life can sometimes feel as disconcerting as those old black-and-white cartoons from the 1930s, where every household object is endowed with frenetic sentience.) I want to compare her to songwriters like Kate Bush or Neil Young or Robyn Hitchcock, although that's ridiculous,

---

most viewers were turned off by the grim nihilism of the first season. I can't get any of my friends to watch it. One friend said, *Are you talking about that show that makes you want to put out a cigarette in your eye?* Yes! That's the one! But you have to push through that brutal first season. (I loved it from the first episode, but I'm not you.) The second and third seasons continue to explore themes of grief and loss, but as the story takes increasingly whimsical turns—often darkly humorous—the initially grim tone gives way to something more expansive, more spiritual: the bittersweet wonder of being alive in a mysterious universe, full of terror and beauty. There will be never be another show like it. And, regardless of your sexual orientation, naked Justin Theroux is a sight to behold.

she's nothing like those artists, and in fact, those artists are nothing like one another. But in a way, that's the point. What they have in common is a quality of creative fearlessness, and like them, Spektor is unafraid to follow the whims of her wide-ranging genius down peculiar rabbit holes. In "All the Rowboats"—a kind of inversion of Keats' "Ode to A Grecian Urn"—she imagines museums as prisons, where the rowboats depicted in paintings are cruelly trapped, trying in vain to row out of their golden frames, and the priceless violins displayed in glass cases "have forgotten how to sing." Another favorite—"Us"—seems at first blush to be the do-or-die swan song of two persecuted lovers, wondering how the world will remember them after they are gone. On closer inspection, however, the song turns out to be about the ghosts of Lenin and Stalin, bitterly scowling down at the gum-chewing Western tourists who gather in post-Soviet Russia to gawk at their statues. Absurd and satirical—and yet it's so moving! How does she do that? She has a particular knack for exploring the loneliness of suffering, but even those songs, the ones that take on themes of grief and depression directly—like "Firewood," or "Jessica"—are leavened by compassion, humor, and the possibility of redemption. Life is filled with loss—but that's not all life is. And hey, if there's no silver lining in the clouds, at least you can look for a good punchline. Spektor writes the kinds of songs that can bring a strange comfort to the dark nights of your winter gloom.

I listened to those songs now, as I had listened to them often over the last few months, but I soon realized I wasn't looking for that kind of comfort. What I was feeling wasn't sadness but despair.

Natasha had already gone to bed. In the hall outside my office door, Luna sat unsleeping with wide open eyes, staring down the dark expanse of a tunnel I could not see. I needed to feel the painful, leaden thing trapped inside my chest, the thing I'd been trying to distract myself from with booze and pain meds and television shows. I needed to face the very real possibility that these might be our last days with Luna.

So I cued up a different song, a song that I love but never listen to because it upsets me. It's called "What Sarah Said," and it's by a terrific alternative rock band saddled with the ridiculous name of Death Cab for Cutie.

It's a real tearjerker.

The song is written from the point of view of a man lingering in a hospital waiting room outside the ICU, where someone he loves—I've always imagined this must be his wife—is unconscious and in the final stage of some serious illness or injury. There is nothing he can do to help her. All he can do is remain here, pacing through this awful place of fluorescent lights and vending machines, counting down the hours as he waits for her to die. Bearing witness to her death is his final act of love.

"What Sarah Said" is a masterpiece in miniature, a six-minute vignette that perfectly captures all the anguish, helplessness, and attenuated dread endured by anxious loved ones in hospital waiting rooms every day. I keep it in my Spotify library because it's such a jewel of a song, but whenever it rotates into play, I always hit the skip button. It reminds me too much of the hours I spent in hospital waiting rooms when Natasha had her endometriosis surgeries. These were not ICU waiting rooms. Natasha's recurring condition had compromised her health, and brought much pain into her life, physical and emotional, but it was not life-threatening. Both of her surgeries were laparoscopic and performed successfully by a surgeon with an excellent reputation. But those experiences made it possible for me to imagine what it *would* be like, if Natasha had been in danger of dying, and I do not like imagining that at all because it forces me to acknowledge the stark fact that someday—if Natasha and I don't die together—one of us will die first.

I can't bear to think about that.

But now I faced the imminent possibility of a different loss, although I hoped I was mistaken. It would be a profound loss, a death in the family.

Scoff if you like. *Sentimental* is the label we tend to slap on anyone who gets too worked up over an animal. The word implies a gooey excess of feeling, an indulgence of emotion wasted on an object of no true value. Hardheaded pragmatists tend to deride the concerns of animal lovers, and their scorn is undoubtedly reinforced by the way animals are represented in popular culture. Plush dolls, Disney cartoons, Hallmark cards, children's books, cereal advertisements. Those are the animals our civilization lavishes with adoration. We've conflated the actual flesh-and-bone creatures with whom we evolved—fellow travelers on the long Darwinian road out of the primordial muck—with the whimsical anthropomorphic characters we invent to tell ourselves stories about ourselves. But those fictional projections make it that much easier to deny the personhood of real animals, to think of them as René Descartes did, as soulless automata without interior subjectivity, mere biological machines on which one could happily perform vivisections without ethical objection, since any resulting manifestations of pain could be dismissed as illusory, a simulation of distress without an entity to experience it.

But Descartes was just repackaging a longstanding common-sense notion and dressing it up in Enlightenment-era philosophy. Having strong feelings for an animal—or animals in general—has always been considered a silly indulgence, something you should feel a little ashamed of. In private, of course, human beings have always formed deep and meaningful relationships with animals, found communion and companionship outside of humanity's walled garden of language and culture. It comes quite naturally to us.

But I understand the need to scoff. As an unspoken policy of the human race, we've agreed to trivialize these interspecies friendships because they reveal all too clearly that animals are sentient beings, just like us, endowed by nature with thoughts, emotions, and individual personalities: a moral truth too hard to square with the everyday cruelties we inflict upon the animals we exploit—for labor, research, clothing, sport, and food, including, of course, the food we feed the animals we care for in our homes. The mute and unceasing misery of animals is woven into every aspect of human civilization, and the cost of empathy is too great to bear.

Still, the heart knows what it knows. Natasha and I had Luna, and Luna had us. This happy fellowship had endured for many years, in three apartments, across two boroughs. She came into our lives during the most painful period of our marriage, not long after Natasha's miscarriage. The trials and frustrations of IVF had left us raw and alienated from one another, but Luna's arrival brought delight into our home, a welcome relief from our mutual resentment.

Luna saved us, Natasha once told me. She wasn't a substitute for a child, please don't think that; it's insulting to all three of us. Luna has always been her own being, shaping our lives as we shaped hers. We knew she wouldn't live forever, but who does? Over time, we will lose everyone we love, one way or another. Knowing that doesn't make it any less painful. Luna's death would be hard and bitter for us, and we would grieve for a long time.

I have emphasized Luna's ferocity, and her gluttony, but I haven't done such a good job of characterizing her affectionate nature. She greets us at the door whenever we come home. She follows us from room to room, plopping herself down wherever we happen to be just because she likes to be near us. She comes running, full of concern, when one of us cries out in pain from a stubbed toe. When I am working at my desk, she is my writing partner, who occupies a chair of her own, right next to mine. Sometimes I'll glance at her and find her gazing at me with the most intense, unguarded expression of adoration and love. No human being has ever looked at me that way. I'd miss that most of all.

But maybe Natasha was right: thinking this way was premature. I often anticipate the worst, hedging my bets against the whims of the universe. But Luna really did seem to have taken a turn for the worse since the morning. She did not look good to me. I was terrified that we were approaching the moment I had secretly dreaded for eight years, going all the way back to that freezing winter day when we'd plucked her off the street and Natasha had given her a name. The moment when I would have to make decisions for Luna that she was powerless to make for herself. I did not want to have to be forced into that calculus of unhappy choices, subjecting her to the misery of an invasive medical procedure in the hope that she'd recover, or choosing instead to grant her that mercy rarely offered to human beings, a swift and final exit from suffering. But I had agreed to take on this burden long ago. Because that's the deal we make, those of us who take animals into our care, and let ourselves love them: that we will *see them through*, all the way to the bitter end. There's nothing sentimental about it.

I clicked *play*, and the opening notes sounded, those undulating, descending piano chords that somehow capture the sense of witnessing a life force drifting away as if carried off by an outgoing tide. I was in two places: here, at home, with Luna and my wife in warm cloister of our snowbound apartment; and *there*, in the antiseptic glare of that dreadful ICU waiting room: the humming of soda machines in empty halls, the chatter of the overhead television, that oppressive hospital odor that Ben Gibbard, the songwriter, so aptly identifies as the smell of *piss and 409*—

Piss.

Huh.

I clicked *pause*. In the middle of my journey down Weepy Lane, I had been dimly aware of a growing pressure down below. My bladder was alarmingly full. I could feel its squishy contours wobbling inside me.

A cartoon lightbulb flashed above my head. I rose from my chair as if compelled by an exterior force. I walked into the hallway, where Luna sat in her bed as she had for the last several hours, unmoving, eyes open, staring that unnerving death-stare. I gently picked her up, carried her to the litter box, and placed her inside. She immediately squatted and an unprecedented torrent of urine gushed out of her, soaking the gravel until it puddled around her legs—

—and then I understood something that should have been obvious before. The Night of Terror, Dr. Boy, the night nurse and her catheter. The unquenchable post-surgery thirst. The all-encompassing, excruciating pain I had experienced that night was not the localized pain of routine laparoscopic surgery, with its three tiny incisions and a bellyful of carbon dioxide. *It was the all-encompassing, excruciating pain of a nearly bursting bladder.* I'd guzzled quarts of water after my surgery, but opioids had dulled my body's ability to detect a full bladder. As I slept for hours, my bladder swelled like a thirsty tick. Within the narrow chamber of my abdomen, my engorged bladder competed for space with a compressed volume of gas and something had to give. That deadly internecine struggle set fire to my nervous system, overriding the narcotics and yanking me out of sleep. Under those extraordinary conditions, I'd been unable exert even the slight muscular pressure required to expel my own urine—which explained why the catheter had brought such incredible relief.

Luna finished her business, daintily shaking the wet gravel from her feet as she stepped out of the box, and I hurried to the bathroom to take care of my own urgencies. As I leaned over the bowl, pissing for what felt like half an hour, I thought of two corollaries to my recent insight. The first concerned toilet training: the socialization of bladder control is so firmly entrenched in the subconscious that we will resist the urge to urinate, no matter how powerful, in unsanctioned locations—such as a hospital bed—even when we are sleeping, incapacitated, or under the influence of narcotics. (This apparently also holds true for cats, who seem to be born toilet-trained.) The second corollary followed, as I considered the case of the career professionals who specialize in narcotic stupefaction—junkies—and how often they seem to be found sitting in puddles of their own urine. *That must be something you have to teach yourself to do,* I marveled as I zipped up. *An acquired skill, like finding a fat vein or snatching an old woman's purse.*

Luna had returned to bed, and I was relieved to find her sleeping, eyes shut, no longer staring down that invisible tunnel.

I checked her litter box. Her prodigious cataract of urine had turned half the clumping gravel into a block of cement. You wouldn't think a ten-pound cat—well, maybe eight at this point—could hold so much liquid.

She'd also had diarrhea again. How could she produce so much shit when she'd hardly eaten? It was another biological conundrum, the exact reverse of Immaculate Digestion.

After I finished cleaning out her box, I returned to my office chair. *No more sad songs,* I resolved. Okay, but what would I do with myself now? Go to bed? With my heart all chewed up like this, I'd never be able to sleep. I contemplated the remaining half-tablet of oxy sitting on my desk. Ugh. I felt I'd had enough of the dreary world of opioids. Honestly, I've never understood their appeal. Why bother when booze and cocaine are widely available and demonstrably more fun?

My phone chirped. I stared at it warily. It was nearly midnight—with a blizzard raging outside—and good news seldom arrives at that hour.

It chirped again. With a sigh, I unplugged it from the charger and punched in the security code. Two messages from an unknown number.

> How is Luna? Sorry got message late. Hope she is ok, I am worried abt pancreatitis. Dr. Katski.
>
> If she's sleeping more it might be bc of the Buprenex.

Dr. Katski! I was deeply touched that she had texted me at this late hour from her personal phone, probably while lying in front of the television with unbrushed teeth.

I now recalled her work with animal charities, how one time I'd taken Luna to an appointment and had found the waiting room stacked with cages of stray cats. The receptionist explained that Dr. Katski regularly donated her professional skills to treating cats who'd been rescued by local trap-neuter-release organizations. And then I remembered another time in her office, when Natasha and I had recounted the story of how we'd found Luna on the icy sidewalk, covered in motor oil, and a tear suddenly rolled down Dr. Katski's cheek. She'd wiped it away, embarrassed, and told us that a few months earlier she'd had a harrowing experience rescuing a stray kitten who'd gotten trapped and injured in a car engine.

Dr. Katski always seemed so blasé, but she really did care.

I began composing a reply, which took a while because I had much to tell her. Of course, it would have been easier to just call her—now that I had her personal number in my phone, all it would've taken was a tap of an icon. After all, the human voice is far more efficient medium for conducting a conversation, and Dr. Katski and I were old enough to spent most of our lives in an era when talking over the telephone was a perfectly mundane event. And had this been just two or three years prior—in a slightly earlier stage of the smartphone Armageddon—that's probably what I would've done. But somehow, with no clear indication of when the line had been crossed, calling someone up for a live conversation had become a deeply intimate act, reserved for spouses, elderly relatives, and customer service representatives. Directly dialing a number was now the social equivalent of showing up unannounced on someone's doorstep.

So I hunched over my $700 hunk of modern technology and struggled to encode my thoughts into what must be the most inefficient means of communication since smoke signals, swiping and pecking on a tiny virtual keyboard with adult-sized thumbs, backspacing over typos, clarifying the random autocorrect substitutions that magically deranged the most commonplace phrases into crackhead gibberish.

In this halting manner I provided Dr. Katski with a semicoherent narrative of everything that had gone on with Luna since the day before. The distressing effects of the Buprenex, the deluge of urine, the persistent diarrhea. And most importantly: the empty blue bottle in the fridge. Due to the back-and-forth lag inherent to texting—messages piling up ahead of responses in usual disorderly jumble of asynchronous dialogue—it took a few rounds for Dr. Katski to understand this last point. We didn't have the leftover antibiotics I'd told her we did.

I asked if she could call in a scrip to the animal hospital. Yes, she replied, but she wasn't sure they'd be open with the travel ban in effect. I confessed that I'd already called them. I omitted my use of profanity and my threats to torch their online reputation, but admitted that

> we got a little emotional, they may be pissed @ me and natasha :(

Dr. Katski's reply had the reassuring steel of a clinician devoted to her patients:

> She has a gastrointestinal issue with food. I'll call them.

I poured another glass of wine while I waited, distracting myself with news articles I'd already read. After ten minutes or so, the phone chirped.

> Ok they refilled it :) Wasn't too easy but they'll do it. Sensitive tummy, she'll feel better once you start that.

Dr. Katski!

And now I remembered the crowded fundraiser for a Brooklyn animal charity that Natasha and I had attended a few years earlier. The event was a cocktail party and silent auction held in a popular Park Slope restaurant. As we were getting drinks, we spotted a well-dressed woman wearing a glittering tiara and a fur stole draped across her shoulders. That weird transgression caught my eye, but as she drew closer, the stole turned out to be a cat, long-haired and very much alive. The cat wore a red bow-tie. The woman was Dr. Katski, and she moved through that crowd like a Hollywood star at a red carpet gala. In the Brooklyn universe of animals and the people who loved them, Dr. Katski was legend. She had clout.

Dr. Katski had convinced the animal hospital to supply us with a stopgap quantity of antibiotics. We could pick it up in the morning. She'd get me the rest when her office opened on Monday.

It was nearly one in the morning. Luna was asleep in the hall, and Natasha was asleep in our bedroom. Dr. Katski's *deus ex machina* arrival on the stage of my despair had me feeling all keyed up, but it really was time to go to bed. I had something good to hold on to, however small. I washed down the oxy with the wine left in my glass—I know, I know, but this is what opioids are good for—and shut off my computer. On the way to the bedroom, I ran my hand gently over Luna's head, careful not to wake her. I turned off the light and crawled under the covers next to my wife.

The drugs hadn't kicked in yet. For a while longer, I lay awake, watching thick currents of snow stream past the windows, and I thought of my childhood, when I'd slip out of bed to press my nose against the cold glass, transfixed by the aching beauty of it all, the magic and wonder of falling snow and the promise of a world renewed.

On Sunday morning, we woke to an eerie silence. Brooklyn had vanished. Outside our windows, a white empire of snow surrounded the building, a mute landscape of extraterrestrial beauty, all soft curves and powder. No traffic, no pedestrians, no dogs. No delivery bikes. The stoops and parked cars and newspaper boxes all buried under unbroken mounds of white. Even the traffic light outside our bedroom window had been powdered over, the signal lights softened into fuzzy halos of colored luminescence. Light flurries of snow still swirled down from the sky, swept upward on gusts of wind twisting through the empty streets. I peered down the avenue. All the shops were closed, except for that one bodega on the corner, the one which only closes two days of the year, for Eid, at the end of Ramadan, and for the other Eid that isn't at the end of Ramadan.

According to the news, Winter Storm Jonas had dumped over 27 inches of snow on New York City—the largest recorded snowfall in its history.* Supposedly the city had sent out plows to clear the roads, but if so, they had yet to reach our neighborhood. The subways were still closed, the travel ban still in effect.

The animal hospital is two miles from our building. On Luna's behalf, I would've happily walked to the Bronx and back if that's what it took to cure her, but Natasha thought it unwise for me to venture out into the slippery streets. If I fell, some newly-knitted internal fissure might rip open, and I wouldn't notice until I began shitting blood. So Natasha would make the journey alone.

After breakfast, she prepared to set out by putting on every article of winter clothing she owns. Long johns, two pairs of wool socks, insulated rubber boots. Two sweaters. Two scarves. She dug out the long-neglected box of ski paraphernalia from the back of the closet and proceeded to put all of *that* on, too: snowpants, balaclava, goggles, ski gloves. Over this bulky ensemble, she struggled to squeeze into her heaviest winter coat, a thick, floor-length black affair with a deep hood that—charmingly—makes her look as though she's just stepped out of a Tolstoy novel. Not today though. I had to help her stuff her arms through the sleeves.

"You look like the Michelin Man," I observed.

"Phhmph brmmphth," she replied from under the layers, by which she either meant *thank you* or *fuck you*. She opened the front

---

* Later, it would be downgraded by weather nerds to some lesser honor, like third- or fourth-greatest snowfall. But that weekend, Jonas still wore the gold.

door and waddled out. A gust of freezing air shot in from the hallway. I knew then that the building door downstairs was still broken and had been left wide open. The foyer was undoubtedly adrift with feet of snow.

"Phone me when you get there," I called after her. "Have fun!"

"Phhmph brmmphth," she muttered, carefully inching her way down the stairwell.

I closed the door and put on the kettle to make some tea.

❀ ❀ ❀

A little over two hours later, Natasha trudged through the door, tired, wet, plastered with snow from head to foot, looking like she'd accompanied Admiral Byrd on a harrowing Antarctic mapping expedition.

She took a moment to catch her breath. "Mission accomplished," she announced.

I helped her out of her coat.

Natasha's four-mile Klondike hike had yielded Luna enough antibiotics for exactly one day. Tomorrow, I'd go back to Dr. Katski for the full prescription.

❀ ❀ ❀

Beauty rarely lasts long in this town, and the postcard loveliness of freshly fallen snow in New York is as ephemeral as a soap bubble. By Monday, Brooklyn was no longer a world of white.

There was still plenty of snow, of course—whole cars were buried under cubic feet of it and would likely remain so for weeks. But it was nasty New York City snow, slushy and gray, pocked with dogshit and cigarette butts. The plows had come through, leaving insurmountable hillocks of snow and dirt at the pedestrian crossing of every street, which, by noon, had been trampled into murky black pits of half-frozen sludge you had to pick your way around if you didn't want to fill your boots with an icy gallon of congealed grease and urine. I was glad not be burdened with a yowling cat in a carrier as I mucked my way to the vet.

At the front desk, Dr. Katski came out to speak to me while her assistant got the rest of Luna's prescription ready. I thanked her for texting me over the weekend, and for calling the hospital.

"Of course!" she said. "I was worried about her. How's our girl doing today?"

"Not great." One day of antibiotics hadn't made much of a difference. Luna still had no interest in food. I supposed that was to be expected. I had hoped for a miraculous recovery, but the real point of Natasha's journey had been to get Luna started on a course of drugs as soon as possible.

The assistant brought out a bag containing the antibiotics and the anti-nausea drops, and Dr. Katski gave me the obligatory rundown on how to administer them.

I had what I'd come for, but I was reluctant to leave. I wanted something more from Dr. Katski—hope. Did she really think the drugs might turn things around? Would Luna recover? Even as I asked, I knew that these were not questions Dr. Katski would be able to answer. Sure, she might have private opinions concerning Luna's prognosis, but what good would it do to share them with me? The future's uncertain and hope is the thing with feathers. Best to stick to diagnoses and treatments, and leave the rest to fate.

"Let's see how it goes over the next few days," she demurred. Dr. Katski couldn't give me the certainty she knew I wanted, so instead she made some suggestions about enticing Luna with favorite foods, feeding her by hand, and a number of other strategies that she knew I was already doing, but it was something to say. And she reminded me that pain was the underlying cause of the anorexia.

"I know the effect of the Buprenex scared you—"

"She looked like she was dying," I said flatly. "She couldn't even make the effort to pee. And it didn't make her want to eat."

"Try giving her less. She's probably more sensitive to it. Cats are like people—some are lightweights."

I nodded grimly. My reluctance to try it again was obvious.

"Half a dose," she said. "See how she reacts. You could even give her less if that's too much."

I didn't want to ask, but I had to ask. "What if nothing works? How many days do we give her?"

Dr. Katski didn't want to commit to a timeframe. "Let's see how she does," she reiterated. "A few days, then call me with an update."

"And I guess the next step is the hospital?" I said helplessly.

She nodded.

"It's just the feeding tube thing." I took a breath. "I don't want her last days to be—I mean, she wouldn't understand—" I stopped myself. I was getting close to tears again, just thinking about it.

She nodded. "I know."

We stood there for an awkward moment while I struggled to contain my emotions.

Dr. Katski broke the silence; she'd thought of something. "You know, there's an anti-anxiety med we could try. Sometimes it helps their appetite. Let me see if we have any in back."

A few minutes later, she returned with a small pill bottle. "They only come in people-size," she explained. "I had Maureen cut one up into eighths."

She opened it so I could see the contents: eight tiny blue slivers, no bigger than fingernail clippings.

"Try it." She shrugged in that bafflingly inappropriate way. "Maybe it will help."

❁ ❁ ❁

As soon as I got home, I opened the bottle. Dr. Katski had given me a small bag of Pill Pockets—semi-soft cat treats, designed to hide pills. I tore a doughy piece off one, pushed one of the blue pill slivers inside, and rolled it around my palm like a piece of Play-Doh until it was the size and shape of a pea.

I got Luna, sat her on the couch, wrapped her up in the towel. I wasn't going to bother with the Buprenex, despite Dr. Katski's advice. I wanted to see how she'd do with the other stuff first. I pinched her jaw and shot a dropper of antibiotics down her gullet. The stuff is bitter, and Luna shook her head in disgust, spraying milky droplets all over the place. Next, a dropper of the anti-nausea stuff. By then, even in her weakened condition, she struggled to pull away, and I had to rewrap her. I pinched her jaw again and popped in the little doughy ball containing the blue sliver. I held her in place until she swallowed it.

She slunk out of the towel and jumped to the floor, shooting me a reproachful look before she crawled back to her bed.

She didn't sleep long. About a half an hour later, she stirred out of bed. I'd been in my office when I noticed her movement, so I got up to see if the pill had affected her.

It definitely had.

Her eyes were wide open and fully dilated. She gazed up and down the hall with a strange ferocity, as if stalking a hidden enemy. Lashing her tail, ears flattened against her skull, she staggered into the living room with an unsteady gait, weaving back and forth as she walked. She looked like an angry drunk.

She headed immediately for the kitchen. With her tail swishing furiously, she parked herself in front of her bowl and gobbled down the entire contents.

My heart soared.

But she wasn't done yet. She reeled back into the living room, where I stood watching in astonishment. As she passed by, I reached down to pet her. To my shock, she lunged at me, but missed and fell to the floor. She scrambled to her feet, and scanned the room until she found what she was looking for—another food bowl I'd placed next to the dresser. I had them all over the house, hoping to tempt her where she went. She made a bee-line for the bowl, crouching down and devouring every last morsel.

Now she headed towards the bathroom, where I had placed another bowl. She'd remembered where they all were. I ran ahead of her to remove it. She hardly eaten in a week and she'd just sucked down two full meals in a span of minutes. I didn't want her to puke it back up. When I took it away, she swiped at my hand. She ran back into the hall, presumably to look for more. I hurried through the apartment, gathering up the remaining bowls before she could find them. She glared at me as I carried them into the kitchen. Then she began running insanely around the entire apartment.

Under normal circumstances, shortly after Luna has been fed her customary late night snack—usually followed by a trip to the litter box to evacuate her bowels—she often engages in a bizarre celebratory ritual, galloping crazily through the apartment at breakneck speed, as if chasing an invisible mouse. These antics are often accompanied by a great deal of eerie, deep-throated yowling. Long ago, I'd been concerned that these disturbing moans might be a sign of distress or fear, but eventually I came to understand them as an expression of pure feline joy. A Google search confirmed that this deranged post-prandial behavior was common enough to have earned its own term of art: *the midnight crazies.**

That was the behavior Luna seemed to be engaging in now, but with severely compromised coordination. Swaying like a Fleet Week sailor barging out of a saloon, she lurched wildly from room to room until she smacked into the leg of the coffee table. She shook herself indignantly, wobbled back into the kitchen, made a leap for the table, miscalculated, and crashed to the floor in a furious heap. After much tail lashing, glaring, and vigorous washing, she swaggered back to her bed, circled twice, and promptly fell asleep.

Holy shit.

I picked up the phone to call Natasha.

I waited until Natasha returned from work that evening to offer Luna her dinner. Although I'd given Luna the antibiotics and anti-

---

*Also known as *the zoomies, fur-and-blur,* and *The Poop Dance.* although it seems that some cats zoom before they poop, some zoom after, and some cats zoom without regard to poop. There's a technical name for this batshit behavior—Frenetic Random Activity Periods (FRAPS)—and all sorts of evolutionary theories about why cats do it, but it remains yet another feline mystery. They really are weird little buggers.

nausea medication, I'd refrained from giving her any more of the blue slivers. I wanted to see if her earlier meal had broken the cycle.

The moment I cracked open the can, Luna jumped up and darted into the kitchen, meowing plaintively.

I set down the bowl and we watched her eat.

"Wow," Natasha exclaimed. "That must be some medicine." She picked up the bottle and squinted at the label.

"Huh," she said. "Wait a sec." She went into the other room to fetch her purse, and by *purse* I am referring to a standard-issue NYC women's handbag, meaning a fifty-pound designer accessory capable of holding roughly the same volume as an army rucksack. I am frightened of it. It violates the laws of three-dimensional space, and contains an unseemly universe of redundant objects I'd rather not know about. Natasha plopped it on the coffee table, disgorging items. Two cellphones. A wallet and another wallet. Pocket tissues, postage stamps, paper napkins, sanitary napkins. A Virgin Mary medallion, allegedly blessed by Pope Benedict XVI. Hairbrush, toothbrush, glasses, sunglasses. A waxy assortment of lipstickery. Lanyards, ID badges, and The Keyring of Too Many Keys. An apothecary of items related to her various health issues, past and present: an EpiPen, another EpiPen (expired), Benadryl capsules, Claritin RediTabs, birth control pills (no longer used but still carried), Bayer Low Dose aspirin, extra-strength Advil Liqui-Gels, and—resting at the very bottom—a small prescription bottle which Natasha dug out and held up to the light.

"I thought so!" she said triumphantly. "The vet gave Luna Xanax." She handed me the bottle so I could compare it to Luna's.

Alprazolam.

It sounded like the name of a magical kingdom.

But now the four children cheered in delight, for just over the hill gleamed the blue spires of Alprazolam, that happy kingdom ruled over by good Queen Xanax, famed throughout the seven lands for her kindness to men and beasts alike . . .

IV. PUNCTUATED EQUILIBRIUM

> To wade in marshes and sea-margins is the destiny of cer-
> tain birds, and they are so accurately made for this, that
> they are imprisoned in those places. Each animal out of
> its *habitat* would starve. To the physician, each man, each
> woman, is an amplification of one organ. A soldier, a lock-
> smith, a bank-clerk, and a dancer could not exchange func-
> tions. And thus we are victims of adaptation.
>
> —Ralph Waldo Emerson
> *The Conduct of Life*

HAT ONE SLIVER of Xanax was all it took. Luna had completely recovered, her greedy appetite restored. She looked fine, she acted fine. I'd continue to give her antibiotics for the next eight days or so, but otherwise it was as if none of it had happened, the prolonged period of self-starvation, the visits to Dr. Katski, the numerous attempts to coax her into eating, the snowstorm. In the arrogant, self-entitled manner of her kind, Luna gave no indication whether she was pleased or grateful to have her health restored. Why dwell on the past? Early Tuesday morning, she resumed her daily campaign of ruining my sleep, pouncing into bed with a jarring thump, pacing up and down the slopes of my slumbering carcass un-til I grumpily tossed her to the floor and shuffled off to the kitchen to satisfy her demands.

Things were looking up. On the night of Luna's recovery, I de-cided to stop taking opioids altogether. I considered flushing the rest down the toilet but those things have a high street value and you never know when a bottle of painkillers might come in handy, so I stashed them in a drawer with my other expired medicines. After my morning coffee, I felt a warm stirring within, familiar and wel-come. I grabbed a magazine and headed off to see what offerings the day might bring. I kept my expectations low, but I'd barely skimmed the opening paragraph of Shouts & Murmurs when the production line creaked into action. The morning output was irregular, below quota, and generally fell short of factory standards, but the workers' strike was over. I was back in business. *Good job!* I felt like I deserved a sticker.

I went into the kitchen and poured another coffee. My cat was good, my pooper was pooping, and I'd said no to drugs. It was time to resume normal life. Maybe, I thought, as I carried the mug to my desk, I could do better than my normal life, which, fully considered, largely consisted of bad habits and complaining. Maybe I was due for one of those *life-altering experiences* people are said to have after a major traumatic event. My routine surgery hadn't truly been *a brush with death*—Luna's illness had been far more harrowing—but it was as close to death as I like to brush. Surely my time with Dr. Boy was unpleasant enough to serve as a springboard for *meaningful, lasting change*. I could get my shit together, stop watching so much television, start finishing all the projects moldering on my to-do list. Maybe even start practicing yoga. Volunteer at a charity. Floss.

I got out my notebook, prepared to envision a bright future of worthwhile undertakings. As I thought about my life, my head became crowded with all the festering crap I'd been putting off for months, distracted by the holidays and my usual winter malaise. Ugh. I'd have to wrap up my old life before I could begin a new one. The shiny new Bucket List would have to wait until I'd worked through a more plodding list, the List of Shame & Neglect:

   i. *email*
   ii. *household drudgery*
  iii. *clutter & bother*
  iv. *unnecessary obligations*
   v. *trivial urgencies*
  vi. *procrastinations*
 vii. *disasters-in-the-making*
viii. *downward mobility*
  ix. *dreams deferred*
   x. *gym membership*

I fired up my computer. The journey of a thousand miles would begin with a single click: *open inbox*. 8,342 unsorted messages. About a third had been flagged for follow-up. Another third unread. I hoped no one had died.

If sorting backlogged email had a flavor, it would taste like chewing gum found stuck under a bus seat. An hour into it and I was thoroughly demoralized. The promises I'd failed to keep. The friends I'd ignored. The exiled Nigerian colonels; the presumptive offers to enlarge my penis. I felt spiritually taxed and, I realized, physically unwell. In spite of flushing out the pipes, I still felt bloated, and I had a strange burning sensation deep inside the area where I assumed my appendix had once resided. That was new. The nirvana of Inbox Zero could wait. I needed a nap.

In the evening, over dinner, I made the mistake of telling Natasha about the burning sensation. Predictably, she overreacted. *What kind of burning? Where exactly? How bad?* These weren't questions with precise answers. The burning was the physical equivalent of a word you can't quite recall. It was more of a placeholder for pain than an actual pain.

"You should call your surgeon tomorrow," she said.

I assured her I would so that she'd drop the subject.

The next morning, while she was getting ready for work, Natasha asked me if I still felt any pain. This was unfair because I hadn't had coffee yet. My guard was down. "It's not exactly *pain*," I mumbled, a tacit admission that I still felt *something*.

"Should I take the day off?"

"No, no," I said. *God, no.* I poured beans into the grinder. "It's nothing, I think it's just in my head."

It wasn't. I drank my coffee while staring hatefully at new email notifications on my phone, and the burning sensation flickered inside me like a question mark at the end of an ellipsis.

My toilet adventures were uninspired but gratifying. I sat at my desk and opened my email client. There were more pressing matters than whipping my inbox into shape, but at least this task had a foreseeable endgame. Only 6,894 messages to go and I could think about having a life. The burning persisted and took on definition.

When I sat, stood, or bent over, I felt a sharp twinge, as if someone had playfully pinched my large intestine. It seemed like something I could live with, if I had to.

Around one, Natasha came home early from work. She'd been worried about me. She expressed her concern by badgering me until I reluctantly described what I'd been feeling.

What happened next is exactly what happened before. Natasha offered to check in with Dr. K and I gave my consent. She called, described my symptoms, and then, without consulting me, proceeded to make an appointment as I stamped and howled like a deranged psychotic, forcing her to cancel the appointment she'd just made.

I know—*weird*, right? It's strange the way life, against all probability, often presents the same sequence of events over and over, like a repeating motif in a novel or a piece of music. It can make you wonder if some not-entirely-benign entity is orchestrating your life, perhaps as an experiment, or merely for entertainment. Kafka had an almost theological obsession with this notion: the universe as a custom-made mousetrap, designed just for you. The science fiction author Philip K. Dick often explored the concept of simulated realities, finding it fertile ground for his paranoid themes.* And of course, there's *The Matrix*, in which oddly recurring events are explained as *glitches*, fleeting evidence that the every-

---

*"This is a cardboard universe," he wrote, "and if you lean too hard or heavily against it, you fall through." That line comes from *The Dark Haired Girl* (Mark V Ziesing, 1988), a collection of Dick's previously unpublished letters and essays which I do not own, have not read, and have no plans to acquire because it is out of print and quite expensive. A variation appears in *The Selected Letters of Philip K. Dick 1972-1973* (Underwood-Miller, 1991), also out of print, expensive, and unread by me. Nonetheless, the quotation has gained wide currency on the internet, appearing in tweets and memes, posted in online quotation collections, fondly alluded to in magazine articles and interviews. It even served as the inspiration for Christopher Miller's 2009 novel *The Cardboard Universe: A Guide to the World of Phoebus K. Dank* (Harper Perennial), which, I gather, satirizes Dick's works and the obsessive, cult-like nature of his fans, but I haven't read that one either. Liberated from context, Dick's cardboard universe quotation has achieved an existence independent from its creator, propagating itself in new forms and contexts by people who have never read the original source—or possibly any of Dick's books at all—and thus self-reflexively offers itself as an example of the very sentiment it expresses.

day world is a shared hallucination—a kind of virtual reality video game—programmed by malignant, artificially intelligent machines. *Life is but a dream.* The Wachowskis' deeply gnostic vision (wrapped up in an action-packed sci-fi blockbuster) has continued to have enduring and widespread influence in the decades following its 1999 release, perhaps because everyone increasingly experiences the world through the mediation of digital technology. In recent years, it's become fashionable among Silicon Valley types—Elon Musk is a fervent evangelist—to insist that we probably really do inhabit a computer-simulated universe, where, much like the palm-tree backgrounds of *The Flintstones*, moments and events get recycled and redeployed in order to save processing power, and, I suppose, money, assuming money is important to whoever it is who lives in the universe simulating the universe we live in. Whenever I find myself mulling over this idea, I wonder if the universe simulating our universe is, in turn, simulated by another universe. It really might be turtles all the way down.

In the simulated reality I currently inhabited, Natasha and I were furious at each other for the same reasons we had been furious at each other exactly a week ago. I had a potential issue with my surgery, and today was Wednesday, the last day of the week that Dr. K saw patients. Natasha wanted me to go and I didn't want to. This time around, I no longer had the excuse of enemas, snowstorms, or a sick cat. Better to turn the focus back on Natasha, who'd once again tried to schedule an appointment against my wishes.

"You don't respect my wishes!" I raged. "What's going to happen when we're old? They'll want to do things to me I don't want them to do, and you'll let them do it! When will I learn that *I just can't trust you?*"

Uh-oh. The moment I said it, I knew I'd gone too far.

Natasha's chin quivered. "You can't trust *me*?" She looked away and lowered her gaze. "How can you say that to me?"

She was dangerously close to tears. Time to slam on the brakes and make a quick U-turn.

"I'm sorry. I didn't mean that."

"I skipped a meeting to come home early. I was trying to *help* you."

"I know."

"You hurt my feelings."

"I'm really sorry."

She sniffed, folded her arms, and sat quietly a moment, weighing the sincerity of my apologies.

"Sometimes," she said, "you act as if I'm trying to sabotage you, and—" Her voice caught in her throat, and she took a breath. "It's upsetting that you think I would ever deliberately try to hurt you."

Deliberately! That was the operative word. I didn't think Natasha would deliberately want to hurt me. She hadn't left those knives hidden in the dishwater on purpose. I did think Natasha might *subconsciously* want to hurt me, but that was a thesis best left unexplored for now.

Tactics: I could apologize for hours (and I had so much, in general, to apologize for) or I could just turn it all into a big joke.

"Well," I said, "you did pour boiling water all over my foot."

This light-hearted quip didn't have the ameliorating effect I'd hoped for.

"I didn't!" she cried. "That wasn't me!"

I was confused. "What do you mean?"

"The nurse did it! I saw her bump the tray when she was leaving the room!"

"The nurse? But I thought—"

"I know what you thought. But it was the nurse."

"Then why didn't you say anything?"

"Because you blame me for *everything!*"

And now she really was crying.

After I apologized, I made Natasha a cup of tea, and then apologized again for good measure. But she'd had enough of that; she wanted to talk about the weird not-quite-pain I had and the appointment she hadn't been allowed to make with my surgeon. Chastened, I told her the truth. I was afraid that if I showed up in Dr. K's office complaining of a persistent pain, she would check me back into the hospital. Natasha pointed out—exactly as she had the week before—that if I got worse over the weekend, I'd have to check myself into a hospital anyway, and, in her professional opinion, the weekend was a terrible time to be in an emergency room.

"You should at least see somebody," she said. She meant that I should make an appointment with a general practitioner.

The thing is that I don't have a GP. If I don't want to see a doctor when I'm sick, I certainly don't want to see one when I'm healthy. The only time I ever get a checkup is when I'm already suffering from some malady distressful enough to require medical attention. In such cases, I just book an appointment with Natasha's current GP. But Natasha didn't have a GP either; she hadn't found a new one since she'd broken up with her old one over that whole pulmonary embolism debacle the year before. She'd consulted with specialists at her hospital in the aftermath of that event, but hadn't yet lined up a regular primary care doctor.

So the next day, Natasha set about to find me a GP at her hospital who could see me at short notice.

She called me around lunchtime, sounding very pleased with herself. After consulting with various colleagues and physicians, she'd identified the very best general practitioner at her hospital.

"He's really popular," she said, "and booked for, like, *months*. But I'm kind of friends with his secretary, so I got you an appointment for this afternoon."

"Great!" I said. "Thanks for taking care of that." After I hung up, it occurred to me that Natasha's plan to help me avoid having to see my doctor at the hospital was to arrange for me to see a different doctor at another hospital.

But at least he wasn't a surgeon.

❁   ❁   ❁

Which is how, late on Thursday afternoon, I found myself in the office of the most popular GP at Natasha's hospital despite the fact that he was booked for months.

The doctor—a portly, well-dressed man in late middle age, with a neatly trimmed mustache and a grave but courteous demeanor—ushered me into a seat facing the wide expanse of his mahogany desk. In total silence, he studied my paperwork while I stared at a wall plastered with diplomas and awards. He was a family doctor, but nowhere in his large office did I see a single photo of his own family, or any photos at all. A man who kept his personal life entirely separate from his professional life. Let us call him Dr. Gravity.

After a short interview, Dr. Gravity led me to a well-appointed examination table of hand-tooled leather for a quick round of palpation.

"Excellent stitch-work here," he noted, visibly impressed.

I blushed. "Everyone seems to like them."

He snapped off his gloves and delivered his diagnosis. I didn't have a fever. My incisions were not inflamed. Still, I'd complained of pain in the appendix area, so—*just to be safe*—he wanted to do a CT scan.

I swallowed. This was unexpected. I'd been hoping for a pat on the head and the reassurance that everything was just fine.

✿　✿　✿

Dr. Gravity instructed me to leave the hospital altogether, and then re-enter through the emergency room to register myself for the CT scan. As Natasha soon confirmed, this circuitous roundabout satisfied some bureaucratic checkbox, the details of which eluded me.

I wasn't thrilled by this turn of events, but once you step into a hospital, events rapidly chain themselves together. One thing leads to the next, like a conveyor belt in a slaughterhouse. I very much wanted to leave, to return to the relative safety of my apartment, but then I thought, *Well, you're already here, might as well get the scan, right?*

It's that kind of thinking that can really fuck you in a hospital setting.

Natasha met me outside, quickly got me registered with the ER, and then conducted me through a labyrinthine series of halls and elevators until we arrived at a tiny waiting room hidden in some quiet alcove of the radiology department. After carefully instructing me on how to find *the good bathroom*, she rushed off to take care of the paperwork and other arrangements.

Back to the temporal metaphysics of the hospital, where time is a syrup. I checked my email for no reason, and then checked it again. I made small talk with an elderly woman worried about her 70-year-old diabetic brother, who was somewhere down the hall being poked at by doctors.

A nurse dropped by and handed me the nasty CT cocktail. While I was sipping it, a young couple with a small, sick child joined us, and sat down, murmuring to each other in anxious tones. They spoke almost no English, but the father tried to ask me a question. I was pretty sure I understood. Through a series of grunts and gestures, I explained how they could find The Good Bathroom. Nodding gratefully, they left with their son. I don't know if they got lost, or they encountered the doctor they were waiting for, but they never came back.

The woman with the diabetic brother left to see what was taking so long. She never came back either.

A long time later, THE SERBIAN came to fetch me.

He was the CT technician, and of course he was young and strikingly handsome: tall and swarthy, with a shiny mop of jet-black hair and the kind of bluish five o'clock shadow no razor can scrape away. What struck me most, though, was his wary, haunted demeanor. THE SERBIAN had a way of glancing sideways at you and quickly looking away, as if he knew of some terrible fate in store for you that he'd been forbidden to disclose. A nefarious plot was afoot, but he was powerless to warn you, he had his orders. He was polite and deferential, and never spoke more than absolutely necessary.

Come this way, Mr. Gore.

Change in here, please.

Now lie down on this platform and please do not move.

His soft voice carried just a hint of an unidentifiable accent. I do not know if THE SERBIAN was actually Serbian. I suppose he may have hailed from any land of swarthy young men—Bulgaria, Macedonia, Queens.

❁   ❁   ❁

By now, many hours had passed since I had first arrived at the hospital that afternoon, most of it sitting in this tiny waiting room. During my tenure here, various medical personnel who worked with Natasha had dropped by to say hello and introduce themselves.

This should have been reassuring—everyone knew who I was and where to find me—but it made me nervous. Natasha administrates two large departments and consequently comes into contact with nearly everyone who works at the hospital—doctors, nurses, technicians, managers, receptionists. As far as I can tell, she's well-liked. From the moment I'd stepped into the building, hours earlier, all sorts of hospital people had gone out of their way to find me and shake my hand, and I could sense a buzz of giddiness in the air. As in any place of business, even a minor departure from the normal day-to-day grind—a box of donuts on the receptionist's desk, a new coffee machine—tends to stir up levels of interest wildly disproportionate to the objective merits of the novelty on hand.

And so I began to understand that Natasha's work friends were a little excited about my visit to their hospital for this post-surgery adventure. It was if Natasha managed a restaurant and I'd dropped by for a meal. Under those circumstances, you can imagine that everyone from the chef to the busboy might try to ensure that I had not just a nice dining experience, but a truly superb dining experience. *Oh, but you have to try the Chef's Special tonight, it's excellent! Here's our signature cocktail! These oysters just arrived this morning from Prince Edward Island! Let me refill your water glass!*

The problem is that the restaurant Natasha manages is not one I particularly want to eat at. At a healthcare establishment, they aren't going to give you complimentary oysters, they're going to give you a complimentary prostate exam.

Don't get me wrong. I'm grateful that Natasha's colleagues like her, and when you're in a hospital, it's nice to know that your special connection means you're far less likely to get chewed up in the gears of the machine. Even so, you really don't want people whose tools of the trade are scalpels and needles to take too much of an interest in you.

But that was earlier, before the workday had finished.

No one has come by in quite a while. The place feels abandoned. The halls of the radiology department are now quiet in the disquieting way that corporate offices are quiet after hours, when the lights are dimmed and there is no one but a single miserable employee working late on some overdue project as the cleaning lady glides from cubicle to cubicle, carting away the rubbish of the day.

I've just realized something. There are no televisions in this waiting room. No magazines either, which is just as well, since there are no tables to put them on. I suspect this little alcove wasn't originally a waiting room. They had half a dozen chairs left over from the real waiting room, and decided to store them in here. *It's not far from The Good Bathroom*, someone probably pointed out.

So where the hell is Natasha? I wonder. I'm annoyed. Where has she been all this time? Ah, but she likes the hospital. This is her natural environment. All her work friends live here. She's undoubtedly back in her own department, talking shop with colleagues, the ones who also like to be here even though they could instead be at home having dinner with their families.

We're not having the same experience. I don't like it here at all.

THE SERBIAN returns, deferential as always, but he looks tired. Are these his normal hours, or am I keeping him here? He tells me that the radiologist is studying my scan and will report his findings to Dr. Gravity shortly.

"And then what?" I ask.

This question is apparently above his pay grade. A flicker of distress in his eyes. He glances up and down the hall. "I don't know," he says in a low voice. "I think your doctor will call you." He hurries away from me.

❄   ❄   ❄

A while later Natasha finally shows up, accompanied by Dr. Beeswax, a bureaucratic colleague she often works with. They are in a jovial mood. Perhaps they've been reminiscing over old quarterly budgets or something. There's no real reason for Dr. Beeswax to be here—his specialty is entirely unrelated to my medical complaints. I know him on a casual basis—he's worked with Natasha for years, and once, preposterously, we went to a Mets game together. So his presence here could be construed as a mere social nicety. But it's easy to see that it's more than that, that he's happy to be here, that my case offers a refreshing change of pace from his customary professional rounds. Dr. Beeswax is like an electrician getting a chance to visit the welding shop. He's having *fun.*

Rocking back and forth on his feet, hands clasped behind his back, he asks me a bunch of questions about my operation. He has colleagues at NYU, and he's disappointed that I can't quite remember the name of my surgeon, because I think of her simply as "Dr. K," and seem to have mislaid the additional letters of her last name. He asks about my incisions, and for a moment, I think he's going to ask me to lift up my shirt, but some sense of professional propriety prevents him from crossing that line.

"So what's happening now?" he asks.

I repeat to him what THE SERBIAN told me, that I'm still waiting to hear results from the radiologist.

"Well, then," he says, clapping his hands together, "Let's go find the radiologist!" And off he goes down the hall.

"Oh shit," Natasha says. "Wait here." She hurries after him.

❄ ❄ ❄

After nearly a half an hour, they return.

"So," Dr. Beeswax says happily, "the scan revealed a *collection*."

This is utterly meaningless to me, but I don't like how bland and innocuous it sounds. Whenever doctors use harmless-sounding everyday words—*growth, procedure, tested positive*—they are talking about something awful.

Collection, Dr. Beeswax explains, is medical shorthand used to describe a pocket of fluid sloshing around the inside of someone's body, in this case mine.

Jesus, I think. So why can't they just say *we found a pocket of fluid?*

It's really nothing to be alarmed about, Dr. Beeswax says, which of course makes me feel alarmed. But since I'd complained about pain—*Oh Christ, why had I done that?*—they want to make sure it isn't an infection. Just to be safe.

I'm reminded of a stupid reality show I once watched at the gym while on the stair machine. *Storage Wars* or something. The collection puddling inside of me is like one of those unmarked boxes auctioned off at storage facilities when the renter has fallen behind on payments. If you want to see what's inside the box, you have to buy it. Until then, there's no way of knowing whether it contains an early draft of The Gettysburg Address or a nest of dead baby raccoons.

That's why they want to do something called a *needle aspiration*. Another term I deeply dislike. It sounds like the title to a Dadaist poem. It means that they want to push a very long needle through the side of my belly to get at that mysterious fluid, the way you might dig around with a straw to suck up the remainder of a Slurpee.

As Dr. Beeswax explains all this, Natasha has been on the phone with Dr. Gravity. "I'll ask him," she says. She takes the phone away from her ear and tells me that Dr. Gravity has generously offered to let me stay in the hospital overnight.

"Why would I want to do that?" I ask.

"Well, that way they can get you started first thing in the morning," she explains. "You're lucky—they have a bed available."

"I'm not doing that."

"But—"

"I'm not doing that."

Natasha shoots me a disappointed look, but tells Dr. Gravity I'll just come back tomorrow.

On the cab ride home, she tells me that Dr. Gravity is furious at Dr. Beeswax. Why? I ask. Because, she explains, Dr. Beeswax wasn't supposed to talk to me about my radiology results before Dr. Gravity had a chance to. I'm not Dr. Beeswax's patient, I'm Dr. Gravity's patient, and Dr. Gravity should've been the one to introduce me to unpleasant new medical terminology.

"So I don't have to get the needle aspiration?"

"Oh no, you still have to do that. They both think that's a good idea."

As the cab pulls up to our building, Natasha says, "The radiologist is pissed, too." Dr. Gravity yelled at him for sharing my results with Dr. Beeswax, even though he had my permission, so now the radiologist is mad at Dr. Beeswax for asking in the first place.

Natasha sighs. "It's okay—I'll smooth things out tomorrow."

This sort of thing, so far as I've ever been able to determine, is actually Natasha's true job.

The next day, I return to the hospital emergency room in the early afternoon. With great reluctance. Better not to think about it too much, just put one step in front of the other. It's Friday, and the waiting room is packed. People like to have their accidents on the weekends.

I join the long line for the front desk and text Natasha. She soon arrives, looking very administrator-like. It's not just the dark pantssuit or the ID badge dangling around her neck. There's just a different aura about her in this place, the aura of competence and power, of someone with real authority.

This aura has a noticeable effect on other people. Even if they have no idea who Natasha is, they sense that she might be someone important. Better safe than sorry. When we reach the front desk, the receptionist glances at Natasha standing next to me and immediately launches into a determined effort to seem helpful, friendly and efficient, which gives her the slightly crazed persona of a hotel concierge who has just realized that the expertly-coiffed woman requesting a room for the night is, in fact, Beyoncé.

We find, remarkably, two adjacent seats in the crowded waiting room but I've barely sat down—*#notmyprivilege*—before we are summoned into the triage room.

Vital signs: taken, noted.

Now onward through double doors into the bustling delirium of the emergency room. It's like barging into the noisy kitchen of a popular restaurant during the dinner hour, a place of controlled chaos and crisis-driven activity, individuals swarming like ants in every direction with intense urgency and single-minded focus.

In the gullet-like antechamber that opens into the emergency room, a wide semicircular counter encloses what is clearly a kind of situation room. Half a dozen hospital personnel are crammed behind the counter, staring intensely at computer screens, poring over clipboards and iPads, grasping at phones that never stop ringing. Overhead, several large monitors display rows of color-coded information that I can't make heads or tails of, but which remind me of the departure boards at airports.

And, indeed, directly below them stands a harried-looking young doctor with the unshaven, ulcerous, baggy-eyed demeanor of a stressed-out air traffic controller, his eyes darting from monitor to monitor, one hand pecking frantically at a keyboard while the other presses a phone against his ear.

Natasha introduces me to this doctor—he's the ER's Chief Resident—forcing him to momentarily tear his eyes away from the monitors so he can grunt a hurried acknowledgment. He nods at me distractedly, and then gets right back to whatever he was doing, because *dammit, people, lives are at stake!* But I understand perfectly the purpose of this seemingly pointless introduction: Natasha is red-flagging me, putting a halo over my head, making sure the dude running this frenzied enterprise knows that I'm a Very Important Person—at least to her—and that she'd very much appreciate it if nothing truly terrible happened to me during my visit here.

We round the corner, and enter into the ER proper, and . . . and Jesus, it's just fucking awful, isn't it?

It's a Civil War battlefield, a bleak tapestry of prone bodies and muted groans. It's a factory farm in a PETA brochure, a dank and dreary arena of suffering flesh welded in place with tubes and wires. It's a Goya etching come to life: *Gloomy Presentiments of What Must Come to Pass.*

It's a goddamn *mistake* is what it is. What exactly am I doing here? In the back of my mind, a nagging urgency has been ringing like a muffled alarm clock since yesterday afternoon: *this whole thing makes no sense.* Of *course* I have pain on the right side of my abdomen; less than two weeks ago a pretty surgeon took a knife and sliced out the swollen protuberance throbbing at the end of my large intestine. Oh, okay, fine, *laparoscopic*, so she used some sort of robotically-guided Roto-Rooter to snip out the offending flesh, but in any case, underneath those magnificent stitches: *I have been wounded.* And—*fuck you very much, Dr. Boy*—I've stopped taking my potentially addictive pain killers since Monday. **Click.** The volume control is no longer on mute. So of course: *I feel pain!* And you know what? It's not even that bad! It's like a three, at best! Hardly worthy of an Advil!

The course of action I must now take is crystal clear. I stand here on my own two legs, captain of my own destiny. I am now going to stop in my tracks, disengage my hand from Natasha's, and I will turn to her and apologize for putting her to so much trouble over nothing. And then I will calmly walk out of here, past the ulcerous Chief Resident, the triage room, the bustling scrum of the waiting room, walk through the sliding doors into the pale winter day, and when I reach the street, I will raise my hand high into the air and keep it there until a taxi pulls up to the curb to take me home.

Just then, a nurse comes forward to greet us, a stout middle-aged woman with cherry-red hair, who smiles broadly and places her hand on Natasha's arm. "Natasha!" she says. "I thought it might be you! I saw your name on his chart."

She leads me to my rollie and tells me to sit.

❀   ❀   ❀

Yes, Natasha knows the red-haired nurse. She used to work with Natasha in a different department, and now she's the Head Nurse here. They are old friends.

Natasha introduces me. I smile and shake hands.

"I've heard so much about you," the Head Nurse says.

"Should I be worried?" I quip, always the charmer. Small talk commences. It's like being at a cocktail party, if you happen to frequent the kind of cocktail party where the woman you've just been introduced to casually snaps on nitrile gloves and proceeds to draw three vials of your blood.

They've moved on to work gossip now, and then Natasha—still chatting gaily—wanders away with the Head Nurse and my blood. I have no idea where they're going.

A new nurse arrives. She's young and pretty. Doe-eyed with long thick braids intertwined with purple ribbons, bunched into a kind of bouquet behind the graceful curve of her neck. She speaks with an attractive West Indian lilt, and flashes me a broad, sincere smile that suggests she probably is a genuinely lovely person even when she's off the clock.

Should I go on? I only met her once, for less than ten minutes, and, aside from a sentence or two further down, she plays no additional role in this story.

I suddenly feel exhausted. This is going to be my future, isn't it? In the twilight years to come, as I grow older and my health inevitably declines, there's going to be more and more of this. Hospitals, rollies, ogling the 24-year-olds who come to collect my bed-pan. Only *ogling* isn't really what this is all about it, is it? That would imply eroticism, that I'm lusting after these young women, enter-taining some sad, ridiculous fantasy of seduction, or—at the very least—that I'm filing away their salient details in the filthy shoebox of my mind reserved for masturbatory rumination.

That's not what's happening. I can assure you that here in the ER, surrounded by the infirm, the injured, and the diseased, sex is the very last thing on my mind. But during my whirlwind tour through the healthcare system of New York City, a certain theme has emerged that's impossible to ignore.

So yeah, I'll admit I've been fascinated by the beauty of all these young hospital workers I've randomly encountered. It's been a bit unsettling, even to me. I don't remember the hospitals being popu-lated by so many strikingly attractive people in the past. But there's something I've realized. They aren't just beautiful and young. They are beautiful *because* they are young. You don't appreciate the incan-descent beauty of youth until you are no longer young. Was I ever that beautiful? Yes, reader, I was. I know it now. I didn't know it then. Like Yeats, in all those grand, late-in-life poems we were as-signed in high school, at a time in life when we couldn't possibly un-derstand the emotions the aging poet was grappling with, mourning over the vanished beauty of Maud Gonne, the great unrequited love of his youth, as well as his own "pretty plumage"; wishing he could transcend the "dying animal" of his body and escape into the age-less beauty of mythology and art. I'm not as old as Yeats was when he wrote those poems—he was in his sixties—but I'm much closer to that age than I am to the age I was when I first read them in school.

But now I stand across the chasm of the years, and encounter-ing all these young attractive people—women and men both—stirs up in me not a feeling of lust or even envy, but a feeling of exile. *I look at them from across the divide.* That's the phrase I keep thinking of. *Across the divide.* As though I have crossed a border, my passport re-voked, my citizenship stripped. From the other side, I stare across the divide at smooth, candid faces still unravaged by time and think, I was once one of you, a denizen of that enchanted land of ambition, romance, and cruelty.

That is no country for old men. Well, at least I finally grasp the brutal sentiment lurking behind that line, the opening to "Sailing to Byzantium." That poem used to puzzle the shit out of me. If I'm being honest, it still does. But less than it used to.

The lovely, doe-eyed nurse hands me my hospital gown and tells me to change. When I'm done, she opens the curtains, hooks me up to the machines, and walks away, back into the fleeting transience of her own young life.

✿ ✿ ✿

I don't feel like lying down, so I sit on the edge of my rollie and peer through the half-open curtain.

I'm feeling a little less edgy now.

Whenever I have to take Luna to the vet, there's always a bit of a struggle when I'm trying to get her into the front door of her carrier. The secret, I've learned, is not to use force. No pushing or shoving. I sit on my knees and hold her between them, locked in place directly in front of the carrier. She can't back up, there's nowhere to go but straight ahead. After a minute or so, she realizes that it's pointless to resist. With a slight heave of resignation, she rises to her feet and walks in, and I latch the door after her.

Similarly, now that I'm latched to an IV stand, I feel calmer, my powers of observation less distorted by panic and rage. This place is not really like a Civil War battlefield. It's more like a parking garage: a dim-lit place of low ceilings and flickering green fluorescence. You may recall that several pages back I employed a virtually identical metaphor in describing my arrival at NYU. But that place was huge and cavernous in comparison, and looked as though it stretched out for blocks in every direction. This hospital is much smaller than NYU, so the space that extends beyond my curtain is less like a parking garage in, say, the Mall of America, and more like one of those grimy hourly garages you find crammed under midtown apartment buildings. From where I sit, a single wide low corridor extends into the flickering distance, crammed with rollies, wheelchairs, utility carts, IV stands, blinking machines. Everything has wheels: this is a place of no fixed locations. Everything is designed to be moved, and then moved again, so that other things can be moved.

Like parking slots, there are curtained bays lining both sides of the corridor, clearly allocated for one semi-private rollie at a time. The curtains are useless. There's no semi-privacy here. Rollies have been shoved into the bays two or three at a time, jutting out at awkward angles, and more spill out into central space of the corridor, double- and triple-parked. Scattered about randomly, there are some heavy, institutional waiting-room chairs for guests—oddly, the only objects that do *not* have wheels—but there aren't many, so family members who wish to sit tend to perch on the edge of the rollies occupied by their loved ones. Most of them are hunched over, fiddling morosely with their phones. Medical personnel are everywhere, dodging and weaving through the obstacle course with the unconscious agility of rush hour commuters in Grand Central.

I'm not sure why I have this whole slot to myself. I don't think it's a VIP thing, there's no way my low level of *#privilege* has that kind of sway in this place of pragmatic expediency. I'm near the entrance, so maybe they keep this slot available for incoming patients as a kind of staging area.

This is not a mystery sufficiently intriguing to capture my interest. I take out my phone.

☼   ☼   ☼

A heavy-set man with the grizzled look of a retired boxer has come to roll me away. I lie back and he stands behind my rollie, releasing some sort of brake with a heavy clang. Getting me to where I'm going is a complicated operation, but he's got some serious chops, deftly executing pirouettes and K-turns, spinning me this way and that in a series of maneuvers that is difficult to understand from the dizzying center of it all.

As we progress down the hall, turning round and round, I'm exposed to a whirling kaleidoscope of patients. For a second, my face is inches away from the face of an elderly Chinese woman in a black knit cap with a Pittsburgh Steelers logo, propped up in her own rollie. She stares at me indifferently, and as we abruptly veer away, I catch a glimpse of a teenage girl—her granddaughter, I guess—sitting on the end of the rollie just past her grandmother's feet, wearing pink earbuds and a day-glo green t-shirt proclaiming that she is LICENSED TO CHILL. Another K-turn, and for a passing moment, I see the older woman I'd spoken to in the radiology waiting room the night before, and that must be her diabetic brother in the rollie next to her. He looks skinnier and grumpier than I'd imagined—but of course he's grumpy, he's spending his Friday afternoon in the hospital. On the floor beneath them is a small boy pushing around a toy ambulance.

We turn again, so that I am facing a long wooden bench that runs along a cinderblock wall, and that's when I first see them.

The Elegant White Couple.

It is only for a moment—we are in the middle of what seems to be a 270-degree turn—but it is as though they are illuminated by a beam of golden light. They are that striking. How to describe them? They look as though they've stepped out of the pages of *The Great Gatsby*. Or more accurately: as though they've stepped off the set of a movie adaptation of *The Great Gatsby*. I don't mean that they are in period costume or anything like that, but rather that the kind of clothing they wear is tasteful and timeless in a way that brings to mind the casual elegance of the Jazz Age, and might well have been put together by the head of wardrobe.

The young man looks to be in his mid-twenties, tall, slim, and clean-shaven, wearing khaki trousers, polished brown loafers, and a tailored white shirt opened casually at the neck, sleeves rolled back part way, revealing the slim gold band of a wristwatch; a creamy sports jacket hangs draped over his left arm. A lock of honey-colored hair falls over his pale brow as he murmurs into a cellphone with the restrained, ashen composure of someone relating the details of a medical emergency to a family member.

He is obviously talking about her. She sits on the bench next to him, hunched over and clutching her left arm, rocking back and forth in agony. Her death-white face is contorted with pain and splotched with tears, and yet she too, even in this tormented state, is transcendentally striking. Dark, shoulder-length hair falls around her face in two perfectly angled drapes, like the wings of a raven. She wears a loose-fitting, short white dress with a drawstring waist and a slightly frilled plunging neckline. Her outfit seems strangely unseasonable for the dead of winter; it's more like something you'd wear to play croquet at a summer lawn party, presumably at some estate in Martha's Vineyard. There's a coat folded up on the bench, and next to it a pair of shoes—a set of coral leather pumps. Her feet are bare. I wonder where they were before they were here, or where they were preparing to go. A film set? A museum benefit? A yacht? It's difficult to imagine them in a grocery store.

It's not just the clothing, or even their attractiveness. They are both very good-looking (you can tell that even though both of them are in a state of great distress) but not extraordinarily so. There's just some ineffable quality about them, that charismatic aura of Significance that emanates from certain movie stars or (occasionally and more rarely than you'd think) the very rich. They might be either of those things, or both. They aren't flashy.

You see them and you suddenly feel that you are no longer in your own story, but in theirs. An extra on a set, a passerby. You fall into the role of witness. That some beautiful and profound tragedy is unfolding before your eyes, and your incidental presence as a bystander is an undeserved privilege.

I stare at them, transfixed. I realize that I am experiencing something like envy. But it's the wistful sort of envy you feel about things you know you will never have, never could have had, the way you might envy owners of private islands, or extraordinary geniuses, or Olympic skaters. No amount of money, fame, or talent could imbue me with that kind of charisma. It's like the Christian concept of grace, a thing bestowed. You are born with it, or raised to have it, and my life is not, and never has been, that kind of life.

I feel guilty for feeling this way. They are obviously having an extremely shitty day.

❀ ❀ ❀

After a short ride in an elevator, my rollie has been deposited in a small antechamber leading into the Department of Radiology. There are about six other rollies in here—or rather, *stretchers*, since only one of them is occupied.* An ancient woman under a blanket, shiny blackbird eyes set in a mass of wrinkles, her mouth slack and wet. I recognize in her features the distinctive characteristics of advanced Alzheimer's, a disease Natasha's father suffered from during the last decade of his life. The old lady's family is gathered around her, a bearded, scholarly-looking man, a woman in a powder-blue hijab, a long-haired teenage girl in casual street clothes, a younger boy with improbably large sneakers, sitting on the edge of the rollie, furiously manipulating some hand-held computer game. None of them are speaking to one another; they are waiting for someone, or something, whatever the next step is in their hospital journey. I don't know these people, I can't really guess much about them or their lives—what language they speak at home, where they take their family vacations, whether or not we would enjoy one another's company at a prolonged social gathering—but I feel a strong empathetic connection to them nonetheless. This is easy to do in a hospital, because everyone here is feeling the same thing that I am. They are all wishing they were somewhere else.

I walked through this room last night, I realize, when I was in the unnerving company of THE SERBIAN. It opens right into the main reception area—I can see the front desk from my rollie—and just beyond that, the double doors that lead into the CT scanning room, where I am going to have my PROCEDURE, a very ugly word that is somehow much more terrifying than OPERATION. I have not been administered narcotics, so I am thinking quite clearly, and what I am

---

*I've grown sloppy with my profligate use of the term "rollie." When I coined it earlier, I defined it as "the living and the mechanical joined in unhappy union," but over time I seem to be using the term interchangeably with the mechanical object itself. How can you *be* a rollie, while also *sitting on* a rollie? If a rollie, by definition, requires a human occupant, can a rollie be empty? I don't know. I'm not a doctor.

thinking about are the words BIOPSY and NEEDLE and COLLECTION. Now that the moment is approaching, I am starting to think in ALL CAPS a lot.

Natasha walks in. I'm not sure how she knew to find me here. Possibly she was following in the serpentine wake of my rollie, but she also just seems to have an uncanny knowledge of my whereabouts at all times.

I don't get a chance to ask. Two nurses of different sizes and colors have apparated at the foot of my bed. The larger one (she's tall and somewhat stout) is white and older, perhaps in her mid-to-late fifties. The smaller, skinnier one is black, and much younger, maybe mid-twenties, and she has a giddy effervescence that she can't quite contain. She's all bright-eyed and bouncy, as though she really, truly loves this job. Or, maybe, as though she's just *pretending* that she really, truly loves this job because she's discovered that makes it somewhat easier to get through those exhausting back-to-back shifts.

Natasha has the usual effect on these nurses, they are both nodding and smiling way too much. She knows the older one already, and greets her by name, and then introduces herself to the younger one.

"If possible, I'd prefer him back in one piece," Natasha jokes.

"Don't worry," the older nurse says. "We'll take good care of him."

Natasha smiles, and briskly strides away. I kind of hoped she might stick around a while longer, but she's already halfway down the hall, off to run the hospital.*

I am sitting on the edge of my rollie. The two nurses are smiling and they are saying things to me.

I'm currently experiencing a certain level of unreality because cognitive dissonance is setting in. I'm trying to be social and friendly with these nurses I've just been introduced to, but it's challenging because I'm not wearing any pants, which is not my normal attire for socializing, and I'm also trying not to think too much about my PROCEDURE because I think I should instead pay careful attention to

---

*Natasha: "I don't run *the hospital*."

what the nurses have to say in case there's some crucial information or instructions, and all of these conflicting directives are causing my brain to stall, like when your computer freezes from having too many YouTube videos open at once, and I find myself momentarily and annoyingly in a Zen-like state of detachment, observing the nurses in the disinterested way you might observe actors in a foreign-language movie with no subtitles and no discernible plot.

The younger nurse is like a cartoon character. She's fun to watch. She's small and wiry, with big brown eyes and a quirky, mischievous mouth, and the loose curls of her hair have been shaped into a kind of triangle—wide at the sides, pointy at the top—which makes her look as if she's wearing a pyramid. She's flirty and jokey, and her version of a cheery bedside manner is so hyperactive and frenetic that I feel certain she's been prescribed Ritalin at some point in her life. She's like an improv comedy actress who never quite knows how to turn it off. She tells me her name is Shy. I'm unsure I heard this properly and ask her to repeat it.

"No, no, you heard right, it's Shy, S-H-Y, Shy," she says in a rapid-fire banter that suggests she has been saying this all her life. "I know, I know, I don't seem like someone you'd call *Shy*—everyone says so—but that's-my-name-don't-wear-it-out, and it's easy to remember because I'm *not* shy, even though that's who I am."

She looks a little alarmed as she runs through this breathless explanation, as though she's not quite in control of what comes out of her mouth.

The older nurse looks exactly like someone who's been a nurse all her life. She's tough-looking, red-faced, with hair the color and texture of straw. She carries herself like an armored tank, and I can bet she's Irish or Polish or some other hard-drinking Catholic ethnicity because I grew up in suburban North Jersey in an era when it still had a strong working-class tinge, and the no-nonsense, hard-drinking Catholic nurse was a popular flavor of mom. When you played over those houses, you knew were being watched like a hawk, and God help you if you lit one little bottle rocket in the backyard, or got caught in the bathroom comparing willies. I think the older nurse is named Carol, but I've already forgotten and I'm a little afraid to ask.

To my surprise, though, she's quite personable, and even a little flirty herself, and then I think, well, sure, she's actually close to your age, give or take a few years. She's not *across the divide*, she's my contemporary. We could've attended the same high school prom, and for all I know, we did.

The older nurse has scanned the code on my ID band, which pulls up my chart on a wheeled monitor stand. As she examines my vitals, she hands a tablet to the younger nurse, which apparently provides a long checklist of questions to ask me. Why I think I'm here, what illnesses run in my family, how much I drink per week, whether or not I enjoy the use of intravenous recreational drugs. It feels like the fortieth time I have answered these questions in the last two weeks.

The younger nurse, while recording my answers to the checklist, has been consistently addressing me as *Taylor.* This is a pretty common mistake, so I let it slide, but the older nurse is frowning as she consults my chart.

"Hold up a sec. Your name is *Tyler*, T-Y-L-E-R, not Taylor, right?" she asks.

I admit that this is the case.

"Tyler," the older nurse says, in very much the no-nonsense tone of the North Jersey moms of yesteryear, "I know you're a nice guy and you're just being polite by not correcting her when she uses the wrong name, but you have to be very careful in a hospital about stuff like this. What if there's someone named Taylor here who's getting something completely different done—like having a pacemaker installed—and we got the two of you mixed up?"

I swallow, and concede that this is a very good point, and one I had not really considered. Although, perhaps I should have because just over a week ago Dr. Boy had similarly threatened to give me a new kidney for failing to take these preliminary questions with the utmost seriousness and exactitude.

The younger nurse, too, looks chastised and nervous, and I realize now that she is subordinate to the older nurse, and possibly being trained. Her reaction to nervousness is much like my own in uncomfortable social situations: she begins babbling and joking even more, and in the process gets a whole slew of information incorrect.

Not only does she start calling me Taylor again, but she then decides that it is my last name instead of my first name, and then she mixes up my birthdate, transposing the month and the day. I'm of course now terrified to let any of this pass, and quietly correct her on each of these occasions, and I can see a kind of *Oh shit!* panic bubbling up in her eyes behind the jokes, and both of us are hoping that the older nurse didn't pick up on these mistakes, because I like Shy and I think she'd be a blast to hang out with at a party and I certainly don't want her to get in trouble, but I'm also kind of wishing I had a different young nurse attending to me before my PROCEDURE because this one is too nervous and jokey and possibly dyslexic, and I really, really don't want to wind up with Mr. Taylor's pacemaker.

The radiology technician has arrived to escort me through the double doors. It is THE SERBIAN. He was here late last night, and he's here this afternoon, and perhaps—like the concierge in the NYU urgent care center—he's always here. I am once again struck by his furtive efficiency. His nervous, sidelong glances, his demure, taciturn demeanor. What is the source of his secret terror? He acts as though his primary patient is Joseph Stalin, and it's only a matter of time before he jabs a vein too hard and winds up facing the firing squad. And then I wonder: is he like this with everyone or is it because I'm a VIP? Is Natasha *Stalin?* I don't think she can be Stalin, she's important but not Stalin-important. I've been under the impression that she's more mid-level apparatchik than Soviet Premier. But maybe she's closely connected to Stalin, or at least that's what THE SERBIAN has been led to believe.

It's strange and a little distressing to me, these glimpses of Natasha in her place of work, and the apparent authority she wields. It's different at home, where I treat Natasha with the jaded disrespect so often reserved for a beloved spouse with whom you've shared a home for decades, bickering over which drawer the can-opener goes in, accusing her of putting my wallet in an unfamiliar place when she was tidying up, because dammit, I always, always, leave it right here in the bowl by the front door, so—*oh, wait a sec, it's here in my other jacket, but can you please stop moving my shit around all the time?* Well, maybe it was like that for Stalin, too, coming home after a long day of collectivizing peasants and signing execution warrants, only to get yelled at by his wife for leaving his underwear on the bathroom floor.*

I am beginning to realize that I have a very limited understanding of the woman I have been married to for nearly twenty years. After all, she spends far more waking hours here in the hospital than she does with me. Arguably, the person she is here at work is her *true* self, or at least constitutes a far greater portion of who Natasha really is than the woman I spend evenings and weekends with. The Natasha I know has an infectious, riotous laugh, easily provoked. She calls her mother and her sister in Trinidad on a daily basis, and they nearly always make her laugh. She loves animals, children, concerts, margaritas, pepper sauce, and sex. She can be irritable and bossy, she's somewhat clumsy, and she is sensitive to criticism. She's surprisingly a bit of a slob, but she also has an uncanny ability to locate any lost object, which comes in handy since I lose things so often. She talks too much, nearly as much as I do. She's friendly and pleasant but can be reserved with strangers and doesn't make new friends easily—that's my job—but once she does, she's a fun and deeply loyal friend, and the reason why (I've long suspected) we continue to get invited to dinner parties and social outings in spite of the fact that I talk too much and sometimes forget to listen. She makes surreal, amusing collages out of magazine clippings and gives them to friends on their birthdays. She can point to any piece of jewelry she owns, costume or fine, and tell you exactly who gave it to her and on what occasion.

But the Natasha of the hospital is not someone I know well. She used to talk about work a lot at home—too much, in my view, especially in the early years of both our marriage and her career—but I made it uncharitably clear that I didn't enjoy listening to the minu-

---

*Then again, Stalin's wife eventually shot herself in the head. The official cause of death, however, was declared to be appendicitis.

tiae of her workday, so now she limits herself to the major highlights. I have trouble understanding who she is here in the hospital, or even what exactly she does. She handles all sorts of matters, great and small, logistics, operations, finances. I know that she's in charge of a lot of people, that she manages large budgets, that she hires and fires people, that she attends meetings and gives presentations, organizes birthday and retirement parties, and occasionally is required to attend certain functions and ceremonies outside of working hours. I've heard about some of these things—while yawning and drumming my fingers—but I've never seen her do them. I know that some people here like her a lot, and I know (from what she's told me) that others do not, but she holds her own while skillfully avoiding getting entangled in institutional politics. I suspect she's very good at what she does. But that's just her resume. Who, exactly, *is* she when she's here? How does the Natasha I know at home become the Natasha who administrates whole hospital departments, and how much do they have in common?

How would I feel about her if she wasn't my wife, and I worked here?

Well, that's a very speculative question because there's no fucking way I would ever work in a hospital.

My imagination fails me because I have no frame of reference, nothing in my life to compare to the kind of work she does. I've generally been underemployed my whole adult life, cobbling together a series of dead-end temp and freelance jobs that I usually wind up quitting, if I don't get fired first.

The most authority I've ever had in my working life was teaching a creative writing class to adults, who used their final student evaluations to complain that I kept leaving the classroom for smoke breaks.

THE SERBIAN injects me with the stuff that makes you feel warm and like you have to pee, but for some reason I don't feel the need to pee this time. The warming sensation, though, is oddly pleasant. What's not at all pleasant is lying on your back on the narrow platform, partially inserted into the portal of the Kubrickian CT machine, while THE SERBIAN tells you to lie very very still as he moves the platform back and forth because he's lining up your actual insides with the CT scan they took of your insides last night, so that they'll know exactly where to push in the needle without rupturing your kidney.

A nurse has entered. I can't see her well because of my horizontality, but she's a calm and serious black woman in late middle-age, entirely disinclined to joke around, and her West Indian accent is somehow reassuring to me, because she strikes me as belonging to a certain category of older West Indian women I have often encountered during trips to Trinidad with my wife, the type of capable, detail-oriented woman who can single-handedly organize a large church fundraiser with only a day's notice, and I feel entirely confident in her professionalism.

THE SERBIAN checks and double-checks the equipment, and then the doctor shows up, a photogenic young Asian guy in scrubs who looks like the kind of guy who probably belonged to a frat in college, and he definitely belongs to a gym because the dude has some enviable biceps. He's speaks with the slightly elided vowels of a stoner, but he doesn't seem like a stoner, so maybe he's just from California. I can totally picture him surfing. I bet he owns puka beads.

My belly and right side get wiped down with antiseptic, and I get a shot of local anesthetic in my side. We all wait a while for the anesthetic to kick in, and it is somehow as socially awkward as a prolonged ride in an elevator with people who are suing you in court.

So, now, using something like a video game joystick, the doctor will attempt to guide a HUGE FUCKING NEEDLE into the right side of my abdomen—the way I might try to guide the grappling hook in one of those arcade games to win a shitty novelty watch—and will then proceed to push it through the multivariegated layers of MY INSIDES until he reaches the COLLECTION that is puddled somewhere around where my appendix used to be.

There's a monitor where, if I want, I can watch what's going on, and much of my concentration is spent NOT looking at that monitor, because I definitely do not want to know what's going on, although it is no doubt fascinating, because I'm pretty sure that if I can actually *see* the needle pushing through my side while *feeling* it pushing through my side, I will involuntarily flinch or squirm and then the monitor will capture the exact moment when he pierces my gallbladder or spleen, or whatever the hell is in there.

As you might imagine, it's painful to have someone push a long needle through your belly, so the doc explains that to minimize my discomfort, they will periodically administer doses of local anesthetic as the needle inches forward. Since I'm doing my best not to look at either the doctor or the monitor, I don't fully understand how all of this works. I have no idea whether this is all done with a single needle, capable of both pushing out anesthetic and sucking up fluid from my insides, or if there are two needles, and he has to periodically withdraw one to insert the other. Or maybe they're both in me at the same time, like a pair of knitting needles, which is something I don't really like to think about because one needle at a time is enough. In any case, this is the part that takes the longest. Now and then, as he slowly works the needle forward—with a side-to-side wiggling movement, queasily suggestive of fleshy resistance—I detect a painful pinch, disconcertingly hard to locate because it is deep inside a region of me that is not ordinarily subject to pinching, and when this happens I tell him *I feel that* and every time I do, he says *OH REALLY?* as if he's genuinely surprised, and then he has to squirt more anesthetic into me and wait for it to take effect.

During the whole procedure, the nurse stands in the vicinity of my head, murmuring reassuring things to me. *Good, good, you're doing fine, not much more to go now, that's right, you let us know when you feel it, you'll be out of here in no time.* I am immensely grateful for her presence.

Once the path through my insides has been properly numbed and traversed, sucking out the collection takes a second or two, and now there's the doctor standing over me holding a vial of warm clear fluid with a sickening pinkish cast. "This doesn't look infected at all," he says, frowning.

Then he shrugs and smiles boyishly. "Oh well, I guess the lab will tell us."

❄ ❄ ❄

Someone wheels me back into the main parking garage for rollies, which now seems to have twice as many patients as before. Wow. There are an awful lot of prone bodies, you wouldn't think they could all fit in here. The weekend is gearing up.

When I'd come in earlier and panicked, I'd thought of images of Civil War battlefields. But on this return journey—since the worst is now over—I've been thinking instead of Woodstock, that other iconic field strewn with bodies. It's not so much the Peace & Love part as it is the overcrowding of half-dressed people in various states of pharmacologically-impaired consciousness. Here and there among all the newcomers, I spot a few familiar faces from my earlier trip—the old woman in the Steelers cap (but her granddaughter is nowhere to be seen), the grumpy diabetic brother, looking grumpier than ever. Ah, and a momentary glimpse of the Elegant White Couple. Well, just her actually. She's now sitting on the edge of a rollie near the center of the corridor, talking to a nurse, it looks like. She's still clutching her arm, but she seems calmer than before, maybe they gave her something.

If it were up to me, I'd have a hard time picking my way through this crowd and finding a place to park. But I'm a rollie, so I'm enjoying the luxury of being free from my own autonomy. It's like being in a driverless car—all the important decisions have been relinquished to an unseen agent. I didn't even get a look at who's pushing me around this time. I'm wheeled almost all the way back to where I was before, near the entrance, and after a lot of tight turns and reversals, I'm shoved halfway into one of slots—halfway because another patient was already in it, and they had to angle her rollie out a bit to fit me in, so neither of us are fully in the slot, but it hardly matters. The curtained slots are only an abstraction at this point. The whole corridor is packed with us, a sea of beds. I'm reminded of that disturbing scene in *Willy Wonka & the Chocolate Factory*, where all four of Charlie's grandparents are crammed together in a single room, living out the remainder of their years in bed.

❁ ❁ ❁

A guy in scrubs wheeling a small cart shows up—a nurse, I think—to switch my IV bag. He's a young, dark-haired white guy with an extraordinary amount of chest hair poking up through the V-neck of his tunic. I think he's either putting me on antibiotics or taking me off them. He told me, but I was distracted by the chest hair, and I don't feel like asking him to repeat himself.

He asks me how I'm feeling.

"I'm okay," I tell him. "Although I don't love having this thing in me." I indicate the IV tube running into my arm.

"Oh yeah? Why's that?"

"It just feels skeevy knowing there's a metal needle stuck inside my vein."

"It's not a metal needle," he tells me.

"No?"

"No, it's just a little flexible piece of plastic tubing. I'll show you." He fumbles around in the drawers of the cart and produces a small conical item packaged in a transparent plastic wrapper. "It's in a protective cap, but you can kind of see the catheter inside it."

It's just as he described, a short, tapered length of flexible plastic tubing, about the same thickness as a hypodermic needle.

"Huh," I say. "I wish someone had told me that a week ago!"

He nods, distractedly. He's looking with concern at something going on at the end of the hall. I follow his gaze, but it's not at all clear what impending crisis he needs to thwart.

"Gotta go," he says.

It takes a little effort to rejigger my brain's longstanding misconception about how an IV feed is set up, but within a minute or two the slight, nagging pain I've been feeling from having a metal needle stuck inside my arm vanishes altogether, never to return.

What a relief. I lie back and look around. I'm going to be here for a while, I suspect.

When they angled me into this slot, they positioned my rollie in such a way that I am directly facing the occupant of the rollie in the bay opposite from me, a yard or two away. This person is an obese teenage girl wearing a short frilly party dress of birthday cake pink. Why isn't she wearing a hospital gown? I don't know. She is propped halfway up in her bed, listening to music on pink headphones. A family-size KFC bucket is wedged in beside her, and a huge cellphone, bejewelled with gold and pink sequins, is balanced on her ample belly. She is gnawing on a drumstick while tapping out messages on her phone. There are crumpled napkins and styrofoam containers scattered all over her stretcher. She looks very comfortable, as if she were in her own bedroom. Her thick legs are spread wide and bent at the knees. It is difficult not to stare, since we are facing one another, but I am trying very hard to not look at her because her skirt is hiked way up, and to look at her is, I'm pretty sure, to look directly at her genitals.

For this reason, I have a strong compulsion to observe all the other people around me. It's not so easy, when you're propped up in a rollie, to look anywhere but straight ahead, but making the effort is preferable to spending the next couple of hours staring up a teenage girl's skirt.

I swivel my head a bit and look around. To the left, there's a group of middle-aged black women clustered around me, mostly on rollies as far as I can tell, and they are chatting in a West Indian dialect. It's the kind of conversation a group of women might have in a laundromat. The subject seems to be a particular Brooklyn neighborhood they all know well—from the context, I'm guessing Bed-Stuy or thereabouts—and how it has changed. They're talking about all the stuff that was there for years and is now gone, bodegas, shops, hair salons, apartment buildings, all swept away in the tidal wave of gentrification.

Someone brings up an after-school program sponsored by the Salvation Army. "Oh yes," says another. "I remember that, it was the best one back then. I had all three boys in that one; the girl was too old."

Somewhat to the right of my feet, is a white woman sitting in a hospital-issued wheelchair. Not the Elegant White Woman, you'd never confuse them. This woman is randomly splotched with tattoos—arms, legs, neck—and seems to have no teeth, although she isn't elderly. She looks like she's done quite a bit of hard living, though. I've been watching her a bit while eavesdropping on the West Indians, and she seems like an annoying type, frequently pestering the nurses for little things—water, snacks, having her chair adjusted and her phone charged—and then berating them when they don't respond quickly enough to her demands. You can learn a lot by observing how someone treats service workers in any capacity—waiters, retail clerks, taxi drivers, secretaries. Judging by this woman's interactions with the staff, she strikes me as one of those reckless, narcissistic personality types who navigate their lives like a coked-up sportscar driver weaving through rush hour traffic, careening from crisis to crisis with little regard for others, blaming everyone else along the way for the resulting carnage of severed relationships and damaged lives. Oh, I recognize the type. I suppose you can find such people in all walks of life—college dorms, movie sets, the White House—but in my neighborhood, I'll usually find them hanging out on stoops and benches because I live up the street from a methadone clinic.

While I've been here, she hasn't been participating in the West Indian women's conversation, but when the after-school program is brought up, she gets excited and chimes in.

"I remember that place!" she says. "It was right next to the supermarket!"

She speaks like a duck—like Donald Duck, actually—and I guess it's the teeth, but there's also something weird about her accent that I can't quite place. It's a variety of white Brooklynese, but it's layered over another regional accent, and I somehow know that she's not originally from NYC, but from some blighted corner of Cleveland or Dubuque or wherever, one of those rusted-out industrial centers in the hinterlands where people drink shitty beer and speak with squashed vowels and twangy inflections. But I don't really know the regional accents of the rest of the country all that well, I've lived in or around New York City most of my life, so for all I know she could be from Philadelphia. Or Vancouver.

To be honest, she looks a bit like a duck, too.

The West Indian women respond with a muted cordiality. I'm sensing that they are not thrilled that she's joined the conversation, and my guess is that their misgivings are not about ethnicity or class—or not primarily about those things, anyway—but because they, like me, have detected something vexatious about this woman, that to be involved with her is to be involved with a lot of tiresome self-aggrandizement and drama. And I suppose they've been parked here with her longer than I have, and if she's already made such a negative impression on me in the half hour I've been here, I can imagine how they must feel.

These are a lot of suppositions to base on a fragment of an over-heard conversation that I can only partly follow, but I have nothing else to do. I really want the nice pocket-size Moleskine notebook I carry everywhere, but it's in my canvas messenger bag—alas, we all live up to our own stereotypes—which is in a plastic bin attached to the back of my rollie. I'm perfectly capable of standing up and fish-ing it out, but I don't feel like doing that. Like Charlie's Grandpa Joe, I've already surrendered to the ennui of living in bed. So I can't take notes. I think my phone must be in the bin, too.

The Duck Woman, now that she has an audience, has launched into a long, cloying homily about motherhood, and as she gets in-creasingly animated, she grows more and more ducklike. Raising kids, *Gahd*, it's so hard, she quacks, you know what I'm talking about, ladies . . . so much work when they're little, trying to raise them right (*twying to waise 'em wight*) but they grow up so fast, and it's so faacking heartbreaking (that *faacking* carries the clear trace of another city in its vowels, and it's driving me crazy that I can't place it), it's so faack-ing heartbreaking when they finally grow up and move out.

There's a long pause, and then one of the West Indian women laughs sardonically and says, "Move out? Ain't nobody gonna *move out*. Them children all still here in my house, eating my food."

All the other West Indian women laugh.

The remark seems to have deflated the Duck Woman, and she falls silent. Order has been restored. The West Indian women resume their conversation, talking among themselves. I've sat up a bit to get a better look at them, and I realize that the woman who just made that joke about her kids living at home is not a patient. She's wearing ordinary clothes, not a hospital gown. She's sitting on the end of a rollie, but it's actually occupied by a skinny old guy propped halfway up, hooked to an IV stand. He's not paying attention to any of this. He's peering over his reading glasses at a word jumble book, pencil in hand.

I don't really understand how this situation can exist. How is it that a group of women from the same neighborhood, who all seem to have known each other for years, have all wound up in the emergency room on the same day, at the same hour? Is it something that they schedule? Is it, like, a standing appointment, like every other Friday at two pm, they all arrive here at the hospital and stand in line for the ER?

I'm bored again, and for a moment I find myself absently staring straight into the V-shaped tunnel of the obese teenager's legs. I quickly avert my gaze back to the Duck Woman. She's staring at her phone with a sour look on her face. She hasn't done anything crazy yet, but I think she certainly has potential.

My interest perks up when a short bald man in a baggy denim jacket approaches her. The resemblance between them is striking. I hadn't realized that the Duck Woman looks just like Popeye, but now I know she does because—aside from her long, stringy hair—she looks just like this guy, and he looks just like Popeye. Wide forearms, long torso teetering over bowed legs, a big, round coconut head, prognathous and banana-nosed. Haphazardly tattooed, like her. And, to my delight, he *also* speaks like a duck, with the same unplaceable accent lurking under the Brooklyn. How did he lose his teeth, too?

Is he her brother? Her son? I genuinely can't tell. They both seem ageless, and not the good kind of ageless. They could be anywhere from thirty to fifty-five, and it's impossible to say if one is older than the other. The thought that he could be her husband or boyfriend is just too disturbing to contemplate: that somehow, through prolonged association and poor dental hygiene, their appearances and mannerisms gradually converged . . . no, no, I can't even go there, it's too frightening. They *have* to be siblings, I think, but then I think . . . *or mother and son* . . . because, dammit, it kind of works either way.

He's speaking to her in a low tone with some urgency, and also—because there's no more privacy here than in a crowded elevator—with a degree of obfuscation. So they're having a conversation something like this:

"I called . . . *them.*"

"Who?"

"Who do you think?"

Blank stare.

He leans over and murmurs something.

"Oh! Okay, so now what?"

"Well, they won't . . . do it. Not without those . . . *papers.*" Ah! Papers!

"What?" she says, outraged. "For shit's sake, these people!"

She looks around and murmurs something in his ear, and then raises her eyebrows quizzically.

"No," he says, frustrated. "You're not *listening.* I told you already. You need—" At that moment, he happens to glance in my direction, and I look away a beat too late. His voice drops to a whisper. Shit. This is very frustrating, now I can't hear him. I need closure here. I need to know what they're talking about, even though I have a feeling that once I find out it will be much less interesting than I've anticipated. This is what purgatory looks like.

Oooh. Money is mentioned.

Something something "at least $700." This sum represents an obstacle, she's shaking her head furiously and murmuring something back. The name *Marissa* floats up, signifying nothing.

He shakes his head, and holds up a hand. "Know what? In that case, I gotta make some more calls. There's still—"

He glances at me again. Crap, I'm totally busted.

"—*stuff* I can do. You know what I mean." He strides away purposefully, and then doubles back. He's forgotten something. Murmurs to her. She fishes around in a large Duane Reade shopping bag and hands him a card. It looks like an ID, but I can't quite see it. He turns to leave.

And then someone *screams.*

Oh God, it's horrible.

It's like the scream of someone being stabbed to death.

An inhuman, ear-piercing, blood-curdling, hair-on-the-back-of-your-neck scream, and it cuts like a searing hot poker through all the chaos and noise of the emergency room, *and it goes on and on and on.*

Every single head in the entire emergency room whirls towards the source of that terrible scream.

My heart thumping hard, I follow the collective gaze towards the far end of this vast chamber.

It is the Elegant White Couple.

She is sitting on a stretcher, rollie, whatever it is, set low to the ground.

A doctor in a white coat leans over in front of her.

Her left arm is stretched straight out, raised in the air as if she is reaching for something on a high shelf, and the doctor is grasping her forearm with one hand and her upper arm with the other.

Her head is thrown back over her shoulders and her screaming face is not the face of a human being, it is the raw primordial face of pure pain.

The young man stands a couple of feet behind the doctor, and the look on his face is horrifying to behold, his eyes bulging with terror, his mouth a petrified O. His hands involuntarily rise up above his head, fingers outstretched, as if he's trying to prevent them from acting of their own accord. His whole body is shaking.

Whatever terrible thing just happened has already happened. The doctor now slowly lowers her arm and gently bends her elbow so that her forearm and hand come to a natural position resting across her lap.

She stops screaming, and her body slumps forward, as if a rope has been cut. She lets out a kind of low-pitched guttural wail, and then begins sobbing uncontrollably.

The young man rushes to her and presses her face against his body, his hand stroking the back of her head. He is crying, too, and his face is as pale as hers.

For a moment, the entire hall remains frozen, and then a soft rustle ripples through the room as everyone turns their heads away, as if we all have collectively realized that it would be indecent to stare at them any longer during this deeply private moment. There's some scattered murmuring, and then, as if a volume control has been unmuted, the whole place goes back to chattering, bustling normalcy.

But there's something in the air, an uneasiness. No one within earshot says anything at all about what just happened.

The West Indian women have renewed their conversation, but somehow they are more subdued. They are talking about cooking and food, the various approaches they take to certain dishes they all know and like, but the conversation seems halting and halfhearted, just something to do to pass the time.

The Duck Woman's brother, or son, or whatever he is, leaves on his mysterious errand, and she goes back to staring at her phone.

I stand up and pull my messenger bag out of the bin.

※　※　※

Sometime later, Natasha shows up. I'm sitting on the edge of my stretcher, kicking my feet, scrolling through the news on my phone. I've had enough of lying in bed like a sick person.

Natasha has spoken to my doctor. Not the surgeon who sucked out my collection, but Dr. Gravity. It occurs to me that I have only met Dr. Gravity once, for less than fifteen minutes, and yet his influence reaches everywhere. He's the puppet-master, the grey eminence. I imagine him sitting behind his immaculate desk like a Bond villain, a secretive little smile forming beneath his neatly groomed mustache.*

"It looks like they won't get the results from the lab until tomorrow," Natasha says.

I nod. *Fine, whatever.* That needle-jockey doctor definitely implied that my collection fluid isn't infected, so I'm not all that worried.

"So he wants to keep you overnight," she says.

She looks at me to see how I'm going to react to this.

I don't react well.

"*What?* Are you *shitting* me? I don't want to do that!"

"It's just to be safe," she says, pleading.

"*This is not a safe place!*" I hiss.

"Please. Please, just hear me out. You won't be in here," she swears. She's getting upset, too. "They'll move you. You'll get your own room, a private room. It'll be like staying in a hotel!"

As she speaks, I am looking around in desperation, and then I realize that what I am doing is looking for an escape route.

"Listen to me," I say through gritted teeth. "I need to ask you something, and I need you to be straight with me." I'm feeling tears start at the corners of my eyes. "Can they keep me here against my will?"

"No . . ." Natasha admits. "They can't. But it's—well, it's *not good* if you just leave without being properly discharged. Look, he just wants to have you here for observation in case something goes wrong."

"I'm not doing that, Natasha. The whole *fucking* point of this was to avoid being admitted to the *fucking* emergency room over the weekend, and here I am, in the *fucking* emergency room."

I am being loud. A few of the West Indian women glance at us nervously.

"So here's what's going to happen," I continue. "I am leaving. I am going home. I am going to buy a six-pack of Corona, and then I'm

*Natasha: "You're being ridiculous. He's one of the nicest doctors in the hospital. Everyone likes him."

going to watch *Westworld,* and then I'm going to sleep in my own bed. Our bed. So I need you to understand that if I am not discharged in the next fifteen minutes, I'm going to yank this IV out of my arm and walk the hell out of here."

Natasha puts a hand over her eyes in the exasperated gesture known throughout the Internet as a facepalm.

"Oh, *dammit,* Tyler." She shakes her head and glares at me. "Fine! Okay! I'll talk to him."

After she leaves, I stare at the IV tube taped to my arm, which I've come to view as a kind of shackle. I think about what the hairy-chested nurse showed me. It's just a tiny tube of plastic—without the tape, it probably pops right out.

How bad could it hurt to yank it out? They do it in movies all the time.

☼   ☼   ☼

Remarkably, Natasha returns in under fifteen minutes. She finds me perched on the edge of the stretcher with all my belongings packed up, my clothes and overcoat neatly folded beside me, as I sit staring at my watch, shaking with rage.

After sufficiently reassuring me that someone will be arriving very very soon to unhook me from the IV stand and discharge me from the hospital, Natasha tells me that Dr. Gravity has no problem at all with me going home instead of staying overnight.

"He was actually really nice about it," she says, quite obviously relieved that I haven't permanently torched her professional relationship with the most popular general practitioner in the hospital. "He genuinely just thought you'd find it more convenient to spend the night here."

I find this statement astonishing. Who the fuck would possibly find it *more convenient* to spend the night in a hospital when home is just a ten-minute cab ride away? These people who work in hospitals, they really have no fucking clue. Of course *they* like it here—they spent years earning diplomas and degrees and certifications just to get here. This is where they *wanted* to spend every fucking day of their lives. So *of course* they think it's just a dandy place to spend the night, practically as nice as a Marriott. They're the ones *running* the machine, they have no idea what it's like to be caught up in the teeth of it. I have a whole raging fire-and-brimstone sermon brewing up inside of me on this very topic that I'm aching to deliver right here, right now, to Natasha and to anyone else within earshot.

But it doesn't matter anymore. We're going home.

V. Homo Erectus

COME CELEBRATE WITH ME
THAT EVERYDAY SOMETHING HAS
TRIED TO KILL ME AND HAS FAILED

—Words displayed across the Prospect Park Bandshell in
the early spring of 2021, an art installation by Mildred
Beltré and Oasa DuVerney with lines excerpted from
Lucille Clifton's poem "won't you celebrate with me"

R. K, MY MYSTERIOUS NYU SURGEON—I'd yet to see her unmasked—had Monday office hours at a practice in Brooklyn. Yes, over the weekend, I'd finally scheduled my long overdue post-op consultation. It was the first day of February.

At the time of this writing, only parts of Brooklyn are hip. Pull up a map of the borough, and place your finger on the green heart of Prospect Park. Now sweep your hand out north and west, towards the East River, the Upper Bay, and the glittering spires of Manhattan, a gesture that will encompass Park Slope, Carroll Gardens and Red Hook to the west, Williamsburg, Greenpoint and Bushwick to the north, and somewhere between, Brooklyn Heights, Cobble Hill, Fort Greene, and all the other charming, overpriced neighborhoods nestled cheek-to-jowl between Prospect Park and the Three Bridges.

This is the Brooklyn that children in Montana are named for: a brownstone empire of skinny jeans and single-origin coffees. Here, in this mostly peaceable kingdom of community gardens and farm-to-table charcuteries, you'll find warehouses of industrial charm, where be-flanneled lesbians offer weekend workshops in beekeeping and database architecture; here are the cozy neighborhood bars where trust-fund kids and unemployed novelists gather to seek solace and companionship, drowning their sorrows with small-batch IPAs and Prohibition Era cocktails; here, the verdant, tree-lined streets of cafes and church steeples, where angry, bearded cyclists rampage through clusterfucks of Bugaboo strollers and tattooed yoga mommies.

But not all of Brooklyn is Lena Dunham. Locate Prospect Park on the map again, and this time cast your gaze to all that lies on the other side, to the northeast and south. It's a big chunk of Brooklyn, spilling out towards Jamaica Bay to the east and New Jersey to the south. All those less-celebrated neighborhoods—Sunset Park and Midwood, Brownsville and East New York, Canarsie, Bensonhurst and Gravesend—turn their backs to distant Manhattan, and focus on the business of living with an authenticity so genuine (so artless, so dowdy and insular) that they have thus far managed to escape the clickbait-hungry gaze of the lifestyle columnists and trendsetters, and the ghoulish real estate developers who trail close behind, sniffing for blood. Sooner or later, of course, some well-meaning fool will open a community bookstore, or publish an admiring profile of a local pupusa stand. Actually, the way things are going, the developers may not even wait for that.

But for now, these neighborhoods are still the places where the true spirit of old-school Brooklyn endures: the stark, dreary subdivisions of wide boulevards and housing projects, of vast urban-renewal residential complexes that stretch for blocks with nary a Whole Foods in sight. These are the immigrant enclaves of Brooklyn, the neighborhoods to which taxi drivers, short order cooks, and cleaning ladies return after their long, backbreaking shifts, plopping their weary asses on plastic-covered couches to take in a meal with the family in front of the big TV. Fútbol, cricket, Bollywood soaps, followed by arguments, laundry, and homework.

These are the neighborhoods in which doctors are born and raised to be doctors, and these are the neighborhoods to which doctors return, opening lucrative private practices for local clientele seeking consultations conducted in Bengali, Portuguese, Mandarin and Yoruba.

❀   ❀   ❀

Like all Brooklynites, I've had occasion to make excursions out to these practices and the medical labs that pop up around them. Unexamined notions of geography always make you think that *staying in Brooklyn* will be more convenient than *crossing the river into Manhattan,* but this is never true. You'll be taking local trains instead of express, and you'll have to walk a lot farther once you arrive. Brooklyn is designed for inconvenience.

Back in the previous summer, I had made repeated trips to the Brooklyn office of a Mount Sinai orthopedist for my recurring plantar fasciitis.* I had originally been Dr. Orthopod's client many years ago, when I lived on the Upper East Side and Mount Sinai Hospital was a convenient place to hobble to. The pain prevented me from running and playing volleyball and I wanted Dr. Orthopod to give me a cortisone shot, which he did not want to do. The danger, he explained, was that repeated cortisone shots could thin, and eventually collapse, the fat pads cushioning my heel and the ball of my foot.

"Once the fat pads collapse," he warned me, "they're gone forever. I've seen it happen! Walking will be *extremely painful* for the rest of your life."

That did sound pretty awful. *But come on, just this once? Please? And I'll never ask again?*

No, no, no.

But I kept coming back. I let him run all sorts of diagnostic tests, expensive CT scans and whatnot that revealed nothing, and then I'd

---

* If you're over 35, you're already familiar with this condition from painful experience. But if you've never heard of it, the short version is "heel spurs," although that's *totally wrong,* a *complete fallacy* and anyone who tells you otherwise has *no idea what they are talking about.* Dr. Orthopod said so.

beg for the shot again. He gave me a horrid night splint that resembled a ski boot and served mostly as an excellent deterrent to sleep. This went on for months. Nothing worked.

I kept asking. One day, exasperated by my whining, Dr. Orthopod agreed to do it. Just this *one* time, he emphasized sternly. He carefully drew an X in marker on the sole of my foot and prepared an enormous, painful-looking needle.

"But you have to understand," he said, "that you should have no more than two of these *in a lifetime*. And please, please—whatever you do—don't go see a *podiatrist*." He spat out the word with the disgust customarily reserved for pimps and child pornographers.

The shot hurt like hell but it worked. It really was the miracle cure I'd hoped for. The inflammation went away, and the YouTube therapy stretches I'd been futilely practicing at home suddenly began to work. Within a month I was running again. But once you have plantar fasciitis, you will have it again. Over the years I had mild bouts that gradually faded with stretches and the hateful night splint. And then, nearly a decade later, in the middle of a summer of long, glorious runs in Prospect Park, it came back with a vengeance. I couldn't shake it. I didn't want to see a podiatrist. I Googled Dr. Orthopod and discovered he had a practice in Brooklyn.

I knew it would be a long war of attrition to get him to give me another shot. In this respect, Dr. Orthopod was like a girl I'd unexpectedly gotten lucky with, a girl who wasn't interested in me, who didn't even like me as a friend, but who'd nonetheless, one regrettable evening, had an uncharacteristic lapse of judgment and now had to fend off my clumsy attempts to repeat the experience. Because, after all, if Dr. Orthopod had chosen to do it once, *he could choose to do it again.*

Trips to Dr. Orthopod's Brooklyn practice involved long subway rides with many, many stops. I am not a morning person, so I always scheduled my appointments for the late afternoon. This happens to be right around the time that school lets out. I would inevitably board a packed train infested with junior high kids, a screeching madhouse of unsupervised teens running amok through the cars, whirling around the poles like Ritalin-crazed dervishes, pummeling each other with—*thud!*—backpacks, screaming, shoving, giggling, flirting, spitting.

I'd hunker down in an out-of-the-way seat, hidden behind a magazine, trying to remember which of those many obscure stops was the right one. On arrival, I shouldered my way out through a hormonal flurry of candy wrappers and homework assignments, trudged up the stairs, and found myself suddenly alone on the quiet sidewalk of an empty boulevard, somewhere in Brooklyn.

Thank God for GPS. Eventually I'd find my way to a blocky beige building full of medical practices, indistinguishable from all the other blocky buildings filled with medical practices, except that this one contained Dr. Orthopod.

His large waiting room was always packed with Ultra-Orthodox and Hasidic Jews, a gently fluttering sea of black and white punctuated by the metallic gleam of crutches, wheelchairs and walkers. They had schlepped their way here on tricky hips and hammertoes because Dr. Orthopod and his colleagues could dispense medical advice in fluent Yiddish. It was a very popular practice. I took my seat among the devout and got comfortable, knowing that I would not be seen until long after the hour of my scheduled appointment. I had no VIP status in this waiting room.

I had been surprised by the demographics of Dr. Orthopod's waiting room. Dr. Orthopod did not look like the kind of Jew who spoke fluent Yiddish. Dr. Orthopod looked like a failed folk singer. He was tall and gangly with a prominent Adam's apple, the way I've always imagined Ichabod Crane. His long, clean-shaven face was framed by scraggly, shoulder-length hair he habitually swept behind his ears, and his pale watery eyes stared out from round, gold-rimmed spectacles with a reflexive look of reproach. His shabby clothes—baggy, ill-fitting trousers, a faded plaid shirt, a ratty knit tie—suggested a constitutional indifference to appearance, and also, perhaps, a life largely devoid of romance.

It was easy to imagine Dr. Orthopod with a battered guitar case slung over his shoulder, waiting for hours in the rain at a rural bus stop. It was harder to imagine Dr. Orthopod growing up as one of eleven children in a sprawling Hasidic household in Borough Park. But then again, it was hard to imagine Dr. Orthopod as a child at all.

He never did give me the shot I wanted, although he did inform me that I had arthritis in my left foot.

I freaked when he told me. "Are you serious? I don't want arthritis!"

Dr. Orthopod showed me the x-ray. "See that one bone in your midfoot, how it's streaked with white? That's arthritis."

"Oh, God, really?" I was horrified. "Is it going to spread?"

"*Spread?* No, of course not! It doesn't work that way." He swept his hair back. "But if you're asking if you'll eventually get more arthritis, well, yeah, probably."

I stared at the white arthritic bone on the x-ray.

"Are there any, like, vitamins I could—"

"No." He rolled his eyes. "It's normal. You're just getting old."

❁　❁　❁

I stopped seeing Dr. Orthopod after that. He was never going to put out. And I was mad at him about the arthritis. I hadn't been aware of it before the x-ray, but now, whenever I went running—I eventually got better on my own—I couldn't stop picturing that whitish bone lodged in the stony architecture of my midfoot, slowly crumbling into dust like a piece of brittle chalk.

Dr. K's Brooklyn practice was somewhere out in the same medical hinterlands, and so my journey to find the woman who'd removed my appendix had a dreamlike familiarity, the long ride out on an exotic branch of the MTA, the unruly schoolchildren and their backpacks, the sudden miracle of sunlight flickering through the windows as the train hurtled above ground, the gum-stained stairwell that led up to a de Chirico landscape of vast boulevards and chunky, featureless buildings.

The day was bright and cold, and I felt marvelous. It felt like my first real outing since the surgery. I had put on nice clothes for the occasion, my favorite black cable-knit sweater, the good corduroy sports jacket that didn't have food stains or rips in the lining, a freshly dry-cleaned overcoat. Now that my belly had deflated, I'd been delighted to discover that—thanks to surgery and a steady diet of laxatives—I'd lost ten pounds and could finally fit into the new jeans I'd optimistically purchased a year earlier.

I sauntered along the mostly empty sidewalks with a spring in my step and a spirit of adventure, feeling something of that grand sense of dislocation you have when you've traveled to a foreign city and accidentally wandered off the tourist map into the unpicturesque neighborhoods where life actually takes place.

My birthday was coming up. In a few weeks I would turn forty-nine, but—I reflected happily—that was not yet fifty. I had a whole year to go.

❈   ❈   ❈

Actually, the year which had just begun to unfold wasn't going to be such a great one.*

Oh, in many ways it would be like other years, a lot of same-olds and rather-nots punctuated by irreproducible moments of joy and grief. We'd see friends, take trips. Natasha made pottery and I went on long runs through parks and beaches. After a few months, my bowels would return to normal, by which I mean that I no longer spent much time thinking about them. I would, however, develop a revolting and humiliating rash on my scrotum, which turned out to be caused by an allergy to sunblock, oddly on the one place I had never applied it. The world moved on, as it always does. Prince died, Muhammad Ali died. Umberto Eco, Harper Lee, Richard Adams, Carrie Fisher. Emerson died in March; Lake died in December. Milestones, marking the passage of one era into the next. Natasha's grandmother, Nanny, the much-loved matriarch of my wife's sprawling international clan, died that year too.

That was to be expected, the changing of the seasons. But all that year, beyond the foreground of daily life, a creeping dread marched

---

*I know. We're off track again, but bear with me just a while longer, friend. My tale is almost told, and this is our last detour.

through the headlines. Mass shootings, terrorist attacks, climate change, the rise of nationalist nutjobbery in nearly every corner of the world. Brexit happened, like watching a friend drink Drano on a dare. The passionate intensities of social media, 140 nasty characters at a time. Lines of force coalesced, the center couldn't hold, you were going to have to choose sides. All this had been happening for quite some time and yet something felt different. A shifting in the tectonic plates had awakened something foul from its stony sleep. It was hard to avoid apocalyptic feelings that year, with the Lord of the Flies slouching towards the White House. And then in November, the nightmare became real. The election of 2016. A festering turd in the punchbowl if there ever was one.

It wasn't just the United States. Shitbags were running the show across the globe. Haters hated with a new, gleeful ferocity. Some sickness had entered the world. In the beginning, galvanized by loathing, Natasha and I did the things a lot of people did. The Women's March, angry postcards to elected officials, that sort of thing. Attended some activist meetings and quickly realized (much as we had during the Bush years) that activism wasn't really our cup of tea, so we raged and stewed, made modest donations to the ACLU and Planned Parenthood, and signed a few petitions.

Life went on. People died, babies were born, leaks sprouted and ceilings were patched. The next year, we learned that Godot had been diagnosed with terminal cancer and this made us very sad because at some point during all those maddening years of missed appointments and paperclipped faucets, Godot had become our friend. With alarming speed, Godot grew sallow and wasted, but between surgeries and chemotherapy he summoned up the old maniacal energy, slapping paint on doors, building a bench out of discarded scrap. Even when he became too weak to do those things, I'd still encounter him in the halls laboriously heaving groceries—one bag at a time—up three flights of stairs to his ex-wife's apartment, where he now resided. He sure as fuck wasn't going gently into that good night.

In the fourth year of the Turd Emperor, the metaphorical sickness that had entered the world became literal. The Plague Year hit New York like a tsunami. The panicked scramble for face masks and sanitizer, the shuttered restaurants and bars, the confused armies of homeless people wandering the abandoned streets and subways, the morgue trucks. We all experienced it together and yet we were all alone. At night, Natasha and I stood at the window, staring out at the darkened plain of our wounded city. Across the East River, the Empire State Building convulsed in red, blinking like the Eye of Sauron. A melancholy wind from across the sea had blasted away all the certitudes of ordinary life. We had only each other now. No, that's not quite right; we had a third companion in our pod. Thank God for Luna. She still puked with stubborn perversity but the spell cast by Queen Xanax held true and she'd never spiraled back into anorexia. Our friend Valerie was not so lucky. In the early days of the pandemic, one of her two beloved cats died. She was devastated. She lived alone and was terrified that if she got sick, there would be no-body to take care of her remaining cat. For many months, she saw no one. She had her groceries delivered and spent her days alone, bird-watching in the nearby cemetery. That would soon become some-thing of a trend.

The numbers rose. Every morning, I put on my N95 and es-corted Natasha to the subway, waiting on the deserted platform un-til the train came to take her to the hospital. I didn't know what else to do. Some days, against her protests, I'd ride the train to work with her and walk back through the lunar landscape of early-pandemic Brooklyn. During that three-mile trek, I'd sometimes stop to piss against the side of a building—there was nowhere else to go—and sense all around me the disapproving eyes of sequestered families peering through the blinds.

We learned to live with fear. Every hour Natasha spent at the hospital felt like a round of Russian roulette. I was certain she'd be exposed, that she'd become one of the hundreds on ventilators, dropping dead within days of diagnosis, and all day and night, the incessant wail of ambulances racing towards her hospital kept that terror fresh. Natasha feared for her colleagues on the clinical front-lines, pulling eighteen-hour days plowing through an avalanche of the dying and the dead. Huge numbers of staff had contracted the disease. She despaired that she'd never again see her mother or sis-ter in Trinidad, which had closed its borders. She cried when she told me that a cafeteria worker at the hospital—a fellow Trini—had died of Covid-19. Whenever the cafeteria had offered some Trinidadian specialty, he'd save a plate just for her. They spoke daily, but she'd never known his name until he was gone.

It felt like an asteroid had slammed into the planet: an extinction level event. But life seeks out the empty places. As the last dinosaurs shuddered into the dying swamps, small furry creatures crawled out into the half-light and blinked, keen to inherit the earth. For a time in the silenced city, birdsong filled the air. By summer, a new dispensation had taken root. The pandemic transformed the Long Meadow of Prospect Park into a Seurat painting, a grassy archipelago dotted with picnicking families, solitary readers, socially distanced yoga classes, and, nestled near the periphery, secretive clusters of young people huddled under clouds of marijuana smoke. A new city regulation allowed restaurants and bars to open outdoor street cafes, and—despite all the masks and precautions—humdrum Park Slope became as lovely and festive as an Italian piazza. All summer long, like mushrooms after a heavy rain, jazz bands popped up on random street corners.

After the murder of George Floyd, the city erupted into months of Black Lives Matter protests, but even in that great outpouring of grief and rage, there was a strange joy. Helicopters roared overhead, but in the streets below, colorful murals exploded across the plywood fencing of vacant lots, children taped crayoned expressions of solidarity to their windows, and young people of all ethnicities tore themselves away from their screens to gather at the barricades and forge alliances seeded with newfound purpose and meaning. In that barren year of social isolation, the flowering of a new civil rights movement offered the possibility of hope.

That was also the year of the bicycle—and not just bicycles. Cheaper lithium batteries and the rise of certain evolutionary conditions (the reluctance to use public transportation, the increased reliance on deliveries, the urgent need to get the fuck out of cramped apartments) led to a Cambrian explosion of newfangled wheeled contraptions barreling through the streets. Every conceivable configuration of bicycle—electric, cargo, tandem, fat-tired, reclined—jostled for space in the narrow bike lanes with a

Dr. Seuss parade of unicycles, tricycles, skateboards, scooters, go carts and rickshaws. Citi Bike offered free annual memberships to hospital workers and Natasha decided to try it. I purchased a membership so I could join her. We bought helmets and practiced in parking lots, and after a week or so, Natasha started biking to and from work. We soon acquired bicycles of our own. This would have been inconceivable a year earlier; we'd always thought our bicycle friends were nuts to risk their limbs in the meatgrinder of city traffic. Times had changed. I surprised myself by signing up for Revel, an electric moped sharing app. They looked like futuristic Vespas. I only used them for short rides, but what a rush! Even strapping on the helmet was a thrill. Whizzing through Brooklyn in my sunglasses and scarf, I'd pretend I was a handsome Italian professor in Rome, late for an important lecture.

Skiing was out of the question that winter. But we did go sledding. On the evening of the first heavy snowfall, we dug out the old blue plastic sheets from the back of the closet, exactly where we'd stashed them a decade earlier, and trudged through the snowdrifts to Sunset Park. In Central Park, they'd had bales of hay at the bottom of the sledding hill. In Sunset Park, there was an iron fence. Just as we arrived, a little kid on a sled slammed right into it. For a moment he lay still, and his distraught mother came scrambling down the hill after him. He stood up, shook it off; he was okay. *Jesus.* We took careful note of the distance between the bottom of the hill and the fence.

At the top, we decided we'd go one at a time so we could take turns recording the adventure on our phones. I went first. Fighting the wind, I unfurled the plastic sheet and flopped onto it headfirst, gripping the slots in front. With a little kick I was off. *Woohoo! I'm sledding!* I shot down over the snow, reached bottom, and immediately rolled off to avoid crashing into the fence. I jumped up, brushed the snow off my coat, waved to Natasha. This was *fun!* Why had we waited so long to do this?

I clambered back up and got out my phone. Natasha's turn. She opted to sit upright on the sheet, facing forward. I gave her a push, and down she went. *Go Natasha!* Halfway down the hill, she lost control, spinning like a top. As I noted earlier, you can't steer those plastic sheets; all you can do to avoid collision is bail. But she didn't bail. Now facing backwards, she reached the flat stretch at the bottom—and just kept going. *What the hell, Natasha?*

Three yards, two yards, *Oh God*—

Her head smacked against the iron bars and she crumpled to the ground.

I stood frozen at the top of the hill, mouth agape. Had I just witnessed my wife die in the most ridiculous manner possible? I couldn't move. And then she lifted her head out of the snow and cried *Tyler! I need you!* and now it was me scrambling down the hill.

She was, thank God, alive. She had a nasty bump on the back of her head, but her winter hat had cushioned the impact. No broken bones, no blood, no lifelong paralysis. I helped her to her feet, and she told me that she didn't want to go sledding anymore.

I laughed, relieved that she was okay.

"But we can come back another time," she insisted. "I want to do it again."

Because that was just how we rolled during the Plague Year, when death raged all around us. By then we understood: every day was a day stolen, every endeavor edged with risk. You could never win the war against entropy—the house always wins—so there was no sense in putting things off for idealized conditions that might never come. I don't mean to imply that I would spend the Plague Year learning to play the violin and firming my buttocks. *Au contraire.* I would watch every terrible sitcom ever made and gain fifteen pounds. But I knew at last what I really wanted out of life. I wanted to live.

But on this bright February day all of those things still lay ahead and I would not have been able to guess the strange shape of the days and years to come. I was a man of my time, living from one moment to the next, somewhere in Brooklyn.

Stopping frequently to consult the map on my phone, I made my way up a nondescript side street that seemed vaguely familiar, a stretch of dumpy rowhouses with concrete yards and plaster Virgins, a lonely corner gas station which seemed to be the only place to buy coffee, or, indeed, anything. At last I reached my destination, entering the lobby of a blocky beige building that looked exactly like the one in which I had visited Dr. Orthopod the year before, but who could tell? All the buildings looked the same around here. I squinted at the directory behind the security desk and found my way to the elevator.

I had expected to walk into a waiting room packed with Orthodox Jews, but I was wrong. That wasn't the ethnic enclave my surgeon served. Signs posted on the walls were lettered in Cyrillic, and the overhead flatscreen televisions played Russian talk shows and soap operas. The patients sitting around the room may well have been Jews, but they weren't those kind of Jews. They were Russians first and foremost. As I took a seat, pale wintry eyes glanced at me with mild curiosity, and flicked away in dismissal.

A stocky middle-aged woman stepped through a door and called my name. Nearly as wide as she was tall, she labored under a towering helmet of hair shellacked in bright Slavic yellow. She glided like an oil tanker through a labyrinth of short hallways and I followed in her wake.

She stopped at an open door.

"You wait here," she said, and glided away.

I sat on a small stool in the examination room and took out a *New Yorker*.

Out in the hallway, a flotilla of large women with custard-like hairdos of yellow and black drifted back and forth, transportation vehicles for manila folders and urine samples. One of them was momentarily intercepted by a slim young woman in a white coat and denim jeans, who pointed to a clipboard and murmured some inquiry in Russian. I could only see her from the back, but I knew right away that she was my surgeon, the woman with the amused eyes behind the mask.

A few minutes later, Dr. K entered the room. She made a little show of it, a Chaplinesque pantomime, suddenly halting in the doorway as if startled by my presence, eyes wide, holding out her hands in an ironic gesture of amazement.

"Well!" she exclaimed. "Here you are at last!"

I smiled as I stood up to shake her hand. I understood. This was a strange meeting after two weeks of deferred appointments. The only contact we'd had since the operation was through the proxy of my wife's embarrassed, apologetic phonecalls as I raged like a lunatic in the background.

With a puzzled expression, comically exaggerated for my benefit, she studied my face and shook her head in wonder, as if trying to square her earlier impressions of me with the smiling, affable man standing in her office in a corduroy jacket and tweed cap.

I was utterly charmed by the whole performance. It all felt a bit like a 1930s screwball comedy, we'd gotten off on the wrong foot, but now that we understood each other better, we could run off together on some grand adventure and solve a jewel heist.

Of course, she was beautiful—of course, of course!—but I'd known that even before I'd seen her without the mask. I'd devoted all those winter nights to watching Regina Spektor videos on YouTube, and now that I could see my surgeon's face, I found a strong resemblance to the quirky Russian-Jewish chanteuse of my depressive evenings: large expressive eyes, heavy-lidded and rimmed with dark lashes, a thick cascade of dark brown curls framing a heart-shaped face, full lips with a hint of irony twisting at the corners.

But it was more than that. Have you ever met someone at a party, or some other random encounter, with whom you felt an instant and mutual rapport? Someone you felt completely at ease with right away, not as if you'd known each other forever, but as if you *should have* known each other forever, that this friendship had been waiting to happen long before you'd even met? She had a low sonorous voice, with the slightest hint of a Slavic upbringing in the way she rounded her vowels. I felt certain that she knew how to play the piano quite well.

She sat down at her small desk, and invited me to pull the stool over so we could sit together while she pulled up my chart on a laptop.

She frowned and shook her head. "But . . . why?" she wanted to know.

Why had I put myself through all of that, the emergency room visit, the extra CT scan, the needle aspiration?

I explained how my wife was a hospital administrator, how the people she worked with wanted to give me the red carpet treatment, the full Blue Plate Special with all the trimmings.

"Ahhh, okay," she said, nodding. This all made complete sense to her, she was familiar with the phenomenon. "Okay, yes, I see. I know exactly what you mean. But even so—" she scrolled through a screenful of my records "—I'm surprised they did all that to you. I mean, this business with the collection. You just had surgery! There's always a collection after surgery."

This was news to me. "Really?"

She shrugged. "Of course!"

It was a reaction to trauma, she told me, just like a blister. The body sends fluid to insulate the wounded tissue.

"And then the antibiotics! We didn't even give them to you after the surgery." Dr. K sighed. "You know, they can really mess with the flora of the gut—"

"I know," I said. They'd prescribed a course of antibiotics after my procedure—*just to be safe*—and while taking them, I'd devoted many hours to reading all about gut flora on my favorite hypochondriac websites, pondering the virtues of kombucha and trying to determine which probiotic supplements teemed with genuine bacteria and which were merely repackaged Chinese sawdust. I had already begun eating organic sauerkraut and drinking liquid yogurt.

"All right," she said, standing up. "Let's have a look at you."

I sat on the examination table, took off my jacket and sweater, and unbuttoned my jeans, lowering my fly just enough to give her access to my incisions. I raised my t-shirt and laid back. Gazing down the length of my naked torso, I felt pleased with how flat my belly looked.

Dr. K ran a finger lightly over my tiny incisions.

"These are healing nicely," she said.

"Everyone admires your stitches," I said.

"Oh, do they?" she snorted, quizzically raising an eyebrow. She looked pleased nonetheless. She placed her hand on my abdomen, and gently pressed her thumb—just once—into the place where I'd once had an appendix. Then she raised her hand slightly and, with a practiced twist of her wrist, flicked her thumb against the same spot, as if sounding the skin of a drum.

That was all. I zipped up my fly and put my sweater back on. We returned to the small desk.

She sat quietly for a moment, as if formulating what to say. I knew she'd had to recalibrate her ideas about me, that she'd been pleasantly surprised that I wasn't the angry, entitled jerk she'd thought I was. That, in fact, she liked me. I liked her, too. We'd been through a lot together, and now, sitting in silence next to her, I found myself wishing things had gone differently for us. Under different circumstances—another time, another place—I would have asked her to dinner. I think she would have made a very entertaining dinner companion. I suspected that Dr. K was a woman who could make me laugh.

She turned her chair so that we sat face to face. "Everything is . . . fine," she said, hesitantly, almost as if surprised at her own assessment. "But you really should come back in about a month."

Her tone was bittersweet, even reproachful. If we'd been in the romantic comedy I'd imagined us in, this conversation would be taking place at an international airport as final boarding calls blared over the loudspeaker.

Her eyes grew somber and earnest. She wanted me to listen to what she had to say. "If you do come back," she said, "I can examine you again. We can make sure everything really is okay. Then we can just close the file on this case." She smiled ruefully. "And you'd never have to see me again."

I did want to see her again, I really did. But not like this. I gave her my best smile and assured her that I'd make an appointment in a few weeks. She nodded once, and gave me a long look. We both knew I was lying. We rose from our chairs and shook hands.

I'd felt good that day, but the winter is always hard for me. In the weeks to come, I slipped back into gloom, forgetting, as I always do, that spring was just around the corner. My birthday came and went:

I was now officially in the last year of my forties. I spent late nights alone at my desk in front of a glowing screen, drinking too much, worrying about the state of my bowels, listening to Regina Spektor while writing long, melancholy emails to distant friends. From time to time, I'd think of Dr. K. Her candid eyes, glittering mischievously. Her quirky sense of humor, her self-assurance, her sardonic, wistful smile. She'd stolen a piece of me. But I never saw her again.

Acknowledgements

Let's get the apologies out of the way first. My personal essays are written with a heavy dollop of the personal, and people who have the misfortune to have interacted with me in even a minor way are subjected, often unfairly, to my cranky subjectivity. I can't apologize to them all, but I would like, at least, to apologize to all the health-care workers mentioned in "Appendix." All of you, working in various capacities in the hospitals, private practices, and ambulances I passed through during those two shitty weeks of my life, devoted yourselves to keeping me safe and whole with the utmost professional care. Some of you, in fact, quite literally saved my life. In return, I devoted page after page to savaging your professions and the institutions you serve. I'm sorry.

(Cats are not inclined to feel bad about anything, but on Luna's behalf, I similarly apologize to the veterinary professionals who saved *her* life.)

I also owe a posthumous apology to Godot. After he died, we tenants gained a much greater appreciation of the role Godot had played in keeping this ramshackle building from falling to pieces. I soon learned more than I ever wanted to know about our antiquated heating system, and so I've come to think I may have been hasty in my judgments concerning Godot's management of the boiler. He was, in the best sense, the soul of this building, and he is much missed.

Alright, then; on to acknowledgements proper. First off, I owe Jacob Smullyan, my publisher, a debt of gratitude. Though I blew past my deadlines like a drunk teenager in a stolen car, Jacob consistently offered me encouragement, advice, and friendship throughout the entire process. It's a source of pride and pleasure to have my debut collection published by Sagging Meniscus Press, a press founded in the eccentric, courageous spirit of the great independent publishers of the mid-twentieth century, fully dedicated to the mission of publishing "books that want to be themselves." And I'm delighted, too, that *Crime* sports a cover by the late, great Royce Becker—the artist whose distinctive work graced most of SMP's catalogue from its founding. Sadly, mine is one of the last: after a long battle with cancer, Royce died in the autumn of 2020. But where one story ends, another begins. Anne Marie Hantho, designer extraordinaire, has taken over the helm, and has already produced a slew of enchanting covers for SMP. She has also taken on design projects that were left incomplete when Royce died—including mine—so the cover of *Crime* is actually a kind of collaboration. This is an especially gratifying development to me, as she is a close friend of many years.

I am fortunate to count among my friends a number of gifted writers. Heartfelt thanks to William Pittman, Rick Ruth, Angela Starita, Alice Stephens, Sarah Stodola, and David Winner, who waded through early drafts of "Appendix," and graciously offered much useful feedback. (An extra tip of the cap to Rick, for tolerating my occasional theft of his witticisms.)

Thanks to Kevin Fitz, who gave me a monthly column—and the delirious freedom to write about whatever I liked—in *The Fire Island Express* ("Lost at Sea"), and, later, in *The South Shore Express* ("Metropolis"), where many of these essays were published in their earliest form. I'd also like to thank *Express* artist Brad Gore, who regularly supplied those magazines' exquisite cover art, and the gorgeous and whimsical illustrations that accompanied my columns.

Warm thanks to Jenine Gordon Bockman and Jeffrey M. Bockman, the founding publishers of *Literal Latte*, a magazine which has a long history of publishing new writers, and I was once one of them. My first published short story ("Epiphany") appeared in *Literal Latte's* third issue, which led to a long and happy relationship with both the magazine and its publishers; several of the essays in this collection appeared in *Literal Latte*. Not only did I gain a lifelong friendship with Jeff and Jenine, but also with several other *Latte* alumni. I've particularly cherished my friendship with Ben Miller and Anne Pierson Wiese (both enviably brilliant writers, and among the kindest people I've ever known), and with Patricia Lynne Duffy (the author of some of the most elegant and charming personal essays I've ever read), who has included me in so many of the reading events she has organized over the years.

My deep gratitude to Fay Webern, author of the memoir *The Button Thief of East 14th Street* (Sagging Meniscus Press, 2016), who died in Vermont in October, 2019, at the age of 92. She had a long and vibrant life, but I wish she had lived to see the publication of this book. Over the course of our long friendship, she offered me tremendous encouragement, invaluable advice on craft, and gave me an education in her own intellectual and artistic passions—especially mid-century modern art and jazz, and the great Yiddish writers who influenced her own approach to storytelling. She was an extraordinary woman and I am privileged to have known her. I'd also like to thank Fay's daughter, the scientist MarthaLeah Chaiken, who often helped facilitate our correspondence, and soon became a dear friend as well. Similarly, thanks are due to musician Peg Tassey, Fay's friend and publicist, who produced a terrific video series of Fay reading her stories, and who (with her husband Indigo) offered us such warm hospitality when Leigh and I traveled to Burlington to attend Fay's book launch at the Light Club Lamp Shop.

A pint raised to James Prochnik, who is the kind of friend any writer would be lucky to have. (I know I'm not the only one who feels this way.) I suspect that, for him, the creative life is the only life worth pursuing—James is not only a superb photographer, but also a sculptor, a graphic designer, and a writer—and he treats the other artists in his orb like fellow pilgrims journeying together on the same formidable road: there to offer a hand when we stumble into the dust, there to cheer us on when some elusive summit has at last been obtained. His compassion, humor and stimulating conversation have been a great source of inspiration throughout our decades-long friendship.

Gotta give a shout-out to Writing Group: Douglas Belford, Matthew Gilbert, Erum Naqvi, Sarah Stodola, Greg Wands, and Sacha Phillip Wynne. It's always a thrill to gather around the table with this talented crew, open a bottle of red, and invent new worlds on the spot. Every time the results have been astonishing; every time I marvel at how much great work can be written in one evening. Thank you.

My love and lifelong gratitude to my mother, Sherry, a voracious reader who filled our house with books. She taught me to read at an early age, and encouraged my earliest aspirations to write.

I'd be much amiss if I didn't thank Luna, my cranky muse, who sits on my desk as I write these words, staring pointedly at me to make sure she gets her proper due. Every writer should keep a cat. Christopher Smart had Jeoffrey, Samuel Johnson had Hodge, and I have Luna, the best cat of all.

Writing can be lonely, and writers draw much sustenance from the people in their lives. I am not going to be able to thank all the people I would like to. In these inadequate notes, I've tried to limit myself to those who have played some direct role in the creation of this book. But I have been wildly, implausibly fortunate to be surrounded by a large and warm circle of friends, all of whom have enriched my life in countless ways. I wish I could enumerate you all, but you know who you are, and I love you all.

Ah, and what should I say about my lovely wife? It's no joke to be married to a writer, especially this one. Trust me, the debts rack up quickly. Leigh (AKA Natasha) is always my first reader, and the one whose opinion matters most to me. Our lives are so intertwined that she has a hand in all my endeavors, great or small, one way or another. But these words can hardly suffice to encompass a territory vaster than empires. All I can really say is that Leigh holds my heart, and knows all that I owe her and all that she means to me.

Photo by Leigh Gore

Tyler C. Gore has been cited five times as a Notable Essayist by *The Best American Essays*. He lives in New York City.

❅   ❅   ❅

CPSIA information can be obtained
at www.ICGtesting.com
Printed in the USA
BVHW052036290722
643376BV00007B/133